ARCHITECTURE
AND THE URBAN ENVIRONMENT

A Vision
for the
New Age

Derek Thomas

Architectural Press

OXFORD AMSTERDAM BOSTON LONDON NEW YORK PARIS
SAN DIEGO SAN FRANCISCO SINGAPORE SYDNEY TOKYO

Architectural Press
An imprint of Elsevier Science
Linacre House, Jordan Hill, Oxford OX2 8DP
225 Wildwood Avenue, Woburn MA 01801-2041

First published 2002

British Library Cataloguing in Publication Data
A catalogue record for this book is available from the British Library

Library of Congress Cataloguing in Publication Data
A catalogue record for this book is available from the Library of Congress

ISBN 0 7506 5462 7

For information on all Architectural Press publications
visit our website at www.architecturalpress.com

Printed and bound in Italy by Printer Trento s.r.l.

CONTENTS

All great ages of architecture are known by their grand period titles - ours will probably be known as 'Architecture in the Age of Consumerism' arising from the self-indulgent intemperance of the developed world, the declining quality of urban life globally, and a universal disregard for proper stewardship of the natural resources of the planet.

In the planning and design of the urban setting the aim should be to create 'ennobling' and 'enabling' environments. Inevitably this demands a process based on peope-driven dynamics, in other words, based on the perceptions of the users of urban space.

In the context of our environmentally stressed planet, it is not responsible to think of architecture as being 'good' only in terms of past design maxims.

In the urban environment, the failure to meet the cultural needs of the community, the end user, threatens the amenity value of the social environment with potentially dire sociological consequences

The rigorous design axioms of the Modern Movement have caused streets to lose their attraction as gathering places. 'As a consequence individual attitudes to urban space have been radically altered... Functionalism, which laid the groundwork for our loss of traditional space, became obsessed with efficiency.' (Trancik 1986)

Sensory Attributes 121

Nowhere do mathematics, science, philosophy and the natural senses permeate one another so intimately as in the understanding of the character of a piece of architecture and that of urban space.

Architecture in Response 135

Much of what is currently presented under the banner of architecture and, curiously rewarded and applauded by architects themselves, is preoccupied with excess - such as designs which are inappropriate to climate, such as glass curtainwall structures in hot, sun-drenched climates, necessitating complete reliance on high-energy resources.

On Environmental Economics 194

This branch of economics, otherwise resource economics, is perhaps the key to bridging the current huge divide between the expediency of big business enterprise on the one hand and a more conservationist vision on the other.

The Timeless Way 212

The imprint of history shows that from earliest times there have been social inequalities in living conditions. This is generally congruent with the widening gap between the 'haves' and the 'have-nots' as the affluent, through economic and political strength, have gained greater access to resources.

Appendices 214-19

Bibliography and Photographic sources 220-22

Index 223-24

Acknowledgements

No man is an island, least of all authors who owe a debt to the society in which they were born; and as their lives unfold, they owe their view of the world and whatever clarity of perception they possess to the cultural milieu which others provide. I am indebted to my family, to friends and to colleagues, and to many others for their support throughout the production of the book. I can trace its origins over many years; from my formative days as a student, to the moulding I enjoyed in my early years as a fledgling architect followed by maturing experience and further study. Ultimately, through the insights gained, I felt the compulsion to write it down almost as a narrative.

My principal text material gained richly from the work of others who are committed in their own individual ways to the quality of their environment and who are concerned with the issues I attempt to address. I pay tribute to the wider fraternity of professionals and colleagues who share the perceptions that inform the main focus of the book, but above all my sincere thanks are due to my wife Christine, Roger Harrison, Alice and Peter Wilkes, Paul van Niekerk, Quentin Miller, Bernie Oberholzer and my progeny, Andrew and Suzanne, I am most grateful to Mary Anne Botha, whose professional guidance was crucial over the initial difficulties of setting the stage for the main theme and the final structuring of the text.

The illustrative material is largely from my own collection but was generously supplemented by others who went to great lengths, even to the extent of travelling great distances, to capture illustrations so essential to the story. In particular, for their response to my calls for assistance with specific image material, with much appreciation I thank Roger Harrison, Alice Wilkes, Martine Ward, Paul van Niekerk, and my daughter Suzanne Allderman. For those who allowed me to raid their private slide collections, I am indebted to Klaus Scheid and Quentin Miller for their extensive contributions.

For permission to publish material that has enriched the substance of certain themes, special thanks are due to particular professionals, namely, architects Mick Pearce and Ken Yeang, who practise in different parts of the world and who provided the images of their own impressive sustainable architecture, the Eastgate building, Harare, and the Menara Mesiniaga Tower, Kuala Lumpur, respectively. I must also record my appreciation to mathematician Dr Chonat Getz of Witwatersrand University and Elisabeth Lickendorf for permission to publish the images and extracts from the article on the science of *izembenge*. The editor of *S A Country Life* permitted the use of material on cob construction. I owe my thanks also to executives of the BRE building, Garston, UK, who kindly consented to the publication of the images of their environmental building that have substantially informed the discourse on responsible building design. All sources of image material are further acknowledged on page 222.

Many others, simply through their support and our informal discussions, unwittingly heightened my desire to record the insights contained in the themes towards a wider appreciation of the tasks that lie ahead for sustainable development and proper stewardship of natural resources for this and future generations. The collective wisdoms that flow from time to time through the pages have vindicated my own convictions regarding the future role of architecture and urban design in effecting essential attitudinal change at this auspicious time, the start of a New Age.

Derek Thomas
Cape Town
July 2002

'Throughout the Universe there is order. In the movement of the planets... in Nature.... and in the functioning of the human mind.

A mind that is in its natural state of order is in harmony with the Universe, and such a mind is timeless. Your life is an expression of your mind. You are the creator of your own Universe, for as a human being you are 'free to will' whatever state of being you desire through the use of your thoughts and words. There is great power there. It can be a blessing or a curse.

It is entirely up to you, for the quality of your life is brought about by the quality of your thinking.'

Akash's wisdom in 'Time' - a rock opera.
Clark (1986)

INTRODUCTION

All great ages of architecture are known by their grand period titles - ours will probably be known as 'Architecture in the Age of Consumerism' arising from the self-indulgent intemperance of the developed world, the declining quality of urban life globally, and a universal disregard for proper stewardship of the natural resources of the planet.

Modern day individualism and eclectic trends have removed architecture from the root stem of its historic tree while choosing to give expression to assertive consumerism. During the latter half of the twentieth century, a time that has been marked by rapid urbanisation of Western societies accompanied by escalating global stress, urban environments have become impoverished and dysfunctional. Exclusivity in the practice of creating urban space as well as in the design of buildings has been allowed to flourish, so that the absence of both social and environmental accountability have become the ugly sisters of the plot.

The practice of present day architecture appears in a state of indulgence and in the business of self-gratification, even narcissism, rather than in the search for meaningful direction. Often there is a sense of alienation in the rarified environments where architects 'strut their stuff' for their peers. Even though individualistic expression in architecture is almost a right, there is evidence that the needs of ordinary people are not always considered to be within the architect's terms of reference.

Contemporary buildings and urban landscapes suggest not only a lack of cultural awareness but that of any environmental ethos, noticeable through the apparent disregard for the looming depletion of strategic natural resources. Although apathy towards real environmental issues can be seen as a reflection of the times, architects and urban designers should not ignore signals of global stress that are of significant social and ecological consequence. Not only architects and urban designers, but societies at large must develop a more focused vision to meet the changed cultural and environmental paradigms of this, the New Age.

The pattern of architectural history in Western civilisations shows distinctive 'cause and effect' tendencies, where the architectural styles of particular epochs respond closely to social, cultural and economic needs on the one hand, and the availability of technical and technological means on the other. Also politically, from the time of despotic rule during the Egyptian period, the role of the individual has evolved from slavery to present day democratic empowerment of the individual. The historical tree of architectural form and expression tends to be a faithful reflection of these influences. However, modern tendencies in architecture and urban design show a poor response to contemporary, and even traditional parameters, where lessons from the past could show the way. Within democracies, individuals are perhaps for the first time in a position to determine the quality of their urban environments, the architectural response to their needs and holistic stewardship of the planet's resources. Yet New Age architectural expression still remains elusive.

Humanistic and environmental resource principles should become the driving creative forces in architecture and in shaping the urban landscape. A new responsiveness must arise to restore architecture to its rightful place in the public and private realms, from which could emerge built environments that enoble the urban experience.

Architecture that is grounded purely on conceptual philosophising and expression, emulating trends in art and sculptural form, can easily become removed from the realities of daily urban living and no longer be of social relevance. The visionary *extraordinaire*, Hundertwasser delivered an apt diagnosis of the malaise in his call for action to the Western world:

> 'The time has come.
>
> The time of surveillance has past.
>
> The time of waiting for paradise is past.
>
> The time of fruitless talking is past.
>
> The time for action has come.' (Rand 1991)

▼ *Traditional African city in a sketch by G Burchell on expedition in the 1700s. A stable equilibrium through a horizontal relationship with nature and good stewardship of natural resources*

◀ *Houston, USA, 1980s: The vertical character of the archetypal American city, has destroyed physical connections in the city and contributed to the loss of meaningful urban space. The insatiable energy demand of the entire CBD coupled with the enforced dependence on the mobility of the energy guzzler, the motor vehicle, is of critical importance in the New Age*

Apart from the need to engage with social issues, the very technology which was designed to improve our lives, indeed our human habitat, has produced unexpected byproducts such as 'sick building syndrome'. In effect, this raises cause for concern as to how healthy our homes and workplaces really are, since we have in fact relied on artificial, high energy-consuming means to correct what amounts to poor architectural design. Environments that are not energy-conserving, and buildings built out of the exploitation of the world's scarce resources, such as exotic timbers, and using methods which pollute and produce toxic wastes, are contributing to the rape of the environment and performing an assault on our health and our sensibilities.

Hundertwasser also identifies a cure:

'The Architect Doctor: Our houses have been sick for as long as there have been indoctrinated urban planners and standardised architects. They do not fall sick, but are conceived and brought into the world as sick houses...

So a new profession is needed: the architect doctor. The simple task of the architect doctor is to restore human dignity and harmony and nature and human creation.' (Rand 1991)

Architecture should not be a matter of economics only, nor should the aesthetic be the outcome of the indiscriminate use of mechanistic drawing aids. Creativity can also be overpowered by the pressures of expediency.

▲ *Houston, USA, 1970s: Interfirst Plaza: Corporate statement of 55 storeys of polished granite and matching glass - aesthetically aloof while heavily resource-dependent from construction and throughout its economic life*

▼ *Jerusalem: Tourist accommodation at a Kibbutz: Clad in local stone to comply with the regulated aesthetic of the city yet the unrelieved monotony arises from concern mainly for square footage*

LOSING THE WAY Architecture that has abdicated to the false gods of Technology, Expediency and Exhibitionism can negatively shape the society we live in. Such buildings are associated with the Modernists and brought the Movement into disrepute, negatively influencing public perceptions about the worth of all contemporary work. In turn, as a reactionary movement, the Post-Modernists created a rarefied environment for practitioners of an individualistic new order that is yet to provide direction for the New Age.

The decline of Modernism is essentially related to these trends in architectural practice so that throughout the developed countries, the resultant universalisation of style has become seamless with the prevailing culture.

Apart from aesthetic and amenity aspects in architectural propositions, our concern for the resources of the planet are today found wanting in respect of spiritual commitment and committed environmental stewardship. The widely interpreted concept of 'sustainability' in terms of architectural design begins to take on a significant and urgent message.

In the mid-1980s, inspired by James Lovelock's valuable contribution to a better understanding of our habitat, a new awareness emerged through the Gaia movement. In his book, *Gaia: A New Look at Life on Earth*, Lovelock propounds a compelling hypothesis: that the earth and all its life systems are an organic entity. Gaia (the ancient Greek earth goddess) is self-sustaining, and has the characteristics of a living organism. The major man-induced interventions threaten the capacity of the organism to sustain its functions - a demonstrable example being the depletion of the ozone layer and global warming which have induced extremes in climatic behaviour as evidenced during the past decades.

On another front and advocating the use of traditional, natural materials and building methods, the *Baubiologie* (building biology) philosophy became a force for change in German-speaking countries. Born of disenchantment with much post-war building, and of prevalent green awareness and concern about chemical pollution from synthetic building materials, *Baubiologie* combines a scientific approach.

Baubiologie aims to influence the design of buildings that meet our physical, biological and spiritual needs. The house is compared to an organism and its fabric to a skin - a third skin (our clothes the second skin), and fulfils essential living functions: protecting, insulating, breathing, absorbing,

▲ *Dallas, Texas, USA: Hyatt Regency Hotel (1970s): Clad with 7.85 acres of reflective glass that requires conditioned air to offset heat loss and gain daily and seasonally*

ENERGY CONSUMER GIANTS Glass enclosed buildings are major consumers in the energy budget and are not sustainable in terms of their continued dependence on dwindling natural energy resources. Constructed in the 1970s, issues of intergenerational responsibility for resource depletion arise, with negative global ramifications.

▼ *Houston, Texas, USA: Allied Bank Plaza: 71 storeys of glass curtainwalling: Genre of the energy-consuming giant on the endangered list and, with the prospect of resource depletion, facing the possibility of extinction*

As proof emerges of the costliness of past architectural errors, and the cost-effectiveness of the Community Architecture approach - claimed to have been up to five times as cost-effective in the provision of housing for the Third World - then, as yet more projects are commissioned, the research loop could be completed by feeding this information back into the schemes that follow.

Knevitt (1985)

evaporating, regulating, and communicating. A building's fabric, services, colour and scent must interact harmoniously with us and the environment. The constant exchange between the inside and the outside depends on a transfusive, healthy 'living' indoor environment (Pearson 1989). The holistic view of the relationship between people and their buildings has an affinity with *deep ecology*, the American 'non-party political search for Buddhist-type harmony'.

Ironically, mankind has the power - through intellectual and scientific means to maintain good stewardship - to avoid the reckless assault on natural resources. Environmental economics (described in a later chapter) is a long-standing but little understood discipline and even less utilised in the development process where it should reside to good purpose as the economists' guide to thresholds of sustainability.

Le Corbusier, van der Rohe and Gropius, the doyens of the Modern Movement, believed that technology (the machine) would provide most of the answers, including the creation of a more equitable society, but we have the benefit of hindsight to tell us that it has not done so. Technology, though a useful means to an end, is a false god. While present day developments around us seem to be preoccupied with stylistic expression or internalised economic returns on the maximisation of revenue from square footage, there are clues that suggest that social idealism in architecture is not entirely dead.

Knevitt (1985) is well known for his writings through which he promotes 'Community Architecture' as a movement founded on social idealism where the views of residents in new and existing residential environments are solicited rather than ignored. The concept simply means that, as a project comes on-stream, research must first be undertaken to assess users' needs and aspirations in advance of the first brick being laid; and then, on completion the need to establish whether these have been fulfilled. Knevitt believes that once having gained recognition and acceptability and been absorbed by the mainstream of development, the future of Community Architecture will lie in the scope of its practice rather than remain as a purely ethical movement.

Detractors would argue that in its construction, Community Architecture, the myth of what could be termed the 'purified community', in fact suffers the same utopian tendencies as the Modernist architecture that it was set up to overturn. Even though Modernist architecture and Community Architecture are radically different in their means of production, they both bring with them idealised visions of society. However, this elevated view need not be of no value as a basis of engaging with social and

Camden, London, Brunswick Centre, 1965-73: Sports stadium or housing? Conceptual architecture with little potential for community development

CREATING NEIGHBOURHOODS The fact remains that while architecture cannot shape the society we think we want, it can indeed have a dramatic impact on those who have to live with the result. By creating a design process more responsive to the needs of people, a more responsible product will emerge.

Jerusalem, Israel, 1980s: Neighbourhoods commissioned by the Israeli Ministry of Housing to house immigrès from diverse cultures in the diaspora. Creating potential for community life where the exterior is as well designed as the interior

cultural needs. Where communities have not been consulted, the history books record significant examples where entire residential districts were later raised to the ground as failed environments. Pruitt-Igoe (St Louis, Missouri USA, 1972) was perhaps the most notorious of failed urban renewal projects due to 'inappropriate design, misunderstood social needs, and poorly conceived public spaces' (Trancik 1986). Earl's Way, Runcorn, UK, fell into the same category: humanless, rigid and unresponsive housing scheme of the 1970s and subsequently demolished due to its dysfunction and imposed mechanistic qualities.

Community architects have sought links with other individuals or groups - outside their profession - who in some ways represent New Age thinking and practice: the Greens, the Friends of the Earth and other environmental

LIVING WITH THE RESULT Community Architecture might be the route to a new consensus about how to create good architecture and to avoid what is bad - in the eyes of both the profession and the user.

◀ ▼ *Runcorn New Town, Cheshire, UK, 1970s: Earl's Way, conceived by a highly regarded architectural office to house a new community. The lesson is the extent to which architecture, in the grip of elitism, and non-reflective practice has been removed from its intrinsic purpose - to provide shelter, comfort and delight for ordinary people*

pressure groups; those involved with preventative medicine and health care; and other likeminded souls in the environmental professions. As projects become more numerous, so also are they getting bigger - often dealing with whole neighbourhoods or parts of cities rather than one-off buildings. They bring about radical environmental change, being designed within a framework of social and economic or physical regeneration.

Under the banner of Community Architecture a decade and more has passed since Knevitt recommended that architects/designers defer to social expectations in the practice of architecture. The unanswered question remains whether there is much evidence on the ground, either in developed or developing countries, to support that likelihood.

The past era in architecture has relied heavily on the expedient use of technology, sometimes with negative consequences largely due to its dependence on energy to achieve short-term sustainability. There is a growing case for the end of the skyscraper, that genre of North American technological mastery, spawned mainly by corporate narcissism and founded on the belief that 'height excites'. The patterns of the workplace are changing, and changing fast. Conventional offices are perceived to be big, tall, hierarchical, hermetic, modular and efficient but are also located in city centres and served by vast energy-consuming systems of transportation to bring commuters to their nine to five employment. In the age of e-commerce and the Internet, interaction does not require old-fashioned hierarchies. Is the weather-sealed high-rise, energy-guzzling and anti-social city block facing its demise?

'All this leads me to predict a renaissance in city life, although following a far more complex choreography than the crude and rigid temporal and spatial conventions that have cramped so many lives since the middle of the nineteenth century... Architects are faced with the task of inventing the urban landscapes of the 21st century, the salient features of which will be mobility, transience, permeability, interaction, pleasure, sociability, creativity, stimulus, transparency. We might do better to use our imagination than to continue to rely for urbanistic imagery upon the conventional office skyscraper...' (Duffy1999)

The need for intensive concentration of business activity in the typical CBDs will be challenged by New Age communications technology to decentralise into more stress free environments for workers. Corporations will need to engage with more people-oriented development, not purely vertical dimension, to express their competitive edge.

In the age of pluralism, any style may flourish - but when has architecture been solely a matter of taste? The need to accept the dynamics of change

◀ *Houston, Texas, USA, 1970s: Four Leaf towerblock condominiums, a refuge for the affluent from noise and air pollution in the public space. Such urban solutions afford little opportunity for community development*

THE RESIDENTIAL TOWERBLOCK AND THE URBAN CANVAS In the case of the city, nowhere has the split between architecture and urban development been more evident. It has led to a situation in which the possibility of the former contributing to the latter and vice versa, over a long period of time has suddenly become extremely limited. (*Frampton 1992*) is now an imperative, not just a nice idea. Adopting the global paradigm shift in work patterns ordinary people are in a stronger position to demand better private and community environments through which to enrich their daily lives. With a fresh understanding of their entitlement to a better urban landscape and the protection of natural resources on which life depends, ordinary people can bring about change while architects and urban designers must steer their creative endeavours into greater accountability.

◀ Chicago, Illinois, USA: One Magnificent Mile, symbol of the Age of Consumerism and of an era where the legacy of environmental costs remains an unresolved issue. In a world which is fast changing, new paradigms will demand that architecture and urban environments be more responsive to social and environmental realities

This book attempts to define sustainable architectural design and environmental goals for the New Age. Remedies for the social environment and greater commitment to good stewardship of the dwindling biodiversity of this lonely planet remain critical areas for attitudinal change. Further, to be worthy of its antecedents, New Age architecture should strive to become recognised as another epoch of distinction in the mainstream of architectural history.

The Urban Habitat

Planning and design of the urban setting should aim uncompromisingly at 'enabling' and 'ennobling' environments. Inevitably, this demands a process based on people-driven dynamics, in other words, planning inspired by the perceptions of the users of urban space.

A CANVAS FOR ARCHITECTURE

An architect's task can be likened to a journey with various possible routes along which design goals might be satisfied. Success lies in choosing the right one! As with architecture, the detachment of planners and urban designers from the social needs of communities is epitomised in the poor performance of many urban environments. At best the dismissal of the real needs of the users of the urban environment can be described as prescriptive, and at worst as a crime of social dimensions.

Adopting the line that a response to culture-specific expectations should be the basis for planning policy raises another issue, that of human rights. Ironically, participation by urban dwellers in the shaping of their own habitat is a sphere of human rights that has not yet enjoyed much political accountability. The right to a better environment is germane to greater productivity and development of each individual's potential and that of the community as a whole. Where millions in urban situations are forced to live in close proximity and encounter a form of rivalry for their own space, the cultural expectations of the urban dweller regarding the need for privacy, self-fulfilment, identity, bonding of communities, work options and recreational opportunity have not been given the status they deserve.

Cultural expectations are a well-researched field and found to be cross-cultural and universally unvarying. Why then does planning not begin with the end user?

Universal cultural needs

The universality of cultural needs, or 'universal invariants', is an anthropological fact. Given the right emphasis, such cultural needs can drive the urban design process to more productive environments. In both qualitative aspects and as a reference for physical planning they offer direction to architects and urban designers alike. Broadly, invariants encompass perceptions relating to:

      ▘ the aesthetic quality of the urban setting as perceived by the user;
      ▘ varying degrees of social encounter facilitated by the spatial characteristics of the urban setting;
      ▘ opportunity for kinship and social networking.

> Given the fact that they exist, what is the value of personal places? Just as with other types of settings, personal places help to fulfil basic human needs, especially those of security, identity, social contact and growth.
>
> *Steele (1981)*

⧄ the attributes of the physical environment that promote self-identity for both individuals and communities;

⧄ the identity of the place, expressed through distinctiveness of character, the familiarity and the territorial bonding with a place;

⧄ the ability of the urban environment to function successfully as a peaceful place for residence, social amenity, employment and leisure;

⧄ the degree to which the choice for privacy is made possible, particularly in denser urban environments. Opportunity for privacy is considered essential towards healthy community living and, paradoxically, productive social interaction;

⧄ security and health aspects and the way physical arrangements respond to these needs;

⧄ ways of generating a livelihood and responsive physical arrangements to conduct informal as well as formal business activity;

⧄ opportunities for spontaneous and formal recreation towards the enhancement of the urban experience; and

⧄ the degree to which nature penetrates and softens the urban environment and allows access to the open space system for leisure.

▶ *Bath, Somerset, UK: Shopping precinct. Traffic-free and intimate of scale, suiting the prevailing culture of the place*

◀ *Tabriz, Iran: A vibrant Middle Eastern bazaar, affording shelter, safety and an atmosphere of busy trading*

TRAFFIC-FREE TRADING Traditional commercial spaces take on many forms but most, either roofed or unroofed, offer degrees of social encounter and the security of numbers. The ubiquitous shopping mall of Western societies is of a later generation, removing trading from the high street into energy-consuming interiors.

Barcelona, Spain: Cathedral square in the historic Gotic area enables allcomers to perform spontaneous Catalan folk dancing with the local city dwellers

Cultural needs and urban space

Urban spaces can prompt socially acceptable or unacceptable behavioural responses. Therefore, designing urban space should become the physical manifestation of cultural expectations, of which some are more abstract in character than others. An aesthetically pleasing urban environment is more likely to evoke the right behavioural responses than wrong ones. On the other hand the desire for levels of social interaction within urban social spaces is probably less understood as an imperative in urban planning. Researchers, such as Levi-Strauss (1968) and Hillier and Hanson (1984), conclude that spatial patterning has a great deal to do with degrees of social encounter and that social interaction in fact determines the success or failure of the urban social environment.

In the case of 'self-identity' and 'identity of place' physical manifestations generally take the form of defined territory, sometimes characterised by typical downtown ethnic enclaves - such as the 'chinatown' phenomenon to be found in many of the larger cities of the world. Territoriality can

In urban design, does the exclusion of the space user result in dysfunctional urban environments?

Quite often the Townplanner does not know that in an attempt to create order, he introduces a measure of chaos: or that he approaches some urban problems from a biased and fragmented viewpoint. With his conception highly weighted in favour of who shall approve his plan: the policy-makers, the decision-makers, and people of the planner's social status, the plan often ends up giving advantages to a few people, leaving a large majority of urban dwellers at the mercy of the ambivalent ambience.

Urban planning should therefore be framed in terms of doing the best to coordinate organisational and spatial relationships among urban dwellers who are space users within the city.

Uyanga (1989)

satisfy the urban dweller's perception of social equalness and sense of belonging. Also, the identity of a place suggests architectural space, which in turn helps people to orientate themselves in the urban environment.

A sense of feeling safe in a social space has a profound influence on perceptions of the users. The scale of more traditional compact city layouts served the needs of cultures successfully where mobility was either on foot or that offered by slow-moving horsedrawn vehicles. Compact cities permitted surveillance of the street more readily due to the presence and proximity of neighbours, whereas the fast-moving motor car exploded the city boundaries and the scale of the modern neighbourhood. The result is a diminished sense of security which would otherwise arise from the proximity of neighbours. With the motor car came air pollution which, in some cities, continues to threaten the health standards in urban living. Personal health and safety are two important aspects that tend to influence a community's assessment of the quality of an urban environment.

Paramount to the city dweller's sense of well-being is the personal right to privacy. Significantly, the restorative power of privacy at one end of the spectrum and, by contrast, the escape from monotony through the stimulus of recreative social interaction, relies on the hierarchical spatial ordering of the urban open space system.

Physical distance between home and city amenities largely determines choice and in turn the lifestyle of the urban dweller. Being a quality measured in distance travelled, a positive or negative view of urban life depends on how easily and at what cost distance can be overcome without inhibiting choice. It also depends largely on how the urban movement corridors provide for essential amenities other than transport, as to whether the matter of distance diminishes the urban experience or not. Functionally,

Have shopping malls and theme parks replaced the traditional public realm?

Commentators observe 'that they have become the centre of suburban life and that, sealed from the realities of everyday life, these escapist cocoons have become the new public realm. The privatisation of the urban realm has brought about the thematisation of public space. The ways in which the production of images goes hand in hand with the commodification of the public realm is a contemporary manifestation of lifestyle and liveability, visualised in spaces of conspicuous consumption.

Public spaces are the primary sites of public culture, windows into the city's soul. They are an important means of framing a vision of social life in the city, a vision for both those who live there and for those who visit. They are also important because they are physical and metaphorical spaces of negotiation, continually mediating the boundaries and markers of human society.'

The question for professionals - architects, planners, and all of us involved in the production of the urban environment - is how to deal with these new forms of development.

Marks (2000)

◀ ▲ *Old residential quarter in Seville, Spain: Neighbourhood street and square, an urban pattern repeated in many of the old cities of Europe*

SHARED OUTDOOR SPACE Dense traditional neighbourhoods were invariably endowed with landscaped outdoor space which became an extension of the private living quarters. The absence of the motor vehicle permitted social encounter, and private entrances could be taken directly off the pedestrian street.

apart from being a transportation link, a movement corridor is in effect a social space, generally associated with social and economic opportunity. The typical city morphology is characterised by the linear traffic corridors and activity nodes that are generally hierarchical, much like the veins in the leaf of a plant. In the design of such traffic corridors the potential amenity value should be realised in physical terms as the opportunity they afford should not be underestimated and should be reflected in their character and in their urban design detail. In this context, shopping malls are anathema to the vitality of the conventional street.

All shapers of the urban environment have to ensure that where high density populations are being planned, such environments are viable, tenable and sustainable without compromising any of the spatial quality objectives outlined above. On the other hand, particularly for lower income communities, it can be shown that cultural needs are not easily provided for in high-density/high-rise as distinct from high-density/low-rise development. Due to the nature of high-rise environments, that of elevating people *en masse* in high-rise development, perceptions regarding spatial quality can be negative and many such developments have failed at great social and economic cost. In the search for optimum density levels, inspiration can be drawn from socio-spatial patterning of more culturally responsive historical precedents, where high densities are achieved in low-rise situations without any perceived sacrifice of a community's socio-cultural needs.

A working understanding of cultural influences on urban space, evident in good historical examples, is essential equipment for the urban designer and architect in order to respond positively to societal needs.

The urban ecosystem

The city can be likened to a machine, consuming and squandering enormous quantities of energy and materials, producing mountains of garbage and poisonous emissions into the air which the city dweller breathes.

Concerns are relevant even at a single project level, that of a building project or that of planning for metropolitan-wide services, where the indication is that 'landcape architects, engineers or architects usually have no concept of how their projects will affect the environment of the city as a whole... Planners often work within a single dimension - transportation, sewage treatment, water supply - with only a hazy notion of how their actions relate to other spheres' (Spirn 1984).

Those who live and work in the urban environment experience the fact that cities create microclimates of their own. Man-induced environments can deviate significantly from regional macroclimatic patterns. The degree

---

Does the concept of an urban ecosystem follow a discernible value system?

Christopher Alexander in *A New Theory of Urban Design* (1987) introduces the 'formulation of looking at urban design' and its application. He concludes: When we look at the most beautiful towns and cities of the past, we are always impressed by a feeling that they are somehow organic. This feeling of 'organicness, is not a vague feeling of relationships with biological forms. It is not an analogy. It is instead an accurate vision of specific structural quality which these old towns had...and have. Namely: Each of these towns grew as a whole, under its own laws of wholeness... and we can feel this wholeness, not only at the larger scale but in every detail: in the restaurants, in the sidewalks, in the houses, shops, markets, roads, parks, gardens and walls. Even the balconies and ornaments.

This quality does not exist in towns being built today. And indeed, this quality could [sic] not exist at present because there isn't any discipline which actively sets out to create it. Neither architecture, nor urban design, nor city planning take the creation of this kind of wholeness as their task. So of course it doesn't exist. It does not exist, because it is not being attempted.

City planning definitely does not try to create wholeness. It is merely preoccupied with the implementation of certain ordinances. Architecture is too much preoccupied with the problems of individual buildings. And urban design has a sense of dilettantism: as if the problem could be solved on a visual level, as an aesthetic matter.

▲ *Stockholm, Sweden: Downtown development in the 1950s*

◀ *Dallas, USA: Typical downtown in the 1980s*

URBAN CLIMATES High density modern urban environments contribute substantially to urban heat island and internalise microclimatic conditions that assert their own ecosystem. The situation is exacerbated by dependence on heat-generating and cooling technology for comfort. Such urban environments also show little attention has been given to the need for outdoor social space for the users. Lack of sunlight and excessive shade render natural ecological functions impossible.

of change would depend on the scale, colour and texture of the intervention into the natural environment. Equally important, therefore, to the understanding of urban ecology is a more 'tuned in' understanding of the urban climate.

Koenigsberger (1974) identified and listed specific factors which distinguish the induced urban climate from the regional climate:

⬡ Changed surface qualities, such as pavings and buildings, which increase the absorption of solar radiation and reduce evaporation.

⬡ Buildings cast shadows and act as barriers to wind and create channels which increase wind velocity.

⬡ Building mass stores absorbed heat and releases it slowly at night.

⬡ Surface colour and darkness of tone play a part in heat gain and loss.

⬡ Energy seepage: Through walls and ventilation of heated buildings; the output of refrigeration plants and transfer of heat to outside through airconditioning; heat output of internal combustion engines and electrical appliances; heat loss from industry, especially furnaces and large factories.

⸜ Atmospheric pollution: Waste products of boilers and domestic and industrial chimneys; exhaust from motor cars; fumes and vapours, which both tend to reduce direct solar radiation but increase the diffuse radiation and provide a barrier to outgoing radiation. The presence of solid particles in urban atmosphere may assist in the formation of fog and induce rainfall under favourable conditions. The extent of the deviations may be quite substantial - atmospheric temperature in a city can be 8° C higher than in the surrounding countryside and a difference of as much as 11°C has been reported.

⸜ Wind velocity can be reduced to less than half of that of adjoining open country, but the funnelling effect along a closely built-up street or through gaps between tall slab blocks can be more than double the velocity. Strong turbulences and eddies can also be set up at the leeward corners of obstructions.

Vegetation can have a significant moderating effect. By covering the ground with vegetation, the surface of solar radiation contact is transferred to a higher layer and will reduce the heat gain from four to twelve times due to the textural increase in the foliage. Urban landscaping therefore plays a most significant part in providing a comfortable moderated temperature for the urban dweller.

Viewing the urban environment as an ecosystem can promote a better understanding of how energy and materials are transformed into products, consumed and then transformed into byproducts, such as thermal material and chemical wastes. In a typical situation these are released into the atmosphere or into the ground or into natural streams. The more 'internalised' the system can be, the more resource-efficient it will be. For example, in numerous cases in developed countries, the reclamation of wastes for the heating of entire neighbourhoods has been shown to be economically viable.

The successful functioning of the urban environment is not only dependent on the management of threats to a sustainable ecological balance in the city environment, but also the urban environment must provide amenity for the daily and longterm social needs of the inhabitants. It is instructive

The design and planning professions are part of the problem as well as the solution to address the cumulative negative effects of developing within the city.

In the *The Granite Garden* (1984), Spirn observes that 'unfortunately tradition has set the city against nature, and nature against the city... This attitude has aggravated and even created many of the city's environmental problems: poisoned air and water; depleted or irretrievable resources; more frequent or more destructive floods; increased energy demands and higher construction and maintenance costs than existed prior to urbanisation; and in many cities a pervasive ugliness... The city must be seen as part of nature and designed accordingly.'

▼ *The rigidity of typical engineering solutions to settlement, where cost of services is a prime factor that determines the layout*

▲ ◀ *Crossroads in Cape Town, South Africa: The rich visual texture of an informal settlement showing distinct organic desire lines rather than a planned gridlike structuring of space*

SPONTANEOUS SETTLEMENT Informal settlements generally show distinct spatial systems that meet the urbanising needs of squatter populations. Typical of conventional planning are the grid like engineering solutions to formalise the settlement of the urbanising masses, often devoid of any gesture to socially essential functions.

to research traditional examples of urban settlement in response to custom and culture which display distinct spatial patterning.

Socio-spatial patterning

Socio-spatial patterning, strikingly evident in historical and even in contemporary informal settlement (most often expressed physically through its spontaneity of character), presents the urban designer with useful insights. Yet, in contemporary urban design and planning there is a general unwillingness to move away from conventional planning that favours the motor car, and architectural approaches that make statements unrelated to social needs. This situation is presumptuous and prescriptive.

To illustrate socio-spatial patterning, in emergent Africa today the urbanising communities, the vast majority of whom are without adequate resources, incline towards their own familiar traditions based on functional and practical needs and, with striking resourcefulness, tend to pattern their own environments. The patterns are invariably dense. Even in formally planned settlements adjoining modern cities, various ingenious physical transformations by the occupants become evident, for instance dwellings fronting onto movement corridors become opportunities for setting up trading activities in the low income sector. The physical manifestations of squatting and sharing space emerge from a logical response to the limited resources available to whole communities. Spontaneous layouts of such settlements express direct relationships to cultural needs while at the same time the need for environmental solutions is catered for. For instance, striking examples of urban patterns are found in settlements of remote, harsher climatic regions of undeveloped parts of the world. As a useful starting point, such spatial patterns should be an inspiration for those who formally shape new urban environments.

How should present day and future socio-spatial patterning respond to changed cultural paradigms?

In *Architecture for the Future* (1996) Jean Nouvel states:

'Much has been built, and in an utterly haphazard way. Conscientious architects have repeatedly criticised this state of affairs. But what have they proposed instead? Solutions are either too clinical, like Le Corbusier's Cite Radieuse, ecological, like Frank Lloyd Wright's Broadacre City, or plastic, like De Stijl's colour and form chart.

In fact, since the 15th century invention of the city as an architectural object, history has repeatedly demonstrated that the city lends itself less and less to an overall plan; that, on the contrary, it is the result of economic forces operating in a given territory, forces which brook no resistance, least of all that of aesthetic or humanistic *a priori* themes.

Architecture must try to take into account the free flow of images, miniaturisation, automation, speed, the conquest of space, and the emerging symptoms of a new popular culture (rap music, sport, etc.). Nouvel's architecture emphasises material and light over the interplay of volume and space. It tends to dissolve the materiality of the world in a subtle combination of reflections, refractions, superimpositions, dilutions, flashing signs and moving colours. The concept of architecture is going through a process of massive change, barely discernible amidst the haze and dust clouds raised by the urban cataclysm that has struck our planet. Population explosion, industrial revolution and its direct consequences, urban encroachment on rural areas, the global market and global communication with their burgeoning networks: these are some of the reasons which explain why, in the 20th century, four or five times more buildings have been built than in the entire previous course of human history.

The transformation is profound, and the scope of architecture has been considerably extended. Today, the built fabric, which has grown up despite appalling conditions, is the visible consequence of an accelerated sedimentation. The facts stare us in the face: the inevitable has become a reality. Once again, topos (Gr: place) has taken place over logos (Gr: reckoning). New building has been designed in difficult conditions, with barely a thought; the definitive criterion has been above all sheer urgency'.

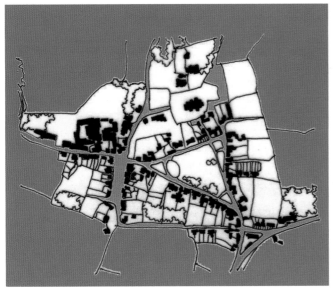

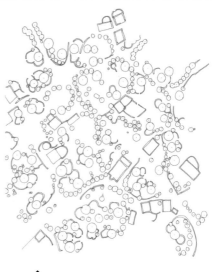

▲ Whittlesea village, UK

◆ Labbèzanga village,

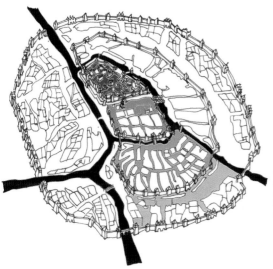

◀ Thumbprint image of early Moscow: The evolving and organic pattern of a city that continually outgrew its original defensive walls around the Kremlin and Red Square in the centre, and accepted in its heart the imprint of Time to determine the present day character

INDIGENOUS SOCIO-SPATIAL PATTERNS All cultures unwittingly display similar spatial patterning and 'organicness' in the physical structuring of their places of habitation. In practice, conventional planning has neither recognised nor exploited the significant link between culture and spatial organisation.

The urban dwellers' appreciation of spatial quality in built environments is visual and practical, and appears to be best served by the neat ordering of elements in terms of interrelationships that show spatial 'organisation'. A common pattern language is evident in all cultures and some notable commentators conclude that 'towns and buildings will not be able to come alive unless they are made by all the people in society and unless these people share a common pattern language' (Alexander et al. 1977).

Depending on the degree of intervention and regulatory planning principles, people arrange space locating themselves in relation to one another 'with greater or lesser degree of aggregation or separation, engendering patterns of movement and encounter that may be dense or sparse within or between different groupings. Second, a community will arrange social space by means of buildings, boundaries, paths, markers, zones and so on, so that the physical milieu of that society also takes on a definite pattern' (Hillier & Hanson 1984). In studies of the phenomenon of spatial patterning, other researchers inverse the order of their analysis and study social and mental processes through what they term 'the crystallised external projections of the process'.

In his search for 'a form that is common to the various manifestations of social life' Levi-Strauss (1968) described as 'authentic' those societies found traditionally in the Middle East, Africa and Europe. Some vivid examples of patterning occur in the layout of older cities and the house types to be found in them. A high degree of commonality often characterises a homogeneous society through the collective dynamic; alternatively, the realities of resource constraints placed on a culture lead to certain outcomes. Two typical examples of such indigenous cities are the old walled city of Delhi and the old city of Baghdad, both of which demonstrate very graphically the attributes of spatial patterning in high-density conurbations and at the same time reflect the socio-economic and a highly developed, 'pre-modern technology' enterprise of the inhabitants. These two cities embody qualities of spatial organisation and urban design worthy of further

The cosmetic treatment of urban spaces renders them ill-shaped and ill-planned for public use.

Urban designers, such as Trancik in *Finding Lost Space* (1986), are outspoken about the issue of 'fitness for purpose':

The usual process of urban development treats buildings as isolated objects sited in the landscape, not as part of the larger fabric of streets, squares, and viable open space. Decisions about growth patterns are made from two-dimensional land-use plans, without considering the three-dimensional relationships between buildings and spaces and without a real understanding of human behaviour. In this all too common process, urban space is seldom even thought of as an exterior volume with properties of shape and scale and with connections to other spaces. Therefore, what emerges in most environmental settings today is unshaped antispace.

▶ *Old walled city of Delhi, India: The black shaded areas represent the voids in a dense fabric of buildings affording shade and security for the inhabitants*

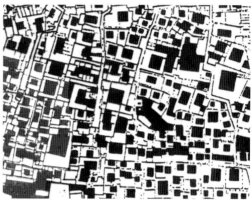

▼ *Old city of Baghdad, Iraq: A hierarchy of pedestrianways leading to courtyard houses, thereby meeting the public and private spatial needs of an urban culture*

DENSE MATRIX OF SPACES AND BUILDINGS Historically evolved cities often embody qualities of spatial organisation and urban design worthy of further in depth study, especially today where higher density living is likely to become the pattern for future urbanisation.

in depth study, especially today where higher density living is likely to become the pattern for urbanisation in the New Age. Although the old walled city of Delhi is in a state of disrepair, this does not reflect on the spirit of the community living there. The city is a working example of a dense, 'self-contained community deriving its great strength from the fact that its structure is a logical outgrowth of viable sets of social and economic rules governing group and individual behaviour' (Fonseca, 1976). In the Mohalla (or residential quarter) of the walled city of Delhi, spatial pattern is expressed in what appears to an outside observer as dark voids between buildings. This belies the real qualities of the environment. Beyond the dark narrow lanes bounded by blank walls are sunny, airy courtyards where private activity can take place. The urban pattern therefore protects the residents by means of two spatial envelopes before a public space is entered, so that social behaviour adjusts from first degree privacy, the interior courtyard; to second degree privacy, the lane outside the door; to third degree privacy, the public square.

Other physical forms of patterning can be more subtle and yet equally significant. Work done on the spatial patterning of the Vaucluse villages of France uses a technique which represents, quantifies and interprets the social origins of spatial design and identifies consistencies in a repetitive 'syntax' (Hillier & Hanson1984). In the traditional village of a region in Africa spatial patterning has been shown to originate from 'philosophical thought' and the 'laws of nature' (Hull 1976).

It is worthy of interest to note that, although spatial patterning is configured culture-specifically and is by nature diverse, a rather basic social space, that is essentially a well-sited uncluttered space, might spontaneously become a venue for creative lifestyle opportunities, and not be considered sterile space to the users. The criterion for success in urban social space is therefore, rather the spatial opportunity afforded for the diverse needs of urban living than overdesign or overplanning. Over time city or town people often place their own stamp on favourite urban spaces through institutional or commercial upgrading, generally in direct response to custom, economic survival, sentiment or habitual usage.

Movement corridors and destinations

Significantly, in the study of socio-spatial patterning the physical embodiment of social custom and functional need is very largely expressed in the urban movement corridors, which are the streets, pedestrian lanes and trafficable open spaces.

In physical terms the urban movement systems in fact represent a cultural storyboard comprised of a hierarchical network of spatial corridors. The differentiated parts and functions are dependent on this circulatory system without which there would be no city. In essence it follows that social

---

Urban ecology deals with sustainable relationships in city development, restructuring, productivity, communication and social life.

At present Denmark has a number of urban ecology projects that have been carried out. To this must be added that the urban ecological way of thinking is influencing both urban renewal and urban construction to an increasing extent.

In 1993 the Danish Minister for the Environment appointed a Consultative Committee on Urban Ecology. The Committee consisted of representatives from different sectors: the Ministries of Energy, Housing, Transport and Environment, the research institutions and the municipalities. The Committee defines the concept, urban ecology: 'Urban ecology describes a particular environmental effort which takes its point of departure in the environmental state of a specific urban area and in citizen participation, while seeking to develop overall solutions to problems connected with the area's resource consumption, environmental impact, and nature. Thus urban ecology focuses on a given

PLACE (a building, a settlement, a neighbourhood, an area, or in principle a whole town) and on a a given group of citizens.'

The Committee recommended a number of ways in which urban ecology in Denmark could be advanced: an urban ecology subsidy scheme could be established; an initial number of larger urban ecology projects for demonstration could be planned and carried out; and a national urban ecology knowledge and presentation centre could be established.

Toward the implementation of urban ecology initiatives, the Ministries established the 'Green Foundation' together with a plan of action largely in the fields of private and social housing. The many urban ecology projects within construction and within the existing housing stock, show that there is both a local and national will to implement projects of benefit to the environmental globally and to human beings locally.

Munkstrup (1995)

ESSENTIALLY FOR MOVEMENT
The rigidity of urban movement corridors will satisfy only some of the cultural needs of a dense urban population - mobility and access. The absence of hierarchical ranking of the traffic routes will distribute the influence of the motor vehicle too evenly through the urban fabric thereby inhibiting the development of amenity and a sense of neighbourhood.

▲ *London: Tower Bridge terminus of the elevated metroline to Canary Wharf: Modern day 'quickfix' expediency to override the discipline of the outdated urban fabric. The loss of spatial quality at ground level is significant*

▶ *Athens, Greece : Focussed on the Port of Piraeus, rigid trafficways lacking hierarchy ignore socio-spatial needs and yield to the tyranny of the motor vehicle*

spaces are integral, nodal and interfacial within this circulatory system of urban settlement. To conceptualise social spaces according to a framework employing the movement corridors and providing them with a social importance and character would be to emulate the success in the layouts of many historic cities.

Simplistically and generally, the components forming the movement systems are hierarchical; some are corridors and others destinations, but both can potentially provide amenity to the urban dweller. All can have distinctive cognitive associations, either private or public.

Stylised, and broadly expressed in ascending order of scale and intensity of use, the urban spatial network elements can be characterised as follows:

- Private social space.
- Open space between buildings.
- The building edge to the street.
- The neighbourhood street or square.
- The street corner.
- The main street.
- The primary street system.
- Natural features.

Private open space is exclusive space, part of the home environment or shared social space of a residential grouping that offers a transitional frontage to the public. Varying degrees of privacy can be achieved through discreet planning configurations.

Open spaces between buildings form an uninterrupted continuum of space, often neglected, that offers design opportunity and amenity potential within the urban fabric and can significantly contribute to the quality of other social spaces. Such residual space, often the interface between neighbours, is equally important as the street for spontaneous communication and civic behaviour. There should be no spaces lost to the community within the urban fabric.

The building edge to social space to a large extent determines the aesthetic and functional qualities of social space. This can take on many forms such as arcaded pavements, stoeps, canopies, awnings or a simple recess in a facade. The potential for social usage of a street or square is linked and enhanced by the architectural character of the building edge.

The neighbourhood streets and squares are important in the urban fabric affording communication, identity and orientation within and between neighbourhoods. Urban form is diverse and varies in character and texture according to the extent of intrusion by the motor vehicle. Entries to properties are invariably off streets or squares, but gateways to neighbourhoods are useful devices to define exclusivity.

The street corner is the confluence of both vehicle and pedestrian movement and therefore usually more intensively trafficked than other urban spaces. Characterised by unusual opportunity for commercial enterprise and social encounter, each junction can become a well-defined 'place'. In the secondary urban movement system, the street corner can invite intensive social interaction. At a primary level it can develop into a main square surrounded by public institutions or become a trading node in the commercial heart of a city.

▲ *Bloomsbury, London: A street of Georgian row houses linking treed city squares*

TRANSPORTATION LINKS AS SETTINGS Three famous cities, London, Amsterdam and Venice, where the building edges to the social space range from the conventional street, to the quaylined canal, to complete water frontages. Each situation affords distinctive character for which each city ahs become recognised universally. In all cases a rich urban canvas is afforded, as demonstrated by the excellent quality of the architecture.

▲ *Amsterdam, Holland: Over centuries the network of 'grachte' has satisfied both the commercial and social needs of the citizens as well as that of transportation*

▶ *Venice, Italy: The almost total dependence on water transport has determined the way of life of the city and provided a unique and successful urbanscape on water. The close-fronting on the canals provides an unusual canvas to which the architecture has responded in a time-honoured way*

Traditionally the main street is afforded distinctive status in neighbourhoods or in small-town life. High up on the status structure, the main street can be a source of local pride and is typically a centre of activity, of culture, education, social intercourse and might serve the locational needs of institutions and commerce. Offering social encounter and cultural status, a sense of identity within the urban milieu, the main street plays an important role in the quality of urban life. Such streets should be provided with wide pavements for safe pedestrian passage together with a high degree of access for vehicles, particularly public transport that is congruent with its functional efficacy.

Primary streets from the main urban arterial infrastructure usually provide for a fast traffic movement corridor, to serve neighbourhoods. They are scaled and relate firstly to the needs of vehicles rather than people. As a link with the wider freeway network of the city or town, they are capable of sustaining both the flow of vehicles and providing cross-urban mobility and interaction within a metropole. For large scale movement of goods and people primary arteries require to be well planned and can contribute to the quality of the urban experience through providing fast and convenient access to destinations. Some of the more memorable examples of the freeway genre are attractively landscaped to mitigate the impact of hectares of hard surfaces and even to promote linear habitats. Linkages such as verges in the primary street system can act as corridors along which animal and plant life can exist and flourish.

Natural features lend meaningful relief in the urban environment by adding to the quality of life of the urban user. Natural features enable the creation of islands or lungs for ecological diversity with good potential for recreation, depending on their scale. Natural areas can become the extension of the surrounding rural areas into the urban fabric.

The social success of the urban canvas expressed through the open space system depends on the response of city management not only to the cultural forces at work, but also to the extent to which social amenity is achieved through architectural responsiveness to that canvas.

DIRECTIONS IN ARCHITECTURE

In the context of our environmentally stressed planet, it is not responsible to think of architecture as being 'good' only in terms of past design maxims.

CHARACTERISATION

Directions in architecture are not readily discernible without the benefit of hindsight. Accepting the imperative of a strong-minded ethos, the philosophical integrity of architecture would be better served if it acknowledged the example of architectural history. In that way lessons from past ages of architecture might provide a useful platform from which a 'New Age' architecture - responsive and responsible and more concerned with the pressing social and environmental issues of today - could emerge.

There have been many prominent commentators on architecture from Vitruvius to Ruskin, to contemporaries like Krier, Venturi, Jencks, Frampton and many others. The architectural roots of the past are essential for its continuity of growth as a creative form; however, in the context of our environmentally stressed planet, it is irresponsible to think of architecture as being 'good' only in terms of past design maxims, i.e. focusing solely on the visual qualities of a building or perhaps its functional performance, at the exclusion of all else. Nor, with trends towards new democratic empowerment, the pressing needs of the urbanising masses globally and modern urban stress, is anyone entitled the think about architecture as exclusive. There is a tendency in latter years, ironically even in parts of the newly developing world, where socially responsive architecture is arguably

◀ *New Haven, USA: Yale University Art and Architecture building (1958-64): Architect Paul Rudolph's bold expression of the secondary elements, such as 'lifts, staircases and escalators, chimneys, ducts and garbage chutes'*

You employ stone, wood and concrete, and with these materials you build houses, and palaces; that is construction. Ingenuity is atwork... But suddenly you touch my heart, you do me good, I am happy and I say:

'This is beautiful. That is architecture. Art enters in.'

Corbusier (1923)

the most needed towards enhancement of the urban experience. Yet the designer's inclination remains removed from the real needs of the end user.

The impoverishment of the architectural aesthetic, in the context of twentieth century design language, has come about partly due to a differing ordering of priorities. For example, compare the contemporary penchant of expressing the secondary elements, 'such as ramps, walkways, lifts, staircases, escalators, chimneys, ducts and garbage chutes' (Frampton 1996) with classical architecture, where such features were concealed behind the facade and the main body was freed to express itself.

In their critical analyses of architectural trends in world architecture, highly regarded commentators have to some extent skewed the goals towards any meaningful transformational ethos. Taken out of context, describing 'our great heroes are our global architects' based on 'the creations of today's global architects are symbols of its maturity' (Pawley 1998) can be misleading as to the role that architecture needs to play in enriching

◀ *Egypt: Temple architecture, the timeless icon upholding the belief in deities in ancient Egypt*

▶ *Coventry, UK: Rebuilding of the cathedral, by architect Basil Spence, symbolised the spirit of a nation recovering from World War 2*

▶ *Rome, Italy: The C o l o s s e u m, classical icon of imperial power and suppression*

CLASSICAL ICONS The look of architectural icons, timeless monuments or public art works from ancient to modern, reflecting the 'artistic-intellectual' expression of vernacular building in response to the cultural or religious needs of their place and times.

VISION

ARCHITECTURE TO BE RECLAIMED BY SOCIETIES AT LARGE TO MEET CHANGED CULTURAL AND ENVIRONMENTAL PARADIGMS

VISION

PROTECTION OF THE NATURAL WORLD AND GLOBAL RESOURCES AND DEVELOPMENT COMMITTED TO AN ENVIRONMENTAL ETHOS

(Left margin, bottom to top): DESPOTIC RULE/DYNASTIC POWER — OLD AND NEW DEMOCRACIES/ANARCHY/THE SOVEREIGN INDIVIDUAL — SOCIAL, CULTURAL, ECONOMIC, POLITICAL INFLUENCES - ENVIRONMENTAL PRESSURES - DECLINE IN URBAN QUALITY OF LIFE

(Right margin, bottom to top): MANUAL LABOUR AND CRAFTS — INFORMATION AND OTHER ADVANCED TECHNOLOGIES — TECHNICAL AND TECHNOLOGICAL INFLUENCES - ESCALATING ENERGY DEMANDS, RESOURCE DEPLETION - GLOBAL WARMING

Social / Cultural influences (left)	Period (central stem)	Technical / Technological influences (right)
	NEW AGE ? 2000+	
Reaction to the Modern Movement as practised by later exponents. Replaced by a culture of individuality of self-indulgent, eclectic manifestations. No declaration of intent regarding pressing contemporary environmental issues	**POST-MODERN** c1980	Non-canonic variety of solutions, adherence to irrational, elitist and exhibitionistic designs with little regard for affordability, sustainability or structural rationality
Prime architectural symbol no longer the dense brick but the open box - free plan flexibility. Rudiments and initial principles of modern architecture betrayed	**INTERNATIONAL STYLE** 1925-	Skeleton construction enveloped by a curtain wall, typified by the tower block on podium
Architectural ideology of unadorned 'form follows function', 'less is more' - purism in simplicity, machine aesthetic, anti-metaphor - utopian with architect as 'saviour/doctor'	**MODERN MOVEMENT** c1920+	First serious confrontation of art with the machine characterised by the 'Depreciation of material that results from the treatment by machine'
Proclamation of the Weimar Bauhaus programme by Gropius envisaged the encompassing of architecture, sculpture and art like the 'crystal symbols of a new faith'	**BAUHAUS** 1919-1932	A culture of teaching of crafts for designing for mass production - collaboration with existing industrial enterprises for mutual stimulation
Collective of European architects believed that 'to raise our culture to a higher level, we are forced... to change our architecture' by introducing glass architecture. Free form and rational prefabricated construction shown as incompatible	**EUROPEAN EXPRESSIONISM** 1910-1925	Promotion of glass to 'elevate culture' leading to strides in development of glass technology
Style inspired by the William Blake Arts and Crafts tradition - cultural acceptance of the use of the machine in design and the expression of symbolism are striking	**ART NOUVEAU** c1880-c1910	Extensive use of the tensility of iron with glass in public and domestic architecture freeing space with iron superstructures over walled enclosures
Territorial transformations 1800-1909: Urban development upgrading to utopian communities. Rising bourgeoisie	**NEO-CLASSICAL** 1750-1900	Steam power, the iron frame, trade with the New World. Technical transformations and development in structural engineering 1775-1939
Reaction to blind worship of Vitruvian rules. A new freedom and desire for originality of style and carved ornament. The movement commenced in Italy	**BAROQUE** 18C-19C	Freedom demanded from orthodoxy of plan, design and ornament. Columns crafted with twisted shafts, surmounted by clumsy curved pediments
Religious and social activity in Europe affected by the invention of printing, use of gunpowder, mariner's compass and immigration of Greeks into Europe. A spirit of enquiry and freedom of thought, energised by intellectual vigour - Classical styles triumph	**RENAISSANCE** 15C-18C	Classical orders ruled. Walls of ashlar masonry laid horizontally, often rusticated - openings with semicircular arches - roofs vaulted with no ribs
Rise of monastic communities - the power of the Pope supreme - the Church became wealthy and clergy proliferated. Growth of towns, commercial activity and rivalry - wealth	**GOTHIC** 12C-16C	Throughout Europe climate varied influencing the choice of detailing - use of materials varied - pointed arch became the structural 'truth'
Decline in Roman power. Civil government and military protection. New states and nations formed in previous colonies in western Europe. Rise of religious enthusiasm and churches, feudal tenure	**ROMANESQUE** 8C-12C	New construction principle - structural equilibrium. Heavy cross-vaulting evolved into lighter 'rib and panel'. Glass in general use during the 9th C - small fenestration in the south and large in the north
Christianity became the state religion of Roman Empire and power moved to Byzantium, Greece, thereby influencing architectural style	**BYZANTINE** 4C-15C+	Architectural forms usually domical on square or polygonal plans - shaded colonnades. Clay for bricks, rubble for concrete, finished in marble
Emperor Constantine - Christianity modelled on Roman basilicas for worship thereby retaining some pagan features	**EARLY CHRISTIAN** 4C-12C	Recycled ruins of Roman buildings and adaptation of fragments quarried from the past
Romans were empire builders with administrative skills - colonisation through conquest - spread of influence of pantheon of deities under the Emperor - love of justice expressed through basilicas. Amphitheatres for contests between man and wild beasts	**ROMAN** 1C BC-4C	Crafted exponents of classical orders. Abundance of marble and stone - terracotta and brick in use - development of concrete and the vault with the Estruscan arch. Regional climate influenced diversity
Symmetry of philosophical thought - artistic sense of harmony and simplicity - worship of deities - colonisation. Buildings were public monuments	**GREEK** 30C-1C BC	Clearcut architectural style through love of precise forms. Structures limited to short spans. Outdoors favoured as expessed in the agora
Culture founded on deities - spiritual belief. Human resource exploited by overlords to build massive royal monuments. Mathematical skills, metaphysical, geological and climatic perceptiveness	**EGYPTIAN** 50C-1C BC	Timeless legacy of eternal pyramidical royal burial chambers. Temples of massive walls, sturdy closely spaced columns and flat roofs. Machineless technical craft. Astronomical knowledge

39

MAIN STEM OF WESTERN ARCHITECTURAL HISTORY AND MAJOR INFLUENCES

▲ *Houston, USA: Transio Tower, early 1980s: Acres of glass curtainwalling typifying the commercial solution and image of corporate capitalism*

▶ *Chicago, USA: Hyatt Regency O'Hare hotel, 1967-71*

the lives of ordinary people. Other disciplines aligned to architecture have sought to capture the essence of 'good architecture' from their vertical, as distinct from a more lateral, perspective. In attempting to define the criteria by which architecture should be judged as either 'good' or 'bad' can become a dangerously selective vision where, in fact, even august representative bodies such as the Royal Fine Art Commission of the United Kingdom (1996) should know better. In not considering the serious breakdown globally of urban social life today, it is with some amazement that even that influential Commission lists the most important design tenets as those based purely on 'order and unity', 'expression', 'integrity', 'plan and section', 'detail' and 'integration'! In its manifesto

'The post-war spread of the International Style signalled its decline as the pursuit of 'pure' architecture mercilessly exposed mediocrity. Few could match Mies van der Rohe and mute curtain-wall facades were soon worn-out clichés. The rehabilitation of form was heralded by Robert Venturi. In two seminal works - two 'gentle manifestos' - Complexity and Contradiction in Architecture and Learning from Las Vegas, Venturi revalorised an architecture that was rich, inclusive and 'impure', deriving its references both from history and from emerging, vibrant, popular culture... Venturi was, perhaps unwittingly, among those responsible for bringing architecture back down to earth, and for putting an end to the discipline's relative autonomy. Then came Ronchamp chapel in the French Jura, which astonished the public..... Le Corbusier, apostle for the machine for living in, author of the ode to the right angle, had produced this complicated, generous and sensual building, full of folds and curves. Architecture was awakening from a long sleep; it shook itself and gazed around and realised that the world was changing. It rediscovered its affinity with the visual arts and evolution over the past century.'

Nouvel (1996)

a commitment to a social and environmental ethos, essential in responsible contemporary architecture, is conspicuous by its absence. Does this elitist attitude generally typify a lack of vision for architecture in the New Age? Will architecture continue to be sacrificed on the altar of the current global myopia about real societal needs? How widespread is this malaise of exclusivity, propagated in the rarefied halls of the privileged? What is the remedy?

Although aimed at furthering a more committed social and environmental ethos, missing yet so essential in responsible architecture, the main thread of this essay is not aimed at diminishing the importance of the aesthetic form. In sharper focus, architecture does deserve the highest pedestal, rising above purely perfunctory technological and material practicalities.

Classical, Vernacular and Modernism

In a treatise on *Classical Architecture and Vernacular Building* (1990), Krier draws distinctions between the cultures of two familiar traditions to feed the discussion on their quintessential differences. Krier observes:

Classical and Vernacular cultures are concerned with producing objects of long-term use against short-term consumption. Classical and Vernacular contrast the collective and the individual, the monuments and the urban fabric, the palace and the house, the public and the domestic.

Classical architecture is the artistic-intellectual culture of the vernacular building. As an Art it is concerned with imitating nature in its principles of beauty and permanence by means of a limited number of symbols and analogies. Classical architecture is a language of construction and tectonic logic; no more no less. It articulates, expresses and adorns construction. Contents other than construction are expressed by other means like architectural sculpture, painting and inscription.

The condition of Architecture to exist as a Public Art is to attain material and above all aesthetic permanence. It is concerned solely with the erection of public buildings, halls and monuments, with the construction and decoration of squares and public places.

Public Art belongs in the public realm, and it thus can reflect the state of socio-cultural health in a society. The path of history is strewn with 'public art' mementoes of autocrats of past times, which when the political order changes, come crashing down at the behest of the ordinary man. The embellishment of public space is not meant to be the canvas for demigods to revere their swollen images, but a place for communities to bring a sense of ownership, through public art, into their urban habitat.

Vernacular building is the manual-artisan culture of building, based on tectonic logic. As a craft it is concerned with the construction of domestic structures, workshops, dwellings, warehouses as well as engineering works. In general vernacular building is concerned with the erection and maintenance of the the urban fabric, of the buildings-blocks forming the streets of the city, its walls and its bridges. Building is a craft culture which consists in the repetition of a limited number of types and in their adaptation to local climates materials and custom.

Krier goes on to explore further distinctions showing what two rooted architectural forms indeed are, and what they are not.

Classical architecture and Modernist architecture are contradictory, antinomic and incompatible propositions - the former based on artisan artistic productions, the latter on industrial modes of production. The Classical denotes the mature, the best, it attains the highest quality and belongs to artistic culture. The term 'industrial' denotes the necessary; it attains a profitable quantity and belongs to material culture. Transcending questions of style, period and culture, Classical architecture qualifies the totality of monumental architecture based on the fundamental principles of Vitruvian 'venustas, firmitas, utilitas' translated into modern terminology as 'harmony/beauty, stability/ permanence, utility/comfort'. These terms are unconditionally interdependent and their links are exploded in Modernism.

Crucible of a most important doctrine giving impetus to the Modernist movement was the *Proclamation of the Weimar Bauhaus of 1919*, with its statement of mission and intent:

Let us create a new guild of craftsmen, without the class distinctions which raise an arrogant barrier between craftsman and artist. Together let us conceive and create the new building of the future, which will embrace architecture and sculpture and painting in one unity and which will rise one day toward heaven from the hands of millions of workers like the crystal symbol of a new faith.

In the promotion of 'environmentalism' in architecture its historical place as a visual art form, a sculpture, a machine for living, a sanctuary, should not, must not, be ignored lest it is no longer architecture.

In setting out to understand the elements of 'good architecture', it is instructive to learn about important ideological and stylistic distinctions, for example differences in aesthetics, cultural purpose and durability, that are to be found in architecture over the ages. A working understanding of the social, economic, political, technical and environmental primers for design expression is essential to perpetuate robustness in the noble art of creating architecture.

By re-examining the catalystic origins of the Modern Movement, and taking a retrospective view of nineteenth century Neo-Classical architecture, certain significant indicators become apparent. The Neo-Classical period comprised 'two closely related lines of the development: The Structural Classicism of Labrouste and the Romantic Classicism of Schinkel' (Frampton 1992). The former school tended to concentrate on prisons, hospitals and railway stations using wrought and cast iron liberally, whereas the latter concentrated rather more on museums, libraries and monuments, indicating the typological association with purpose. Whereas these two lines, nineteenth century Structural and Romantic Classicism existed side by side, the Modern Movement tended toward the former, to the exclusion of the latter. Decoration became anathema to the fundamental tenets of the Modern Movement and eventually the over clinical nature of Modernism spawned the contemporary but reactionary and metaphorical Post-Modernists into being.

Curiously, although there was general disillusionment with the legacy of Modernism, a phenomenon known colloquially as 'High-Tech' burst out like a rash in the 1970s. It was closer to expressing the use of machine-based elements in architecture than had been ever been propagated by the original Modernists. Essentially a nuts-and-bolts industrial aesthetic adopted for use in residences, workplaces and even public buildings, it was populist and trendy and the variations within its influence are still finding a place in the design repertoires of today. So the machine alone was not always popularly perceived as the cause of Modernism's decline.

A new kind of architecture

When modern architecture took shape in the early twenties of the last century, it laid claim to be a new kind of architecture: an objective design discipline, free from stylistic impulse and a concern for mere appearance, dealing instead with an underlying process of enablement where human activities could be released into their natural physical complement. The attempt to reduce human requirements into the merely physical was justified on two main grounds; in the first place the organisational pattern of the biological construction, as in the hexagonal structure of the honeycomb, was thought to be wonderful in itself, and it was this directness between cause and effect which was to be emulated in human constructions.

Maxwell and Stern (eds) (1978)

Modern Architecture, which wanted to play its part in the liberation of mankind by creating a new environment to live in, was transformed into a giant enterprise for the degradation of the human habitat... [the perpetrators] were the architects of trade unions, cooperatives and socialist municipalities [which were] enlisted in the services of the commercial bourgeoisie

Frampton (1996)

Considering that we live in an age where we are totally dependent on the machine and the computer, it would be illogical to expect that our architecture should not derive creative expression from those technologies. Far more important to the attainment of good architecture, is how well we manage the other influential forces (apart from the machine) at our disposal. The West in particular understands environmental economics and enjoys wealth, profound knowledge, technological skills, political empowerment and a relatively much wider freedom of choice than ever before. A critical analysis of where architecture stands needs to examine how we create our living environment so as to respond to threats to health from urban stress and pollution, to environmental destruction, social and human dysfunction. Had the much pilloried Modernist formula provided the inspiration for addressing the negative onslaughts in the urban experience, then it would not have emerged as an architecture of failure. Instead it wrote its own sentence, and in most of the Western world was 'thrown out with the bathwater' by the Post-Modernists, the proponents of subsequent eclectic trends.

In North America, towards the end of the nineteenth century, the stylistic shift away from classicism reflected the new emerging architectural philosophy. It was a period accompanied by liberating engineering technologies. Steel could became the framework for large structures, while the advances in concrete inspired freedom in architectural and engineering design.

During this milieu, and accepting the advantages afforded by the new technological developments, Frank Lloyd Wright was exploring a distinctive grammar of ornament, convinced that a new character was needed in architecture for the growing egalitarian society and that historicist styles

◄ *Barcelona, Spain: The Barcelona Pavilion, 1928-29, by Modernist Mies van der Rohe: Demolished in 1930 and rebuilt to the original design in 1959, it epitomised the new order of Modernism. Sometimes the model has been described as being without practical purpose, and on the other hand as an 'icon of the Modern Movement' due to its freeing of the plan of structural considerations. Apart from structural considerations, through dogmatic functionalism the Modenists set out to liberate architecture from the pseudo-Classical chains of the past*

◀ ▲ *Oak Park, Illinois, USA: F. L. Wright's houses: Thomas House, 1901 and Heurtley House, 1902. Lloyd Wright was regarded as a Modernist, yet he sought to include ornament and style alongside the use of machine technology. Wright believed that the machine could be used intelligently, 'in accordance with its own laws, as an agent for abstraction and purification - processes by which architecture may be redeemed from the ravages of industrialisation'*

from other continents were inappropriate. Later this review of the established order was the route chosen by other strong proponents for change.

In Europe and North America, the founders and practitioners of the Modernist order, Gropius, Le Corbusier, van der Rohe, liberated architecture from the pseudo-Classical chains of its past and opened vistas of creativity through a utopian cocktail of presumptious idealism, deterministic ideology, and dogmatic functionalism. Niemeyer in South America was engaged in exploring the intrinsic plasticity of concrete and shell-like forms to overthrow the constraints of traditional materials and shapes. Unfortunately practitioners of Modernism saw themselves as 'prophets' or 'healers' who embarked on projects to redevelop the established urban fabric with slab and point block structures, most often sited within extensive soulless landscapes.

From our more distant vantage point in time, the Weimar Proclamation of the Bauhaus of 1919 persuasion reads more like a 'settling the scores'

Can the impoverishment of the city be laid at the door of the architecture of expediency, serving solely economic efficiency and political ends?

Frampton in *Modern Architecture* (1996) observes that while all arts are in some degree limited by the means of their production and reproduction, this is doubly so in the case of architecture, which is conditioned not only by its own technical methods but also by productive forces lying outside itself. Nowhere has this been more evident than in the case of the city, where the split between architecture and urban development has led to a situation in which the possibility of the former contributing to the latter and vice versa, over a long period of time, has suddenly become extremely limited.

of long-standing social and political division, reconciling differences between the artists (intellectuals) and craftsmen (hand skills), which prevailed at the time, rather than the birth of a major architectural ideology. From the Bauhaus emerged a recognisable approach, 'from which emphasis was placed on deriving from productive method, material constraint and programmatic necessity' (Frampton 1992). Gropius, whose tenure as director from 1919 to 1928 saw the institution progress through various influences, proclaimed that the definitive philosophy for architecture was that 'A: permanence + B: comfort + C: beauty' should be rewritten as A + B = C, i.e. beauty is expressed through true functionality only. Stylistically Modernism was 'anti' in terms of ornament, representation, historic memory, humour and symbolism basing its faith in the high-rise or point block, asymmetry and regularity. It produced an international style, lacking in either recognisable regionalism or honest cultural expression. Later, this ideology became grist to the mill for the Post-Modernists, due to its glib and presumptious formula for successful buildings.

On the urban design scene at the time, Le Corbusier's proposal for the redevelopment of Venice envisioned the revitalisation of the city for modern living with breathtaking and vicious disrespect for the tangible and fragile ambience of the place. His proposal was to straddle a new infrastructure

▲ ◀ *Notre-Dame-du-Haut-chapel, Ronchamp, France: The pilgrimage chapel, mid-1950s by Le Corbusier: The ode to the rectangle had given way to the sensual curve. With forms derived from Algerian vernacular architecture, the contrast with previous arrogant insensitivities to the traditional, to cultural legacies and even 'place' shows a striking departure for Le Corbusier*

▲ ▶ Pompidou Centre, Paris, France: A new typology built in 1977, that is indifferent to its urban context. Considering its art and library holdings it represents an underprovision of wall surface and an overprovision of flexibility. A symbol of today's conviction that an art gallery is not only an edifying institution, but competing with other attractions for patronage

TECHNOLOGY IS MASTER Evidence of the ambivalence of the architectural profession since the mid-1960s can be seen in products of the time. Through optimising the use of technology the boundaries of the failed Modern Movement were challenged and the projection of architecture as an art form compromised, becoming instead a place of distraction and amusement.

on pilotis across the unique cultural landscape of the old city. Happily Le Corbusier's 'arrogant' proposal for Venice did not succeed in getting to see the light of day. Despite the vistas on options which Le Corbusier opened for the *Villa Contemporaine* concept, his intellectual power left a legacy of insensitivity about the intrinsic worth of traditional cities, yet, even today in the architectural fraternity, sycophantic reverberations still linger about Le Corbusier's infallibility as a visionary. Eventually 'Corbu recognised (this) stress in his own work as a dialectic, a struggle between head and heart, an art not of resolution but of suspension' (Maxwell 1978).

In the editorial of *Architecture for the Future* (Nouvel, 1996), the forces of change are said to be constantly at work on architectural expression:

Are Late-Modernism and Post-Modernism philosophically and stylistically the same?

Charles Jencks in *Current Architecture* (1982) holds that:

Late-Modern space expresses a dignified quietism for several architects, an honest neutrality and agnosticism toward a society which cannot make up its mind what to value. Clearly this agnosticism is not adequate as a general position... but it has a limited honesty and integrity.

Sometimes Post-Modernism is confused with Late-Modernism because, as we have seen, that movement is also a Mannerist play on a former (architectural) language.

Some architects practise both approaches, and there are also inevitably buildings which are transitional... there are, however, many philosophical and stylistic points which separate the two movements.

'... architecture is an art of the future, a perpetual project whose plans are constantly being redrawn... architecture is a slow-moving art, closely dependent on economic, political and social factors, and on changing fashions. It is therefore quite legitimate to attempt to decipher premonitory signs, symptoms, trends in contemporary architecture, from which we might cautiously infer longterm consequences.'

Late-Modernism from 1960 onwards is still alive and well with notable examples stretching from the early 1970s to the 1990s, for example in cities like Paris, the Pompidou Centre (Piano and Rogers 1971-77), and in Barcelona, the Centre for Contemporary Culture (Pinon and Viaplana 1994). The latter building is less well known but uncompromisingly Modernist in as much as the design idea breaks with all conventional approaches in this extension of a historic landmark building in Barcelona, the old Casa de la Caritat. The slick glass skin of the new, with a slightly skewed 'ops' effect, is planted boldly within the wings of the carefully restored courtyard thus providing a modern side while doubling its space visually. The new building acknowledges the eaves level of the original at which point the glass curtain wall is tilted periscopically inwards, in fact reflecting images of ships outside the harbour of the city one kilometre southwards. This design device locates this important cultural centre within the maritime context of the city and is indeed a courageous use of Modernist principles. Aside from this example, the Catalan appreciation of the finer role of architecture towards the embellishment of the urban experience is legendary.

A design idea emerging strongly from the Late-Modern period has been the concept of the giant industrial 'shed', used as a shelter for a variety

◀ *Barcelona, Spain: The Centre for Contemporary Culture (1994). Uncompromising Modernism found in the highly creative design environment of Catalonia is expressed in this contemporary extension to a fine example of the city's traditional architectural idiom. Through this project, the CCCB becomes a mirror of the city's cultural face and restores Modernism's philosophical credibility, without abandoning its projection as an art form*

◄ ▲ *Waterloo, London: The Eurostar rail terminal (early 1990s) by Nicholas Grimshaw, exalting the architectural aesthetic of the 'giant industrial shed'*

of functions. The Late-Modernist designers have developed a new formal typology around the warehouse, the supermarket, producing an aesthetic almost akin to an engineer's approach. Exalting the aesthetic of the giant industrial shed, architect Grimshaw '... has always been driven by his determination to explore the resources offered by industrial modes of production, and to design buildings which feel incontrovertibly "right". Whence the sense of restraint that pervades all his most characteristic projects... The attention he pays to the "human" aspect...moderates any tendency to technical expressivism.'

Grimshaw's monumental structure for Waterloo Station in London is undeniably spectacular in the huge curve it defines to follow the line of the tracks.

Is ornament synonomous with good architecture?

Lloyd Wright believed it is:

As melody is in music, ornament is in architecture the revelation of the poetic-principle, with character and signficance. Ornament is as natural to architecture of the genus Man as the turtle's shell is to the genus Turtle. Inevitable as plumage to the bird: natural as the form of the seashell; appropriate as the scales of the fish or leaves of the tree or the blossom of the blooming plant.

Man takes a positive hand in creation whenever he puts a building upon the earth beneath the sun. If he has birthright at all, it must consist in this: that he, too, is no less a feature of the landscape than the rocks, trees, bears or bees of that nature to which he owes his being.

Endorsement of the role of the machine

Lloyd Wright exalted the role of the machine:

The new buildings are rational: low, swift and clean and were studiously adapted to machine methods. The quiet institutional, horizontal line (it will always be the line of human tenure on this earth) was thus humanly intepreted and suited to modern machine performance. Machine-methods and these new streamlined, flat-plane effects first appeared together in our American architecture as expression of new ways to reach true objectives in building. The main objective was gracious appropriation of the art of architecture itself to the Time, the Place and Modern Man.

Lloyd Wright (1901)

'The functions of the Waterloo International Terminal are analogous to those of an airport, and it has most of the services and facilities one would associate with such a building. Yet it is still very much a railway station, a heroic edifice erected on a centre-city site and hemmed in by constraints... the first monument of a new era in rail transport. There is a sense of "Brutalism" about it and an attempt to use industrial elements poetically. The style has been applied to community and shopping centres, exhibition centres and art galleries, business premises and even the private house' (Nouvel 1996).

There was a strong motivation for Post-Modernists to break down the dogmatic tenets inherent in Modern and Late-Modern architecture as well as those

▲ ▶ *The design language of Post-Modern gave rise to little innovative grammar of its own. This universally employed elevational style is one of the badges of a limited design vocabulary compared with other mainstream periods in architectural history*

▶ *New Orleans,USA: Piazza d'Italia 1975-79*

◀ *New Jersey, USA: Casino: Genre of the 'escapist cocoon' and a 'pointless cacophony' (Frampton 1996) which has become the new public realm*

▶ *Jerusalem, Israel: Housing complex showing a reactionary style which imposes severe physical constraints on the occupants by virtue of its rigid geometric discipline*

ASSERTIVE POST-MODERNISM Post-modern aberrations of architectural language can seem to be a pointless cacophony and hybridisation of architectural elements. In some instances Post-Modern exalts 'baroquish' expression with historic reference producing trendy and undoubtedly profitable escapist 'theme' environments.

▲ *Figueres, Spain: The Dali Museum. Dali's highly individual and cynical design for an experiential gallery to make his work accessible to the general public. Its validity as an architectural statement lies more in its success as a magnet for the inquisitive and art lovers alike than its contribution to a particular mainstream genre*

in the architectural profession, nevertheless there is some overlap. Jencks (1982) observes that Post-Modernism from around 1960 onwards sought to be popular and pluralist in a backlash to the appalling urban manifestations of the Modernists - the soulless, intellectual, elitist exercises which left the user feeling deprived of humour, happiness and goodwill.

The Post-Modernists reacted with double-coded styles, producing hybrid and complex design forms, variable with surprises while merging conventional with abstract. Their work expresses 'pro' representation: metaphor, historical reference, humour and symbolism, and positively exalted 'baroquish' excess. Far from being a 'short-term phenomenon' the response from the user has been positive and enduring. Considering its place in time, and changing paradigms, there is, however, a major deficiency in the Post-Modern individualistic philosophy - that of commitment to, or even acknowledgement of the need for an environmental ethos. Its relevance as part of the vision for the New Age is thus questionable.

There is no such thing as true style not indigenous. Let us now try to evaluate style. 'Style IS the man.' Yes, style is, as should be, largely a matter of innate CHARACTER. But style only becomes significant and impressive in architecture when it is thus integral or organic. Because it is innate it is style genuine - or not at all. Style is now a quality natural to the building itself. Style develops from WITHIN. Great repose - serenity, a new tranquillity - is the reward for the proper use of each or any material in the true forms of which each is most capable.

Lloyd Wright

Frampton's (1992) view is that Post-Modern stems from an 'understandable reaction to the pressures of societal modernisation and thus as an escape from the tendency of contemporary life to be totally dominated by the values of the scientific-industrial complex... The conscious ruination of style and the cannabalisation of architectural form, as though no value can withstand... the tendency to reduce every civic institution to some kind of consumerism... In Post-Modern architecture classical and vernacular "quotations" tend to interpenetrate each other disconcertingly.'

The backlash to all the '-isms' in architecture comes in various forms, but there is now an element of desperation with the way in which architecture has tended to became removed from the real needs of ordinary people. Amateurs and others outside the design professions have produced building alternatives to both conceptual and conventional architecture. Chaitkin (1982) describe the various forms of 'protest' architecture as 'vernacular revival, simplified self-build, and low-grain energy systems - all in the de-industrialised model of an underdeveloped country of communes'. The search for something closer to nature is a strong thread running through the solutions to their discontent. The motivations for these recent past initiatives arose from the disillusionment of middle-class exiles, founders of Drop City in America, who wanted to 'de-culture' themselves through new environments, and to peasants coming to the city, who squatted in the barriadas of South America, for example, while trying to work into industrialised urban society.

Another form of discontent can be seen in the nomadic existence chosen by other objectors to urban impoverishment, which is manifest in a genre of houseboats and mobile homes, very much in evidence in the USA. The wealth of designs can display boundless creative flair within the limits of personal resources, and a strong reactionary philosophy arising in response to the dysfunctional urban environments from which they have fled. Inextricably bound up with this phenomenon is not only the prescriptive approach which has crept into the architect's creative portfolio - through failed environments, an invisible wedge is being driven between urban neighbours. The remedy would be to satisfy socio-cultural aspirations and to deal successfully with issues of mobility, lack of social amenity, economic affordability, sustainability and, not least, contact with nature and natural resources.

Although merely a microcosm of society, these alternative settlements are growing and however one views the cause, they represent the failure of the social, political and economic functioning of architecture, as well as the urban environment to meet their urbanising needs.

There is an element of urgency missing, while the 'peripheral schools' such as the return to Regionalism and the appearance of Deconstructivism, both in the 1980s, take centre stage. Even in its naming Deconstructivism suggests a reinvention of architectural expression by the knocking down the old order. Foremost practitioners of this school, such as Gehry and Libeskind, have emerged as deconstructivists who in the 1990s moved into the field of fractal geometry in their designs for major commissions, such as the Bilbao Museum, Spain, and the Jewish Museum in Berlin.

Even though products of this reinvention have caught the public imagination, the lingering impression about present day architecture is that it is not available for the needs of the common man. This should be corrected through commitment to a new vision for the future position of architecture where in fact it belongs - in addressing long-term public and environmenal interests.

It is baffling that, with all the knowledge and sophistication which serves the social and economic purpose of the developed Western world in particular, a mainstream architecture of relevance has not emerged. The causes are far from simple to address as the solution demands soul-searching, circumspection, pragmatism, and wider user representation at the planning stage, or perhaps more dispassionate methodological

◀ ▶ ▼ *Berlin, Germany: The Jewish Museum (1989-2000): Structured to connect voids along a line that is present but not visible, Daniel Libeskind's design embodies something quintessential to German-Jewish history and culture*

DECONSTRUCTIVISM Arguably the roots of non-linear architectural form, which has links with the fractal character of later architectural design. Other pioneers of Deconstructivism, such as Gehry, developed more organic expressions of non-linearity, culminating mainly in public architecture based on fractal geometry, expressed spiritedly in the design of the Bilbao Guggenheim Museum, northern Spain.

The Deconstructivist form distorts itself. Yet this internal distortion does not destroy the form. In a strange way the form remains intact. This is an architecture of disruption, dislocation, deflection, deviation and distortion rather than one of demolition, dismantling, decay, decomposition and disintegration. It displaces structure instead of destroying it. What is so unsettling is precisely that the form not only survives its torture but appears all the stronger for it. Perhaps even the form is produced by it. It becomes unclear which came first, the form or the distortion, the host or the parasite.....To remove the parasite would kill the host. They comprise one symbiotic entity.

(Wigley 1992)

approaches. Properly facilitated methodologies balancing the subjective preference ratings of the end user against trained planning and design expertise are common processes in modern day participative planning. In this way a greater understanding by professionals of the socio-cultural needs of a community will ultimately lead to more successful and fewer failed urban environments.

Schön in *The Reflective Practitioner* (1983) suggests that the discipline of architectural practice could review its role and adapt:

'The idea of reflective practice as an alternative to the traditional epistemology of practice... to new conceptions of the professional-client contract, the partnership of research and practice, and the learning systems of professional institutions... reflective practice leads, in a sense both similar to and different from the radical criticism, to a demystification of professional expertise.'

Coupled with the reflective approach of Schön, there is the phenomenon of universalisation in architecture which has been instrumental in hastening the destruction of traditional cultures, but so has the compulsion towards the language of derivative architecture and 'theme worlds'. In the vast majority of situations the evidence of this trend is environmentally demeaning mediocrity with subcultural manifestations that have skewed the direction of the architectural mainstream.

Globally, there is as yet no evidence of any leadership, philosophical, political or otherwise, capable of tilting the focus or influencing commitment to another more visionary architecture. Further, for designers of the urban fabric, the time-tested principles of 'harmony, stability and utility' relevant in architecture should also find ready application.

The practice of architecture, including the patrons of architecture themselves, in fact all who are involved with the shaping of urban environment, need to show greater accountability for the spiritual, physical and intellectual well being of those who have to live within the products of their endeavours. In this way architecture could restore its integrity in the eyes of the ordinary people and elevate the qualities of the social environment to enhance the urban experience.

Cross-cultural stylistic imports in Algeria, Kuwait and Saudi Arabia

The oil boom of the late 1970s brought with it significant development in the Arab countries, notably Saudi Arabia. The Arabs, according to their own spokesmen, knew little about town planning and unfortunately looked to the West at the worst stage in the latter's architectural history. The evidence of this is the shoddy imports all over the economically booming Saudi Arabian cities and towns.

It is an indictment of the architects of the West, fortunate enough to have Arab patronage, that they appeared to throw all design integrity to the wind by denying the roots and the cultural values of the place. In the words of a Saudi Arabian architect, Kamal el Kathrawi, 'We need a philosopher - it is not an architectural problem - there is no clear philosophy about how things should develop.'

Algeria, similarly to Saudi Arabia, for decades has suffered the importation of assertive Western individualism in architectural design. The free-standing slab apartment blocks in the coastal town of Skikda, designed in the Le Corbusier mould of 'Unitè d' Habitation' at Marseilles, were imposed on the terrain without any planned link with the bland desertlike landscape. Le Corbusier's model of the free-standing block was 'copied with disastrous consequences in a great deal of subsequent urban development' (Frampton, 1992) alienating people from their culture and contact with the land to which they were accustomed.

Kuwait has lost almost all traces of its old life, the regional architecture having been destroyed and now replaced by the ubiquitous supermarket, parking lots and the like. The work of foreign architects in the early years shows the 'dilemma' - only token gestures with no attempt to merge. Their buildings are halting attempts, for example in black marble and glass, better suited to colder climes. Much of the legacy of the early years, and still prevailing even today, is an unhappy mixture of tokenism, surface dressing, confused expression of values. People have said, 'we are losing our identity'. Progress however, does not lie in replicating traditional styles. The issue is how to accommodate local tradition with modern techniques.

▲ Skikda, Algeria: In the mould of 'unite d'habitation' - apartment blocks inappropriately appearing in the desert

There is much evidence of the 'Post-Modern dream house', essentially Western with an outward aspect, which has replaced the inward-looking traditional Islamic house. The culturally important intricate system of inner courts, each with its own social function - for men, for women and for minding children etc. has been abandoned.

In more recent times the more influential such as Sheikha Hussa al-Sabah, daughter of the late Emir, have through their example returned Saudi architecture to its roots. The commissions of architect Hassan Fahti are a testament of a great philosopher builder, and includes their own culture's ritual needs - genuine, authentic modern and Islamic.

The challenge has been met by architects like Jôrn Utzen, whose Kuwait parliament building is a modern expression inspired by the Bedouin tent. The building captures the imagination of the people by leading them back to their roots. About the building there is a purity of form and dignified stillness. The breeze from the sea continues through the roof over the vast assembly hall, thereby providing a cooling effect which is at the same time energy conserving. The city's water supply is another project where an imported design solution successfully acknowledges the context. Raised towers, designed by a Swedish firm, resonate with the familiar image of tall palms in an oasis. This grouping of lofty sculptures in unison won the Agha Kahn award for design excellence.

▲ *Jeddah, Saudi Arabia: Haj Terminal: SOM Architects America*

There are, however, other more responsive Western architectural contributions to the oil wealth-driven development in the Middle East. Jeddah, 100 miles to the west, boasts the Haj Air Terminal by SOM of North America, proving that even Western architects can be sensitive to the opportunity provided by environmental and cultural indicators. The derivative design incorporating twenty-one enormously scaled tent structures provides a tenable air temperature of 80° F under the tents while the ambient temperature is 130° F outside. The building has great visual strength and is sensitive to Islam's design legacy.

Oscar Niemeyer's approach has been no different to other stylistic imports. His earlier design of the structures for the University of Constantine in Algeria was conceived from a foreign perspective and stands as a monument to the folly of Western architects ignoring the regional vernacular.

Underwood (1994) writes that 'Niemeyer also stressed that, compared to a design with multiple structures, his simplified solution was more economical in cost of infrastructure and maintenance, more respectful of the hilltop site, and more conducive to the interaction of students, and thus pedagogically superior... Critics have noted the lyrical *parlant* quality of the buildings.' In terms of response to climate, these structures were emphatically dependent on energy-consuming cooling and heating technologies, and thus the designs did not consider economic sustainability in the harsh climate into which they have been imported. In social terms, the departure from the highly evolved vernacular architecture of the region is questionable. Niemeyer's structures have placed the so-called socially interactive character in a vertical stack.

◀ ▲ *Algeria: University of Constantine:*
Oscar Niemeyer, 1969-77

Arguably, if high-rise residential projects of the post-war era are a measure of social architecture, vertical layering does not promote good community living. Finally, there is little lyricism to be observed in a structure which dominates its site with uncompromising determination.

Throughout the world, and arising from a new awareness of national identity and cultural worth, there appears to be a stance that the stylistic cast-offs of the West are not universally appropriate everywhere else. Regional vernaculars are being revisited, not only for their technical response to site and climate but also to the evolved way in which the regional culture has been successfully catered for in the past.

Cultural Rhythms

In the urban environment, the failure to meet the cultural needs of the community, the end user, threatens the amenity value of the social environment with potentially dire sociological consequences.

Response to lifestyle

African colonial cities show varied and distinct cultural landscapes. They are generally characterised by European suburbs and central areas, workers' camps, Indian or Arab areas, African elements of great variety, depending on origin and culture and the use of different materials. All is somewhat village-like, dispersed, animated, noisy, colourful, with commerce everywhere: a profusion of shops, markets, stalls, stands and workshops, so that no lane or street was without them. The cities of other cultures display similar characteristics.

At the same time activity shifts among areas - at dawn it is the central market, in the afternoon the small local outdoor markets in each quarter, then shifting markets as itinerant merchants stop on any piece of open land (Rapoport 1977).

The object of this descriptive observation by Rapoport is to illustrate how the cultural landscape of cities and towns can become imprinted by the diverse, shifting needs of a populace. It follows that if urban form is an expression of culture, then 'the city is ideally a series of areas of varied culture and subculture character', and then, Rapoport observes, a number of design imperatives follow:

    \ It is necessary to understand the cultures of the various groups involved and the influences on form of their values, lifestyle, activity systems.
    \ The goal is conflict resolution on an urban scale.
    \ Open-ended design with some frameworks which link and relate them is the logical application.
    \ Open-ended design ideally creates environments which allow more degrees of cultural expression.
    \ Forcing people to modify and evolve is as bad as the inability to do so.
    \ Urban social spaces should permit freedom of social action.

Spaces that liberate

The utilisation of environments as stage sets and props to assist people both in enacting their social roles and escaping from them needs serious discussion in everday life (Goffman 1959). In older cities of the Western world, squares are far more than just so many metres of open space.

▼ *Paro, Bhutan: In autumn the main public space in a large town becomes part of the agricultural life of the region. Using the wind, the harvested rice is separated manually in a time-honoured tradition*

▲ *An Algerian city: Public space, animated, noisy and colourful with the bustle of traders and social encounter*

In Italy, for example, the piazza is a truly social space and represents a way of life, a concept of living. As a physical manifestation of that culture's creative genius, the piazza is not only the extension of the Italians' living space, but also expresses either 'the mediaeval concept of highly enclosed space of picturesque rather than emotional charm', or 'the sophisticated and mathematical centralism of the static Renaissance', or 'the dynamic feeling of mass movement in space of the Baroque' (Kidder-Smith 1956). The Italian piazza, for example, expresses the dignity of man with strong cultural symbolism, a timelessness and therefore a secure feeling of intergenerational continuity in the open space settings.

It is reasonable to expect that given an opportunity, people will shape an appropriate environment for themselves and that 'this is the most important way in which people assert a sense of mastery and control over their environment and that is an important factor in their well-being'. This factor prompts the concept of 'open-ended design' which is 'a form of design which determines certain parts of the system, allowing other parts, including unforeseen ones, to happen spontaneously' (Rapoport 1977). In this way constraints on the particular use of a space are removed and a degree of personalisation of that space is made possible, much like a person's home, where social and cultural values, needs and individuality can be expressed. Such a design approach overcomes the problem of a 'tight fit'. Open-endedness liberates social space for communities to create their own cultural landscape. Such empowerment of the user to play an active role in the shaping of their own urban environment presages greater success.

Sense of community

A sense of community is psychologically rooted in the minds of city dwellers, and often given expression in the form of geographical boundaries within the urban environment. With their almost stereotyped character, typically the ethnic 'chinatowns' mentioned before, usually found in close proximity to a central business district, are important enclaves for strengthening a 'sense of belonging'.

Communities are important for strengthening a sense of belonging, both for the individual and the wider group. Design elements can reinforce a collective sense of community by means of physical separations, the placement of local centres, the diversion of main trafficways, the exploitation of irregularities, or terrain and other differentiations of a physical nature.

Allocating common land for a neighbourhood is in keeping with the concept of clustering described later, and assists in the gradation of 'publicness' that ultimately characterises the urban fabric.

A clear distinction should be made between three kinds of residential neighbourhoods - those on quiet backwaters, those on busy streets and those in between (Alexander et al. 1977). Each neighbourhood should be given an equal number of each type. 'Since the basic issue is one of control, neighbourhoods should be strengthened and reinforced by spatial form, allowing the urban dweller's options to range from the escape from stress to social interaction' (Lynch 1981).

In a residential neighbourhood, the use of main gateways giving entry to clusters is a device creating a psychological shield against overexposure to public activity. The gateways should be solid elements, visible from every line of approach, and could even be a hole through a building.

Alexander et al. define the image of a neighbourhood square as being a public outdoor room, a partly enclosed place, possibly a structure without walls which is useful to, and maintained by, the community.

LIFESTYLE AND ENVIRONMENT The urban fabric of the city is an expression of the cultural life of that society. The American model, where the private vehicle is king, has no resemblance to the older cities of Europe, which are more than merely square metres of open space. Some become internationally famous places to visit and then become part of millions of private photograph albums due to the visual and experiential pleasure they afford.

◀ ▲ *Minneapolis and Dallas, USA, dedicated to the motor car, where the banality of the residual spaces between buildings has no appeal for the urban users*

▶ *Central piazza, Bergamo, Italy: Shared space with the motor car but it remains the traditional meeting place for community life in the town*

◀ *Piazza Signoria, Florence, Italy: A square which has served for seven hundred years as the public meeting hall, forum, circus and execution spot for the city. Also famous as an open air showcase for sculptural works by the great masters*

Today, Western trained architects are cheerfully prepared to embark with confidence, and often incompetence, on the resettlement of diverse ethnic groups and cultures in many countries; they are planning, replanning, rehousing, rehabilitating people throughout the world in buildings often alien to the way of life and in totally inappropriate structures for the climate and environment.

Oliver (1976)

In contrast to what has been described above, in *The Gaia Atlas of Cities* (1992) and described in the theme of 'New directions for sustainable urban living', Girardet comments that 'Le Corbusier was the most vocal guru of modernism, advocating large, angular building shapes to house hundreds, even thousands of people under one flat roof in vast unrelieved landscapes. He cherished new construction technology; concrete, iron girders, and plate glass were considered preferable to brick, timber and leaded windows. Le Corbusier praised the totalitarian approach to city planning that had been adopted by Napoleon and Haussman. Le Corbusier also believed that pure geometry was the solution to planning cities and buildings. He called for the rule of the right angle and the straight line; there was no place for nostalgia and traditional, vernacular shapes. After all, this was the age of the machine and Le Corbusier believed houses were "machines for living in". His proposed blocks had nothing personal and intimate about them; apartments to him were "cells".'

Le Corbusier was only able to build one of his *unitè d'habitation* concepts, but his followers have seeded the concept for him all over the world. Also, 'His tamed natural world was designed to be visual rather then palpable. Le Corbusier emphasised his preference for geometry and industry over nature. In 1925 he went so far as to praise the fact that cities were an assault on nature. It took 20 years and the destruction of World War II for his ideas to come into their own' (Girardet 1992).

The contemporary situation is different and the high-rise slab block for housing the urbanising masses has fallen into disrepute. Using informality

◀ *Jerusalem, Israel: Neighbourhood park, shared social space in a medium density residential environment, affording a sense of community*

▼ *Montreal, Canada: Residential megablock built for the athletes at the 1976 Olympic Games, and thereafter meant to house a residential community*

HIGH RISE CELLS FOR LIVING The high-rise residential block, advocated by some doyens of the Modern Movement have been breeding grounds for socially dysfunctional communities - yet evidence of such housing forms are still being emulated in some countries to house the less affluent.

▲ *Marseilles, France: Le Corbusier's Unitè d'Habitation, 1946-52*

yet user-discipline to achieve safe, convenient social spaces that function independently, collectively, formally or informally, there have been past developments that provide street users, particularly children, with more informal human-scale environments. These have been cases of conscious planning to create in the vehicle driver the feeling of an intruder in a pedestrian domain. In order to accomplish this, careful attention has to be given to the road layout in estate planning.

In Radburn, New Jersey (USA), in the 1930s, Clarence Stein's concept of the segregation of pedestrians and vehicles was implemented. The Radburn concept responded to the increasing hazards from the growth of car ownership. Designed specifically for the safety of children, the idea of traffic segregation seemed to offer a solution to the more hazardous consequences of an increasingly traffic-dominated society, in which a high premium is placed on door-to-door mobility. 'In the UK the Radburn idea revealed that the early expectations of the Radburn concept were

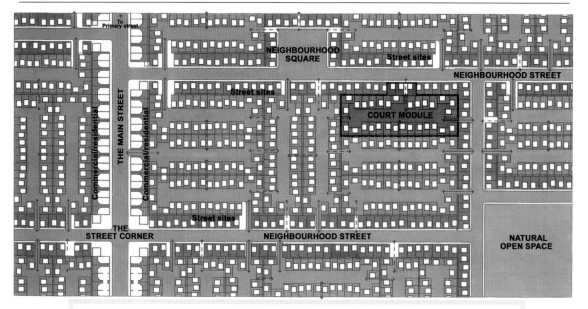

SHARED COURT CONCEPT A stylised layout within a hierarchy of streets, illustrating a graded segregation of pedestrians and vehicles. The spatial organisation provides for privacy and security in the residential zones forming a shield against unwanted public intervention into the privacy. See larger version of shared court module on following page.

only partly met. A generally sound accident record is often counterbalanced by other deficiencies: children play in garage courts; pedestrians walking in roads rather than footpaths; problems of accessibility to facilities; high cost of maintenance; high capital cost and duplication of hard surfacing; and larger areas of land' (Schaffer 1982). However, the upside of the original Radburn concept was more safety for children and flexibility of trafficways.

Linking with the above key points, in the post-Radburn situation greater flexibility in traditional streets was achieved by the application of the *woonerf* concept. More typical in parts of Holland and Germany, it is a concept which combines traffic management through physical constraints in the design of the residential street, with increased opportunity for play, to socialise and for leisure. The liveability of existing neighbourhoods is thereby greatly enhanced.

The Halton Brow scheme in Runcorn New Town, UK, implemented in the 1960s was the first of many attempts to reconcile pedestrian safety with vehicular traffic. Typical features that have been identified as being central to permitting vehicular intrusion into a pedestrian zone should include (Baker, Thomson and Bowers 1985):

⤬ a road hierarchy in the neighbourhood eliminating through-traffic;

⤬ narrow, even circuitous carriageways;

⤬ materials and textures more associated with pedestrian areas, i.e. cobbles, brick paving and less conventional road surfaces;

⤬ shared pedestrian/vehicle access ways or 'shared spaces' and absence of pavements which, as a form of zoning, might suggest separate provision for pedestrians and vehicles and signal vehicle priority to a driver;

⤬ reduced visibility;

⤬ short vistas; and

⤬ rumble strips.

Since the concept was first applied to existing as well as new settings, the impact of the *woonerf* concept on leisure activities has shown that children's play was the chief activity. Eubank-Ahrens (1987) noted that 'although verbal communication among grown-ups did not increase with the redesign of the streets, the latter did have an effect on areas where communication took place'. On the other hand, because of a noted increase in the length of stay by residents in the streets, the amount of interaction observed increased correspondingly. It is noticeable that, 'children (and, indirectly, their parents) seemed to feel more secure, allowing for a proliferation of types of play' and 'children gained more contact with adults, which would not have been possible in playgrounds or other isolated play facilities'. The *woonerf* concept clearly provides more behavioural options for children next to their home base, and thereby contributes to a better quality of urban life.

▼ *Typical shared court module where pedestrians take priority over motor traffic, a layout similar to the 'woonerf' concept*

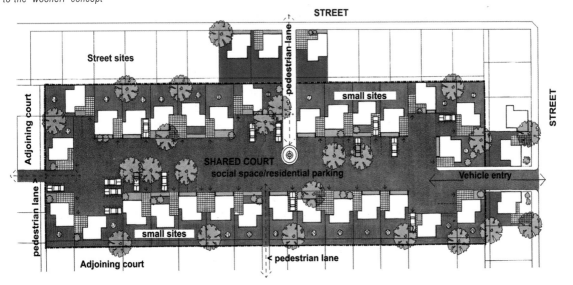

There have been some negative exceptions to the application of the *woonerf* principle in established neighbourhoods. 'In existing neighbourhoods which undergo demographic change, conflicts invariably arise between the established older order and newly arrived residents' as well as by 'the different behaviour of various age groups, which have an impact on the usability of public open space' (Eubank-Ahrens 1987). However, the positives in the application tend to outweigh the negative aspects.

Optimum norms for shared streets

Shared spaces are only possible where traffic flows are fewer than 250 vehicles per hour, and the majority of the traffic has its destination in the area itself. No area of street designed on the 'shared space' principle should be more than 500 metres from a 'normal' vehicular street.

Also, each street in the area should have directional changes every 50 to 60 metres, but additional changes could be necessary (Bentley et al. 1985):

\\ Two-way traffic should be encouraged throughout the area, to reduce vehicle speed.

\\ The section should be kept narrow with occasional widening.

\\ Raised objects should not be higher than 750 mm, to allow good visibility to motorists in case of play activity on the street.

\\ Adequate parking of the on-street type for residents and visitors must be provided. This demands greater attention from drivers, and provides better play spaces when the absence of parked cars liberates the space.

Busy streets and pedestrians

In a busy vehicular street the pedestrian movement zone should be given special consideration appropriate to the intensity of pedestrian traffic involved. In subtle ways a pedestrian zone can be created and demarcated with avenues of trees. Though seating, bus shelters, telephone kiosks and cycle racks may not be justified in all situations at the outset, space should be left for their inclusion even at a later stage.

Typically, in a lower income neighbourhood, private outdoor space is extremely limited. Because backyard spaces are small and usually perform the function of storage areas, family activities tend to spill over into the public domain and thus could be in conflict with the spatial needs of the wider community. The tightness of the private open space fabric may be relieved by the provision of green and suitably paved open spaces, 'located along the highest activity route in the area' to form part of the

▲ *Barcelona, Spain (1992): The wider median is 'afforested' with steel sculptures to lure the urban dweller into a zone encircled by motor traffic. It is doubtful whether the expense of providing such measures can mitigate against the failure of this urban feature to attract patronage*

◀ *Chester High Street, Cheshire, UK: The original Tudor resolution of traffic separation serves the pedestrian well even today. Raised shopping walkways under cover in some sections provide the pedestrian with a greater sense of security than is possible with the conventional pavement/street situation*

BUSY STREETS   The advent of the motor car brought about problems of separating motor traffic from pedestrians in city planning. A traffic island not readily accessible to pedestrians becomes a 'no-mans-land'. Wider pavements or separation by a distinct level change between sidewalk and carriageway are appropriate solutions.

continuum of external space of the neighbourhood and to be readily accessible (Dewar and Uytenbogaardt 1977).

In noisy, heavily trafficked streets, safety can be achieved by providing relatively small embayments set back from the pavement line. These spaces should be located in areas of high pedestrian activity, and where possible raised slightly above street level with stepped or ramped access at frequent intervals. A good example of how such a level change has been employed to advantage is in the main shopping streets of Chester in Cheshire (UK), a concept which has served the town well since Tudor times. To reduce vandalism at night, these setbacks should be brightly lit, and in ideal situations backed by buildings which are occupied during the night hours.

▲ *Athens, Greece: The Acropolis with its Parthenon hold a place of high distinction in architectural history and together became the classical reference for subsequent important architectural schools. The perfect interdependence of the elements, and the agoric character of the social space, strongly express the ancient Greek cultural landscape. In a sense the agora was the living heart of the citizenry*

Outdoor urban life

The agora of the ancient Greek civilisation was a feature of Greek city planning. Innumerable classicists have gone into raptures over 'the glory that was Greece', yet 'no one seems to have recognised that this glory was only made possible by a very special form of town planning: the provision of the agora (public space) at the centre of each Greek city... Agoric planning is founded on the concept that the individual cannot be in perfect health unless he is part of a family in perfect health' (Peck 1982). The agora was a place symbolising democracy, where the inhabitants gathered for political, commercial business and social intercourse, so that as a public area it became the city's living heart.

The Greek view of man's relationship to the world is most readily seen in concrete form, especially in the architectural structures. In describing the Parthenon in its setting on the Acropolis, for instance, Wheeler (1964) noted that 'Neither the building nor its decoration had any inner life; it was a perfect exterior, a perfect piece of man-made geology.'

Just as the sacred ceremonies occurred outside the buildings, so did the structures themselves turn outward with their pedimental sculpture. In this way the ancient Greek culture was expressed in their social spaces offering a physical statement of their preferred public lifestyle.

Agoric planning, according to Peck, involves the application of at least the following conceptual principles to the design of urban space:

⸜ Comprehensiveness: The agora (social space) must contain all the commoner amenities for active recreation, within reason for both sexes, all age groups and all interest and activity groups.

⸜ Centralisation of amenities.

⸜ Attractor planning based on the principle of 'cumulative attraction'.

⸜ Biopoint, biopattern and biodistance planning. Mark a person's biopoints on a map, join them up, and that is the human biopattern. The distance that the urban dweller has to travel to visit all biopoints can be termed the biodistance. If the distances are too long, the urban dweller has simply to abandon certain of the biopoints, which limits choice and detracts from the urban experience.

⸜ Functional unity: Amenities catering for the most basic of public needs.

⸜ Adaptability: The Greek agora consisted largely of one of the most adaptable of all amenities - open space.

Agoric planning was considered vital and essential to urban life - it enriched the individual, who in turn enriched the environment. Urban designers of today could well learn from this example - more significantly, the positive effect well-designed social space can have on urban cultural life.

In the modern context formal outdoor recreation is an important aspect of urban life - sportsfields, trails along a natural feature, botanical gardens, animal sanctuaries and structured playgrounds serving the needs of social development. In many situations a charge for entry could be levied to offset the capital cost of imaginative play equipment.

Security through the presence of others

In cities which have grown centrifugally through ease of mobility provided by the motor car, community life in the suburbs has been found wanting, yet in its hustle and bustle and unstructured supervision, street life in dense communities has something difficult to define - a culture helps to raise kids successfully (Jacobs 1962). The practice of fencing in homes and gardens (for privacy and protection from the street) and the practice of using a motor car for every errand effectively isolates the family from personal encounters with those who live in the neighbourhood.

▲ Jerusalem, Israel: A typical new neighbourhood for the diversity of immigrant cultures being housed around the city with a large measure of success. The Israeli Ministry of Housing met the challenge to provide safe, new residential neighbourhoods, by enabling a sense of community, while achieving surveillance of the public space by the residents themselves

▲ Barcelona, Spain: Barcelloneta, traditional home of the seafaring: In medium to high density residential settings, the effect of deterring the incidence of crime is potentially enhanced

NEIGHBOURHOOD WATCH In high density residential neighbourhoods the surveillance provided by the presence of the occupants themselves is almost automatically a byproduct. In this way a deterrent against crime is achievable, and the opportunity for other forms of mutual support is afforded.

In high density residential situations it is possible to provide a spatial system that provides for the watchful presence of others, either from those living in the street or those in transit through the street. Using the principle that nodal points should always be visible along street axes ensures that there will be a point from where the important foci can be seen. Such a system will allow access to strangers, but informal monitoring by the residents of adjacent dwellings that provides an effective mechanism for policing the neighbourhood. This subtle form of security is no more than a mere grouping of dwellings alone to achieve a self-monitoring environment. Although building in security in this manner does not provide guarantees against crime, the effect of deterring the incidence of criminal activity is greater. The downside could be that, where a neighbourhood watch is established, a loss of privacy could follow.

Territorial needs

The territorial instinct of the individual or the group is instrumental in the development of 'identity with place', an important outcome of satisfactorily designed urban space. Factors, such as in high-density development, effectively threaten the private space of the individual. Overcrowding the carrying capacity of a specific urban setting is a symptom of potential failure in many high-density environments.

There is a more obscure side to the question of providing for the need for own territory. The territorial needs of commercial and corporate business differ entirely from those of the individual or community. The business environment aims to project a strong image of prosperity and is not primarily concerned with the same physical markings of space as in residential neighbourhoods. 'The very idea of modestly fitting into the collective city is antithetical to corporate aspirations and the chest-beating individualism of the American way' (Trancik 1986). The result is the public space, in fact a public asset, is frequently turned over to private corporations for their own purposes. In such instances even though usufruct over a city space or site might be conditional, the city's collective space becomes transformed into a city of private icons.

There are indications that 'open-endedness is also intimately linked with territoriality since it allows personalisation, an important way of defining individual and group domains. By allowing group signs to develop and define rules of occupance, [a code of conduct becomes] not only noticed and understood, but willingly obeyed. Such rules are subtle and frequently understated, and also change subtly, and the designer cannot provide for them - they are best allowed to develop within an open framework where they can then also respond to change in the population of the various areas. It is a principal way of giving to the environment' (Rapoport 1977).

Commercial opportunity

The economic or physical means to 'close the distance', and ease access to the facilities of a modern city, is usually the privilege of the affluent in the modern city, which, by nature of its sprawl, necessitates rapid modes of transport. A city's amenity value is a measure that covers a range of opportunities, experiences and activities that are available to the inhabitants and how these are provided for. Also, the measure of success will be determined by the ease of mobility of the poor and access by people on foot, rather than criteria that are vehicle dependent. 'If essential city facilities and opportunities are so located and dispersed through space

NODAL SITUATIONS   Commercial opportunity normally exists in situations which are nodal, such as at railway stations, or at the confluence of city streets. In large cities, where land is scarce, the architectural response to such activity is generally a building of mass, or height, thus expressing the economic importance of the place.

▲ Osaka, Japan: The Sony Tower, 1976, with mixed commercial uses while providing height for telecommunications for the city and surroundings

◀ Charing Cross, London: Concentrated commercial opportunity over a major underground rail connection

that they are easily available to the poor as well as the wealthy, the entire system is richer' (Dewar and Uytenbogaardt 1984)

People want to be close to shops and services, for convenience, and excitement, but they also want to be away from instrusive services for quiet relaxation (Alexander et al. 1977). To achieve a balance, gradients of density are a good proposition on the basis that community facilities scattered individually through the city do nothing for the life of the city. For that reason, according to some commentators, nodes of activity spread about 300 metres apart provide the most viable concept. Ideally at the centre of the node, a small public square should be created, surrounded by a combination of community facilities and shops which are mutually supportive, the objective being to stimulate vitality within the urban mix.

A feature of older cities is the promenade. The relation between the 'catchment' of the promenade and the actual physical paved area of the promenade itself is critical. A formula would not be universal, except for the qualification that 'a promenade will not work unless the pedestrian density is high enough.' (Alexander et al. 1977).

A common denominator in the activities of the average urban dweller is the quest for some form of night life. A cluster of night spots will create life in the street but the public places surrounded by night life amenities should be well lit, safe and lively. The clustering of amenities will increase the intensity of pedestrian activity at night drawing people out to the same few spots in the town. Transport terminals can create an ideal opportunity for certain kinds of night time activity as they are places for people waiting to embark on public transport, or disembark to be met by others.

Space for informal marketing and jobs

Use of the social space system in the urban situation should be encouraged to promote economic activity. The common turf provided for informal and periodic activities, such as public meetings, spontaneous theatre and busking, periodic markets, fairs and circuses, is an important use of social space.

Unfortunately, 'Most planners conceive of the street as a transitional space and do not allow for it to act as an open space, activity space, or social space, yet it can play an immensely important role in the design and planning of many cities, as we have seen in Mexico, Africa and elsewhere..' (Rapoport 1977).

The social and commercial role of the traditional street has been undermined by the ubiquitous enclosed shopping mall. Widespread applications of the internalised emporium concept 'have siphoned shopping and entertainment

◄ *The plethora of informal trading in London streets is positive evidence that commercial activity is opportunistic and that streets are not exclusively transitional spaces or traffic corridors*

Skikda, Algeria: Street trading is as old as civilisation itself

off the street, which no longer functions as a gathering place' (Trancik 1986). Most often such emporia are situated on the fringe of the urban area so that individual transportation is necessary. In this way they do not make access to the wider market easier, thus drawing distinct socio-economic boundaries between income groups in a metropolitan context.

At no cost in terms of capital investment for infrastructure and accommodation, trafficways and nodal intersections, social space can provide important outdoor venues for small trading enterprises`. In this way such venues can increase income options and assist local economic growth, a strong factor particularly in emergent economies.

The most humane cities are always full of street cafès that provide unique venues for people to mix in public, in streets, parks, squares, along promenades and avenues. Busy streets should allow the front of the cafè to spill out onto the pavement, so that sets of tables and chairs stretch out into the public place. Mobile food vendors should be accommodated so that public seating can be utilized to enjoy a snack while seated. Some rules for food stands include (Alexander et al. 1977):

⤹ They should be concentrated at road crossings where they can easily be seen.

⤹ They should be free to take on the character of the area around them.

⤹ They can be either portable stands, built into the fronts of buildings or mobile carts.

In cities in developing countries diversified forms of informal trading and small business enterprise permits a greater decentralisation of work. As the culture of small business takes root in the local economy the workshop in the home grows and grows in importance. The relationship between a workshop and a public street is a special one, and is potentially a way to enlarge the connection between the worker and the community, from which every member of the community will benefit, provided that it can be seen from the street and that the owner can 'hang out a shingle' (Alexander et al. 1977).

Recreational needs

In all urban societies there is a need for places for healthy recreational spaces. Informal or formal, with or without equipment, the way recreation is practised or enjoyed is part of the cultural lifestyle of any given urban community. Around cities endowed with natural features and specific climatic conditions, hiking trails or skiing within easy reach for urban dwellers might be the pattern for recreation. On the other hand, in situations where winters are long and natural features less prominent, structured amenities might be required of the local government for the urban population to enjoy the therapy of play. These are two ends of the recreational spectrum, both evident in many cities in the world, and depend largely on the level of affluence and the preferred form of recreation.

◄ *Toronto, Canada: In a winter climate such as that of North America, there is a great need to enjoy the short summer sunshine, indicating a popularity of structured water playgrounds*

▼ *Paro, Bhutan: A large town sustained by an agrarian economy based largely on the production of rice. The best agricultural soils are reserved for productive farmlands, the residential needs are located on the high ground, and the commercial needs are sited along a single ordered main street*

Urban culture and natural regimes

The concrete manifestations of urban cultural life typically take the form of vast areas of hard surfaces with buildings sprawled horizontally or raised high in dense conurbations. These man-made urban environments create microclimates of their own and, depending on the intensity of any developmental intervention into Nature, can impact negatively on the macroclimatic conditions of an entire region. The effect is greatest in large towns or cities to the extent that it is justifiable to speak in terms of an 'urban climate'.

Aside from the site contextual considerations, the inevitable climate change, and social and cultural paradigms of the times, urban designers and architects should endeavour to ensure the sustainability in perpetuity of the natural systems within the urban environment. In the next chapter discussion on the conservation of biodiversity in the urban environment and biogeographical and geomorphic principles highlights a mitigative response to negative impacts from urban intervention into natural regimes.

Urban Design in Response

The rigorous design axioms of the Modern Movement have caused streets to lose their attraction as gathering places. 'As a consequence individual attitudes to urban space have been radically altered... Functionalism, which laid the groundwork for our loss of traditional space, became obsessed with efficiency' (Trancik 1986).

The potential catalyst

For all urban development the starting point should be a holistic assessment of the processes whereby the goals are to be achieved. Instead the fields of urban design and planning, as well as architecture, have become ever increasingly specialised, and defensive of the importance of their territorial expertise. This fragmented mode of approach spells potential disaster for the urban environment, and as a consequence a loss of those qualities that enable a better life under urban conditions.

Considering historical precedents, it is most often in the sphere of residential development or redevelopment that reshapers of the urban environment are afforded the opportunity to restore urban environments to vitality and productiveness. In housing specifically, which is directly associated with the round-the-clock needs of the individual as well as the community, lies perhaps the strongest potential for catalytic change or for urban renewal. It is significant that goals for sustainable neighbourhoods and even cities highlighted earlier in this source book can often be achieved through the intervention of new large scale housing projects.

By replacing blighted or downgraded sites, three scenarios for housing development could make urban renewal possible:

⬝ Where residential districts take the form of 'urban redevelopment', buildings in need of renovation would supplement new development and make use of the existing amenity infrastructure and urban landscaping. It would involve retaining parts of the old with the merging of the new into an upgraded fabric. Redevelopment work generally takes the form of an implant into the existing urban structural and social situations, or development of a 'brown field' site within a metropolitan area. The 'fall-out' effect on neighbouring districts and vice versa must, however, be considered as such interventions and may either be the initial spark for revitalising the peripheral area as well, or it may have the opposite effect of rapid degeneration of the periphery into slums. An effective social programme to deal with negative perceptions of the residents of the redevelopment site and surrounding areas should form part of any redevelopment strategy.

Seoul, South Korea: Mass housing developed to accommodate the athletes and officials at the Seoul Olympic Games in 1988

URBAN CATALYST Large scale housing projects can become either the catalyst for urban upgrading, or unfortunate monocultural interventions. Where such intervention is holistic it affords opportunities to address the shortcomings of socially impoverished urban environments of the past.

Barcelona, Spain: The Olympic Games of 1992 provided the city with the opportunity to transform a derelict, under utilised waterfrontage, thereby benefiting the entire city population. Intervention took the form of the Olympic Village with accommodation for 15 000 athletes and officials along the waterfront and included the construction of a new yacht harbour with its extensive promenade and quayside lined with restaurants and shops

⟍ Where residential districts take the form of 'urban expansion', expediency sometimes favours the use of 'green field' sites on the outskirts of town, where controls are not as rigidly entrenched and rapid preparation and completion of housing projects can be achieved to reduce development costs. The downside is that such development is often characterised by physical isolation, functionally separating the town's living areas from the workplace. The dependency on rapid transportation modes becomes imperative, where invariably the construction and upgrading of transportation routes lags behind such development thus creating social and economic hardship for the newly housed communities.

⟍ Where residential districts take the form of 'new urban building', in general such development can be characterised by the 'new town' concept, notably in England and Israel. In England the aim has been primarily due to the pressure of population numbers, or locating people closer to employment opportunity. In Israel the new towns represent specific settlement measures for opening up undeveloped areas such as the desert and for settling people from a diversity of cultures in the Jewish diaspora. In this concept, the basic planning conditions can be self-imposed, and offer scope for 'ideal planning' with central town amenities, jobs, recreation areas and residential districts appearing simultaneously.

The above residential interventions, all primarily aimed at providing for residential community life, represent a potentially effective starting point for upgrading jaded city environments.

Utilising these scenarios, urban designers and architects would be enabled to use their creative energies to address environmental concerns with a renewed sense of social responsibility, linked with their commitment to planning for a productive urban living.

URBAN SPATIAL SYSTEMS

From an urban planning and design perspective, a transportation framework will be integral in the development of urban morphological form. As has been highlighted in an earlier chapter, in new situations a pattern of hierarchical transportation routes will be key to the structuring and growth of the urban environment, as well as the potential for 'capacity' development.

The movement system can become the means towards more efficient land usage through which wider urban functions may be served. In historic or existing urban agglomerations, this form of urban structuring will mostly be a 'given' either in an imposed or more dynamic configuration.

Movement corridors

Movement patterns within an urban environment are broadly represented by the following typical configurations, either in pure or composite form:

▨ Linear configurations which are a primary organising element catering for cars, cycles, people and services. As part of a movement system they are not confined to a straight line, but could be slow or tight curvilinear; they could also be segmented depending on whether they are planned strictly for cars or for people.

▨ Grid systems create nodes at regular intersections, and yield square or rectangular fields of space. A useful city case study of the influence of topography on the grid configuration of streets is San Francisco, where the public transportation exploits the characteristics of a difficult terrain to striking advantage. The needs of the city have exploited the attributes of the topography and produced an energy-efficient transportation system for that city.

▨ Network configuration is in essence a random system connecting specific important nodal points in urban space.

▼ *Edinburgh, Scotland: Like a painting by an old master, the urban design character depicted in this famous view, with Princes street to the right and Edinburgh Castle to the left, is timeless in its appeal, both visually and as the vital and functioning heart of the city*

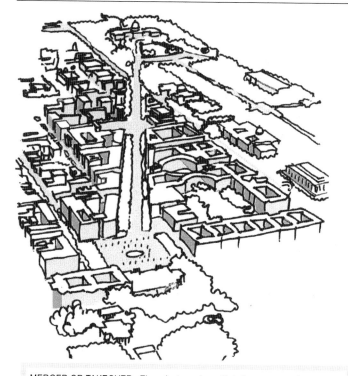

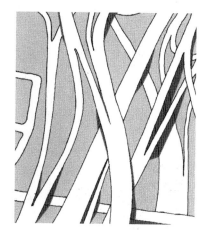

◀ *Washington DC, USA: Strong axial movement corridors absorbing and distributing vehicular traffic through an urban situation, energising nodal activity at intersections and providing social amenity almost throughout*

▼ *Los Angeles, USA: An extreme case: an actual confluence of freeways designed in response to the pressures of private motor vehicles, resulting in socially and biophysically sterile urban space*

MERGER OR TAKEOVER   The private motor vehicle has consumed vast tracts of urban land to speed its passage. Movement systems which are integrated into the fabric of the urbanscapes permit evenly mixed usage of the corridors, whereas the freeway system consumes space with a loss of social amenity. The opportunity in such instances for returning the residual land to natural regimes would at best be a gesture to biodiversity by the creation of linear habitats within an environment otherwise largely given over to hard surfaces.

⬉ Radial systems are capable of providing efficient circulation, providing they are supplemented by concentric circulation and depending on other factors, including topography.

⬉ Spiral configurations are continuous systems originating from a central point and becoming increasingly distant from it. Unless planned to create a specific spatial experience, the choice of such a system would probably be dictated by topography. Italian hillside towns provide good precedents for spiral corridor systems.

⬉ Composite configurations are more common than the preceding pure forms, and the movement systems of most towns have evolved organically from dynamic growth transposed through socially and economically determined desire-lines. The resultant richness of spatial diversity at the intersections of a composite configuration can be well exploited for social and economic vitality.

Contemporary city building, in general preferring the bulldozer to natural uses of the site, is prone to avoid and even eliminate those differences in levels which can add such spice to urban enjoyment. Whether such changes are many feet... a clever play and interplay of heights can provide not only delightful space sensations but determine the very paths and functions of traffic.

Kidder Smith (1956)

Dependent on the type of mobility, such as by motor vehicle and cycles or pedestrians, it is important that a movement system does not destroy the integrity of a public space with which it links and through which it passes. Planning can employ devices to avoid the bisection of a space by a movement system. Alternatively, a movement system could pass through axially, obliquely or along the edge of a space. A movement system can also be planned to exploit three-dimensional topography where changes in urban levels can enhance the urban spatial character. Italian mediaeval towns, such as Assisi and Lucca, or the famous Piazza di Spagna in Rome are all outstanding examples of the power of level changes to enhance the visual qualities and amenity value of urban space.

Essentially, a movement corridor is characterised by attributes which relate to its place in the hierarchy of circulation and the function it performs as a low or high volume carrier of transport or people. Characterising factors include: the form of the spaces through which it passes; the entrances which open onto it; considerations of scale, proportion, light and vistas; the degree of enclosure, either completely open on one side or open on both sides; and the manner in which changes in level are handled.

Meaningful urban space

Urban design theories abound, but three provide a useful basis for the examination of modern urban space, and that of historic precedents (Trancik 1986):

> ＼ The Figure-ground theory: Founded on the relative land coverage of buildings as solid mass (figure) to open voids (ground), this theory highlights the 'unity of opposites'. The object is to manipulate the relationships by adding to or subtracting from or changing the physical geometry of the pattern. The Figure-ground theory is a graphic tool for illustrating

Curitiba and its 'surface metro'

'The Brazilian city of Curitiba has taken the lead in organising a particularly rational public transport system. A city of about 1,6 million people has a unique surface metro, a highly efficient network of fast-running buses, obviating the need for an underground system. The city has built high-speed bus lanes that prevent buses being held up by car traffic. With a bus stop every 400 metres people have convenient access to buses and cylindrical loading tubes allow passengers to pay their fares in advance to speed up the boarding process. One million three hundred thousand passengers use the city's public transport system daily; it is faster and often cheaper than that of other Brazilian cities. The city also has an extensive system of

cycle lanes, and traffic calming in selected streets. Despite high car ownership of one car for every five people, car use is lower than most other Brazilian cities.

New York has taken a close look at Curitiba's surface metro system and hopes to make its own bus routes more efficient. A high-speed bus network could serve to improve linkages between the various transportation systems currently in use in the New York metropolitan region.'

Girardet (1992),

(For Curitiba schematic see page 195)

Mousehole, Cornwall, UK: Many of the older European villages reflect similar configurations where narrow streets, small squares and pedestrianways form a matrix of interconnected social space

and managing mass-void relationships; it is a two-dimensional abstraction in plan view that clarifies the structure and order of urban spaces.

The Linkage theory: Derived from lines formed by streets, pedestrianways, linear open spaces and connecting one element to another. Movement systems and efficiency of the infrastructure take precedence over patterns of defined outdoor space.

The Place theory: Goes beyond the previous two theories in that it adds the components of human needs within their cultural, historical and natural contexts. The unique forms and details of a place's indigenous setting will add richness.

Each of these approaches has its value, but the optimum is one that draws on all three, giving structure in the urban fabric to solids and voids, organising links between parts, and showing response to human needs and indigenous character of the setting (Trancik 1986).

Starting from a more spatial platform, to create public spaces which encourage social interaction, there are two types of relations to be considered; between inhabitants and strangers, and among the inhabitants themselves. Social spaces are defined by some urban researchers (Hillier and Hanson 1984) as either 'convex' or 'concave' in terms of their spatial syntax. The former description (convex) applies if a line connecting any two points on the perimeter of a spatial system does not penetrate outside that perimeter. Concave space implies the opposite.

Taking this concept to a more developed stage, 'convex' zones create potential 'fields' for social encounters which when linked axially result in a matrix of interconnections. This structuring frame will then 'show which segments of the open space system are more integrating, and which are segregating' (Mills, 1988). Further development of this revelation shows that the integration 'core' of the town is 'a reliable predictor of dense movement and encounters' (Hillier and Hanson 1984). By using these deductions of spatial meaning, 'new urban designs can be rigorously assessed in terms of the social encounter/movement patterns they will generate' (Mills 1988).

The function of neighbourhood cannot exist where urban space lacks structure or is dispersed and not connected. It has been found that the layout of social space virtually controls the formation of child play groups and has, therefore, a critical influence on the social development of the children of that neighbourhood. Researchers generally conclude that the typical suburb with the conventional layout of streets negatively affects the development of the child and is an inhibiting factor in the development of social skills. Relative to this thesis, Lantz (1956) researched the correlation between the incidence of neurotic and psychotic levels in a sample group of 1000 men, with a significant outcome. Taking into account, retrospectively, the number of friends of individual men, numbering five and over at the ages of four to ten years, the results indicate a relationship between the higher incidence of neurosis and psychosis where friends at the given age numbered fewer than five. The indispensible need for 'connected play' amongst children justifies more consideration being given to the planning of social spaces to promote the child's ability to bond with peers under relatively safe environmental conditions.

A numerical model on the theme of Lantz's findings would show that optimum 'connected play' is more likely to be achieved where 'at least 64 households are connected by a swathe of land that does not cross traffic' (Alexander et al. 1977). This optimum can be attained through connecting several houses in clusters, even in existing situations, thereby eliminating or reducing the need to cross traffic for interaction within the cluster.

URBAN DESIGN GUIDELINES

Over one hundred years ago, in *City Planning According to Artistic Principles,* Camillo Sitte wrote of the meagre and unimaginative character of modern city plans. His proposals for creating visual order to endow character to public squares included the following principles:

    ✒ The centre of public squares should be kept free of clutter.

▲ *Neighbourhood, Jerusalem, Israel: Due to the adequate allocation of space for informal recreation, medium density housing environments, designed by the Ministry of Housing for immigrants from diverse backgrounds, have been largely successful as neighbourhoods*

BUILDING COMMUNITY LIFE   Formal or informal play areas with adequate space, shade and wind shelter should be located within the precincts of a neighbourhood to facilitate supervision of children at play and encourage the development of community life.

▼ *Cleveland, Ohio, USA: The American model: Kids' play equipment often designed and built by the parents*

⟍ Public squares should be enclosed entities.

⟍ The size and shape of public squares are critical.

⟍ Irregularity is acceptable in the configuration of a public square, and does not necessarily negate visual order.

⟍ A continuum of interlinked social spaces enhances the parts as well as the whole.

⟍ The ideal street should form a completely enclosed unit visually.

After a lifetime of observing city spatial relationships and the successful embodiment of the aesthetic in physical form, Sitte's conclusions, although not presented as absolute principles, nevertheless point to some useful and tested conventions in the attainment of visual order and character in urban space planning.

Public squares free of buildings

Of a survey of two hundred and fifty-five churches conducted by Sitte in the city of Rome, only six were found to be free-standing. What is of great importance for such buildings is that they 'achieve their full effect only when they can be viewed from an adequate distance on a piazza that is not too large' and integration with the space has been carefully resolved. In Italy, successful examples of the placement of important buildings on a public square, where one or more sides forms part of the perimeter, are Piazza del Duomo, Piacenza and Vicenza; San Cita, Palermo; and Piazza del Santo, Padua. In all cases successful perspective is achieved without having deeper space, so that according to Sitte, 'the facade of the building could be viewed as the backdrop to a stage'.

In mediaeval towns, a street intersection in a public square, a well-known feature in contemporary town planning, was the exception rather than the rule, since this would prevent 'any coherent total effect'. The concept of planning the streets to enter the public square from the corners and even at varying angles, more closely approximates the patterns followed in many mediaeval towns. Sitte identifies the cathedral square of Ravenna as the 'purest type of this ingenious system'.

Shape and size criteria for public squares

In analysing the relationship that exists between the size and shape of plazas and of the major structures on them, Sitte identifies two types of square: the 'deep type and the wide type'. The position of the observer in relation to a major building and the proportional relationship between the size of the public square and that of its buildings is important. St Marks, Venice, is a prime example where the ideal spatial resolution has been achieved.

Sitte states that 'strict symmetry and geometric exactitude' are unnecessary to the 'creation of pictorial and architectonic effects... '. Old public squares were not conceived on the drawing board 'but instead developed gradually *in natura*'. Sienna, Italy, has numerous examples of public squares which are irregular on plan and create fine settings for churches and other important buildings. The aim was to 'carve out a deep plaza in front of the church facade and to ensure good vantage points for viewing this major structure'.

The purposeful design of irregular public spaces liberated from mechanical conceptions on the drawing board is a worthwhile option to explore. The worst effects of imposed geometry, such as stiff triangular-shaped public squares or residues of space, which have no functional or aesthetic advantage, should be avoided. To liberate planning from imposed geometry in no way diminishes the importance of visual order in planning urban settings. Irregularity is compatible with goals of visual order, as can be appreciated in the examples referred to by Sitte and as can be seen, in particular,

▲ *Gotic area, Barcelona: Square with fountain in the residential quarter*

▼ *Piazza del Popolo, Rome: Axial confluence of avenues in the grand city plan. Originally planned for the carriage and the wheel it is thus today fully organised for vehicular traffic*

◄ *Bergamo, Italy: Main square with church*

▼ *Milan, Italy: The Duomo, Italian gothic cathedral interfaced with a much used piazza where in close proximity religious and major secular events take place simultaneously*

THE AMENITY VALUE OF TRADITIONAL SQUARES City squares take on many forms, from the informal to the formal. In some older city squares, the church encloses one side; in dense residential habitation the square was necessary to provide light and air to surrounding buildings and outdoor space for social activities. Revered architecture and social spaces are the stage for cultural events, not only as places of worship but as familiar territory for the city's social calendar. Today, there is a danger that squares become traffic concourses at the expense of their value as social amenities.

in the public squares of Sienna, Italy. A lesser known Asian example is the mogul palace at Fatehpur Sikri, where, due to the subtle asymmetry of the building elements in a vast uncluttered space, a sense of visual repose is achieved.

Visual closure and visual order

Streets that are visually enclosed avoid the impression of being a thoroughfare, and provide a better setting for the architecture.

It is not only the public squares of the old towns that merit study but also the configuration of their streets. The spatial enclosure they achieve is equally important to good urban design. Sitte states that, 'The ideal street must form a completely enclosed unit. The more one's impressions are confined within it, the more perfect will be its tableau: one feels at ease in a space where the gaze cannot be lost in infinity.' Straight roads are necessary today and are often of very imposing effect. What Sitte condemns is their mechanical employment, *a priori*, without concern for the configuration of the terrain or other local circumstances. He states: 'If the meandering line is more picturesque, the straight one is more monumental; but we cannot subsist from monumentality alone, and it would be desirable that the builders of modern cities do not abuse the one or the other, but make use of them both as appropriate, in order to give to each district which they lay out an aspect in conformity with its purpose.'

Principles of visual order, which allow diversity without monotony and provide spatial character and integrity, are useful goals in the design of city spaces. Such 'ordering principles' as axial, symmetrical, hierarchical, rhythmic/repetitive, transformative and the use of a 'datum' line device can present the beholder with subliminal evidence of an underlying visual ordering.

The application of principles for designing 'ordered' urban space can be synthesised as follows (Ching 1979) :

   ⊠ An axis can be established by a symmetrical or asymmetrical arrangement of forms and spaces.
   ⊠ There are two types of symmetry: bilateral symmetry which is the balanced arrangement of two equivalent elements about a common axis; and radial symmetry which consists of equivalent elements balanced about two or more axes that intersect at a central point.
   ⊠ A form or space can be made significant by being made visibly unique, by endowing the shape either with exceptional size, shape or location or a composite form of these principles.
   ⊠ Rhythm employs the fundamental principle of repetition, of which

▶ *Agra, India: The Taj Mahal: World Heritage site: Serenity, and a sense of order and peace, achieved through perfect symmetry in terms of layout and the design elements of the tomb itself and its flanking structures*

▼ *Rajahstan, India: The unambiguous and subtle resolution of buildings and space forming the vast court in the palace of Fatehpur Sikri achieves the same visual repose as its symmetrical counterparts*

SYMMETRY AND ASYMMETRY For the 'creation of pictorial and architectonic effects... ', both symmetry and non-symmetry are valid as a basis for achieving a sense of perfect visual equilibrium appropriate to the situation.

the simplest form is linear. Alternatives include grouping of elements by size, shape or detail.

▨ Transformation allows the systematic manipulation of a typical, appropriate, architectural model, geometric form or shape, through a discreet evolution to respond to the specific context of the design at hand.

▨ A datum is a device in the form of a line, plane or volume which has the property of organising a random pattern of elements through its regularity, continuity and constant presence. As a device, a datum must have sufficient scale to perform its function effectively.

The relaxed concepts of Sitte and the geometric principles identified by Ching are not mutually exclusive, but rather provide the urban designer with a set of time-tested conventions for developing a well-conceived urban spatial canvas for architecture.

▲ *Dallas, Texas, USA: Historic cultural buildings lose their importance to monocultural commercial development and become traffic islands or void fillers in the business environment*

▶ *Oxford, UK: The curved High street provides visual closure affording greater appreciation of the tableau of fine detailing of its famous architectural assets, individually and sequentially*

Planned outdoor amenities

Related to the findings of a survey conducted by (Whyte 1982) certain behaviour patterns in small public spaces were observed, supporting the theory of the influence of a space on social interaction.

Children in particular have a better sense of place if the urban neighbourhood contains play environments scaled to their size and humanised by good landscaping, lighting and well-designed equipment. The quality of the urban environment makes a difference in children's conduct and their willingness to learn acceptable social behaviour, leading ultimately to more productive community life. Children learn through their senses - a child at play is, in fact, learning and can learn from the environment in a positive way. Barren urban spaces are the antithesis of what is necessary for satisfactory social development, whereas good neighbourhood playgrounds can stimulate multisensory play. If well designed they can provide the environmental conditions for a child's social intercourse and positive experiential appreciation of the urban habitat.

In the wider public context the urban environment requires planned amenities comprising many familiar forms usually under the umbrella of landscape architecture. Generally these are:

  ⧵ seating, fountains, shelters, steps, kiosks, bandstands;
  ⧵ sportsfields, play equipment and landscaped parks;
  ⧵ trails along natural features; and
  ⧵ botanical gardens and sanctuaries.

Options for recreational space should include a range for both formal (e.g. organised games) and informal (e.g. play space, parks) use.

Whereas formal recreation space should be incorporated as an imperative in an urban environment, in practice such facilities will be determined largely by available space, official perceptions of sustainability, and the ability of the target population to bear the costs. In a study of community needs in the developing world, the *Urban Projects Manual* (Culpin et al. 1983) provides the following synthesis for formal facilities:

  ⧵ The location of the recreation facilities should be as central as possible to the areas which the spaces serve, though this need not be the most valuable area of the project site.
  ⧵ Access will be important, but a location behind commercial, industrial or public facility areas would be suitable, provided that they are safe areas.
  ⧵ Areas for formal games should be reasonably level and of suitable surface.

For informal areas:

  ⧵ They should be provided on a more pragmatic basis.
  ⧵ Locating a large number of small open spaces relating to housing clusters or local access roads will prove to be most economical and socially acceptable, particularly for the supervision of children from their homes.
  ⧵ Hardened areas may be desirable for older children, though these should be located so that activity does not affect other users of the social space.

With a view to a reduction in costs to the public purse, an important factor in current thinking is the issue of responsibility for the maintenance of outdoor amenities. Design proposals should always be sustainable, and

▼ *Barcelona, Spain: To encourage patronage (without much visible success) a forest od steel sculptures provides shade in the central island of a trafficway, Avenue d'Icaria, for the inhabitants of a high density residential environment, the original Olympic Village of 1992*

▲ *Central Johannesburg, South Africa: Public benches in a shady park*

FORMAL PUBLIC SPACE   Organised city environments offer scope for outdoor art forms, such as sculpture and formal landscaping. To be successful, such social spaces should be accessible, have visual appeal, be removed from motor traffic, offer a place to sit in the shade and safe.

developed in accordance with prudent economic policy, which could be guided by any or all of the following:

    ＼ Private maintenance of garden areas in front of houses. This concept could include the house owners' responsibility for the maintenance of the immediate street trees.

    ＼ Maintenance of sports areas by clubs.

    ＼ Maintenance of small public gardens by commercial establishments, e.g. restaurants.

Places to linger

The observation of the survey of small New York plazas that most downtown squares were not used much except for crossing to the other side (Whyte 1982), tends to confirm that streets are 'centrifugal' not 'centripetal'. Unless the amenity value of the place holds some specific attraction for them, people are driven out instead of being attracted in. For example, if the building edge does not provide them with places where they can linger, the place is likely to become a thoroughfare rather than a social space. Both Whyte and Alexander proceed from the standpoint that spontaneous social encounter is the validation of a well-designed social space.

A further identified pattern (Alexander et al. 1977) is the custom that people choose to linger in public spaces where they can enjoy a view toward some feature of interest. People feel most comfortable in spaces which have a 'back' and a 'view into a larger space'. This axiom would apply at all scales from a seat in a garden to a town square with a vista onto a larger space.

To 'colonise' and encourage the effective use of public space it is suggested that the following seating principles will assist (Bentley et al. 1985):

> ∖ Locate seating parallel to pedestrian flows; on wider streets with active uses on both sides, arrange seating down the centre of the space.
> ∖ In squares establish desire-lines for pedestrian flows and then arrange seating to take advantage of the people-watching potential of these positions. Some people like to stand or lean in similar locations.
> ∖ Seating can take the form of chairs (primary seating), or benches and secondary features such as tables, steps, walls or planters. As much primary seating as possible - never less than 10% of the total number of seats. A rule of thumb of 30 cm of seating for each 3 square metres of open space is recommended.
> ∖ Plan choices for seating configuration to encourage both planned and spontaneous social encounter.
> ∖ Avoid locating seats lower than their surroundings, as this reduces their potential prospect onto the social space.

As activities fill the perimeter of a public space it becomes more lively, therefore opportunity for pockets of activity should be incorporated into the edge of public spaces, to accommodate spontaneous activity and cause people to want to linger.

Controls on sun and wind

The progress of the seasons asserts an influence on the popularity of social spaces, a fact which should not be overlooked. The degree of penetration of the sun into a public space correlates with the preference as to where to sit, or not to sit. Sunlight is important, compelling people to follow the sun across a space in the colder months or to avoid it during the hotter seasons. It therefore requires social spaces not to be simply sun-traps for the colder seasons, but to provide for shade when the situation demands. They should be places where people may decide for themselves what 'qualities of the experience' suit their preference at the time.

The levels of sunlight and shade can be assisted by urban design characteristics in a variety of ways such as the size of the open space, level changes, building mass enclosing a space, trees or other features within the space. The ambit of the urban design discipline essentially encompasses the design of all of these design factors in the ordering of urban space.

The absence of wind and draughts is as much a critical factor as the opportunity to enjoy the sun. Air movements around new buildings can radically alter urban environments and create discomfort through gusting and eddying. Apart from the role of urban design, mitigation of the unwanted effects of winds can be achieved architecturally through the design of recesses and similar design considerations for the modelling of the vertical planes of the facades enclosing the public space. Manipulation to obtain desirable and to avoid undesirable micro-effects is, however, more reliably achieved through wind-tunnel testing on models of surrounding buildings and building texture at an early stage.

Windspeed is important because it affects temperature. For example, a 50 kilometre per hour wind at -1° C has six times the cooling effect (chill factor) of still air at -12° C (Bentley et al. 1965). When the criteria for urban social spaces are being formulated, the design guidelines for the buildings on the periphery should take into account:

     ▘ Adverse ground level wind conditions are most frequently associated with buildings significantly taller than their surroundings.

     ▘ Wind-tunnel testing to highlight possible improvements before massing is finalised. Tests can yield useful pointers as to improvements that could ameliorate the negative impacts on open spaces.

Having dealt with shape, scale and climate as major determinants in what constitutes popular social spaces, the designer should also consider the import of studies that have identified a link between the amount of 'sittable' area, and the intensity of use of a space (Whyte 1982).

Researchers tend to concur that the most popular plazas provide opportunity for social encounter through the provision of sufficient public seating. On the other hand, seating designed especially as a 'seat', does not appear to be essential so much as a ledge or a step which can serve as a sitting space. Ideally, when seats are provided they should be ergonomically correct, i.e. comfortable for the user, ensuring well-contoured seats and backs. Sitting configurations should allow people to sit facing another person, or to the side, or back to back, in the sun, in the shade, or in groups, or alone. The physical area for seating measured as part of the total area of an open space should ideally be in the ratio of 1:10 according to the circumstances of case studies conducted (Whyte 1982).

Pedestrian density in a public area

According to empirical observation 15 square metres per person in a public square is considered lively; at 50 square metres per person that same square can be regarded as dead (Alexander et al. 1977). The rule

◀ ▲ *Vancouver, Canada: A downtown public place invitingly furnished for a respite from the bustle of busy streets. Well-located out-of-doors amenities responding to a strong preference for sunny situations after the long dark winter months spent indoors*

URBAN LUNGS A well-conceived and located social space is without equal for its restorative value in busy urban environments. Furnishing of city squares for the convenience of the urban user is an essential part of their success.

▼ ▶ *Arequipa, Peru: Public squares abound providing seating and shade for the benefit of the city dweller*

◀ ▶ *North American downtown social space: Typical accessories include a sculpture lyricising the arts with a strong sense of place and a fountain in contemporary design idiom to fill a void, but offering little invitation to the urban user to enjoy its immediate space*

ACCESSORIES TO PUBLIC SPACES Well-designed urban social spaces need carefully considered spatial structuring but also features that provide amenity, such as seating, fountains and sculptures for the convenience and delight of the users.

▼ ▶ *Florence and Barclona: Traditionally in Europe accessories were seen as a means of furnishing the outdoor city spaces, such as the loggia and sculptures of Piazza Signoria and Gaudi's integrated seat with lightstandard in the Passeig de Gracia*

of thumb suggested therefore is: for public squares, courts, pedestrian streets, any place where crowds are drawn together, estimate the mean number of people in the place at any given moment (P), and make the area of the place between 150 x P and 300 x P square feet (approximately 15 x P and 30 x P square metres).

It should be remembered that a square of 30 by 30 metres will seem deserted if there are fewer than 30 people in it and there are not many places in an urban context where there will always be 30 people. On the basis of the thesis that it is possible to recognise a person's face and a normal speaking voice to be heard across a spatial width of 23 metres, Alexander et al. propose that a public square, except where it serves as a centre to a large city, should be no more than 20 metres across. This applies only to the width; in the length there would be no constraint necessary. With the aim of either encouraging or discouraging social encounter, the issue of appropriate pedestrian density levels is a matter of importance, requiring to be addressed along with all other design aspects discussed.

Pedestrians-only streets

Some urban designers hold that for pedestrian streets to function properly two special properties are needed: first, vehicular traffic must be excluded, and second, 'the buildings along the pedestrian street must be planned in a way which as nearly as possible eliminates indoor staircases, corridors, and lobbies, and leaves most circulation outdoors' (Alexander et al. 1977). Another aspect is that the most comfortable pedestrian streets are those where the 'width of the street does not exceed the height of the surrounding buildings'.

In locations where public activity is sufficiently intense, watching other people becomes in itself one of the most common activities. That this mostly happens at the edge of the space suggests that the perimeter offers a sense of refuge as well as a good prospect of what is going on (Bentley et al. 1985). Also, the prospect onto the activity within the social space could be enhanced if the seating is at a slightly higher level than the space itself, while the width of the pedestrian movement zone must be appropriate to the level of pedestrian traffic involved. A choice has to be made between pedestrian-only streets, where motor traffic defers to people, or public space where traffic intervenes only in a controlled way. In any event, between the pedestrian movement zone and the vehicular space, a linear zone for street trees, seating, bus shelters, telephone kiosks and cycle tracks should be planned.

Parked cars are themselves one of the most effective barriers between pedestrians and moving vehicles.

The residential/public interface

The treatment of the interface between residential buildings and the public environment is of crucial importance to the social performance of an open space. Public and private spaces are interdependent, each affecting the functionality of the other (Dewar and Uytenbogaardt, 1977). Architectural management of this interface should aim at ensuring that:

- ⬊ the clarity of the interface prevents spill over of public activities onto private space;
- ⬊ the private/public interface needs to provide a sense of enclosure, scale, continuity and protection as it is largely instrumental in determining how successfully the public space is used; and
- ⬊ the way in which the interface affects the use of private space. The closer to the street the interface is, and the less complex its definition, the less private it becomes. When the private space is very small, and therefore very close to the street, the interface could become an ineffective device for defining privacy.

Commercial, industrial and community facilities usually 'front directly onto the pavement; residential activity on the other hand requires a much greater degree of privacy and consequently the interface has a zonal structure, creating graduating zones of increasing privacy' (Dewar and Uytenbogaardt 1977).

Pollution-free spaces

Transportation-related air pollutants and their spatial and temporal distribution differ greatly from place to place within a city. Air pollution is a function of the commuting culture, traffic volumes and speed, topography of urban form, built materials and meteorological conditions.

In the urban situation, Spirn (1984) outlines effective design controls in the relationship between buildings and open space that together with

◀ *Jaipur, India: Urban sprawl that necessitates the use of motorised transportation to support productive urban life. Without sizeable green lungs levels of air pollution reach dangerous levels impacting on the health of the city dweller*

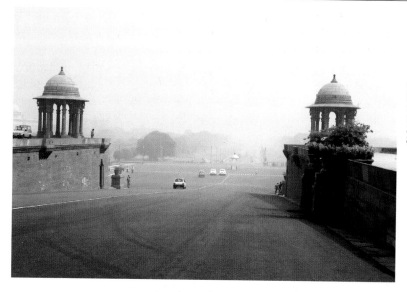

New Delhi, India: View from between the Secretariat buildings eastwards along the ceremonial Rajpath towards the India Gate. During the post-monsoon period, when air pollution levels rise alarmingly in the city, no visual connection between the two is possible

landscaping strategies could promote air circulation and reduce the levels of air pollution:

⊠ In flat, open terrain under calm conditions, air pollution levels are highest adjacent to the road and decrease with distance from it.

⊠ Street canyons lined with buildings of similar height, oriented perpendicular to the wind direction, tend to have poorer circulation than street canyons that are lined with buildings of different heights and interspersed with open areas. To promote air circulation in street canyons, step buildings back from the street, increase openings and vary building heights.

⊠ Wind shadows on the lee of buildings reduce air circulation and provide a place for polluting emissions to build up. To reduce wind shadow at the base of a building, buildings designed with a pyramidical shape or openings are more likely to permit air flow.

⊠ The more enclosed the space the more likely the accumulation of pollutants. To promote air circulation, streetside arcades or canopies designed to be high rather than low would ameliorate the situation.

⊠ To reduce the effects of pollution, create planted highway embankments and woodland growth landscaped to help filter pollutants from the air and the dispersion thereof. It is desirable to locate pollution-sensitive uses away from highway emission zones. Green spaces within the urban setting are dust-reducing and have the property of assisting towards cleaner air by a process of carbon-dioxide fixation through photosynthesis.

The relation of smog to urban sprawl is well known. 'The more sprawl, the greater the energy expended in getting people and materials back and forth between them, and so the greater the air pollution' (Dantzig and Saaty 1973). In the sense that green spaces are dust-reducing they contribute to healthier urban settings and consequently the well-being of urban communities. The aim is to achieve a 'safe' urban environment so that people breathe pure air and with assurance are able to enjoy the outdoors without the threat to their health.

Other forms of pollution, such as noise pollution, potentially detract from the quality of the urban outdoors and should be addressed scientifically at source, particularly where the daily functions of city life are integrated and densely concentrated.

Sense of place and space

Familiarity with a place in specific urban contexts is an important factor evoking either positive or negative responses. Most cities have their showpiece public spaces, but similarly most have their no-go areas. Before the twentieth century places that looked important were important, and places of public importance could easily be identified. In the modern context, this tends to be less so. Some urban designers link the notion of familiarity with legibility, 'which is the quality which makes a place graspable.' (Lynch 1981). Furthermore, 'legibility is important at two levels: physical form and activity patterns'. In outline, important critical factors in the 'legibility' of public space are: the biggest open spaces should be related to the most important public facilities; and the point of a legible layout is that people are able to form clear, accurate images of it. Lynch, who pioneered the topic of image maps in the 1960s, suggests that there are overlapping features amongst people's images of places, namely, nodes, edges, paths, districts and landmarks. It would be wrong to assume that every area should contain all these features. Note that it is the user rather than the designer who forms the cognitive image.

The terms 'hard' and 'soft' spaces are sometimes used by planners. Both have a useful function and contribute to the character of place (Trancik 1986). Hard spaces are those principally bounded by architectural walls often intended to function as major gathering places for social activity, whereas soft spaces are landscaped or those dominated by the natural environment, whether inside or outside the city.

Architecture and landscape architecture must respond to and aim at strengthening the sense of place. Those who comment critically on the spatial attributes of the environments for social intercourse believe that the 'notion of place' is as a result of familiar associations with a place:

⟧ Part of the presence of any good place is the feeling of it embodying and being surrounded by a field of its own sort of space with its special limits and potentials. It is this field that is only interesting today if it implies connection: roads with buildings, buildings with buildings, with trees, with the seasons, with decorations, with events, with other people in other times (Smithson 1967).

⟧ Just as each locality should seem continuous with the recent past, so it should seem continuous with the near future (Lynch 1981).

⟧ A place is a space which is distinctive in character. Since ancient times the *genus loci*, or spirit of place has been recognised as the concrete reality man has to face and come to terms with in his daily life (Norberg-Shultz 1971).

These associations which people form make certain subliminal demands on an urban space for the experience it affords, such as a sense of timelessness and where change only takes place when it is rational. Where a sense of place has a hardnosed meaning is where street traders set up shop Theses notions place a particular obligation on the urban designer to recognise the bonding of the urban dweller with 'place' - a dynamic interaction which is both abstract and challenging.

◀ *Downtown, Johannesburg, South Africa: Street trading, a new means of economic independence for the urbanising masses*

INFORMAL TRADING Democracy brings empowerment and the burgeoning informal trading sector is a pillar for survival in urban situations in developing countries. To be viable commercial opportunities require suitable urban space at nodes of intensive pedestrian activity.

Observers believe that the character of a place consists of both the concrete substance of shape, texture and colour and the more intangible cultural associations - a certain patina given by human use over time (Trancik 1968). This phenomenon arises from the need for people, as cultural beings, to have a stable system of places to depend on, thereby providing emotional attachment and identity with place. The analogy on a personal level is one's own home environment. The universal nature of this dependence on the qualities of a particular space places a very real onus on the urban designer 'to create truly unique contextual places' and to 'explore the local history, the feelings and the needs of the populace, the traditions of craftsmanship and indigenous materials, and the political and economic realities of the community' (Trancik 1968).

A sense of neighbourhood

To foster a sense of belonging in an ideal neighbourhood, perceptions play a significant part and optimum population threshold is an important factor towards effective social networking and bonding. Evidence so far suggests that:

   ＼ people identify with neighbourhoods which have extremely small populations;
   ＼ such neighbourhoods are small in area; and
   ＼ a major road through a neighbourhood destroys the potential for bonding.

The Western experience is that, if the population is over fifteen hundred persons, such a group finds difficulty in coordinating itself to reach decisions about important issues affecting their common interests. Some sociologists set the figure as low as five hundred persons.

Research in the USA concludes that the optimum physical area for a sense of neighbourhood was found to be from one up to three blocks. A more significant factor, however, is that a 'neighbourhood can only have a strong identity if it is protected from heavy traffic' (Alexander et al. 1977). In his chapter on the *Identifiable Neighbourhood*, Alexander advocates that neighbourhoods should not be more than 300 metres across with

'In Saudi Arabia traditional concepts of planning and urban forms show similarities with those found in comparable climatic regions of the world. It is recognised here that the influence of religion created a certain type of organisation and that the need for privacy resulted in special details in the micro-environment of the rural and semi-rural layout. The Arab city or town also developed around centrally located mosques, souqs (markets), khans (guest houses) and hammams (public bath houses) surrounded by housing and other services. However, the organisation of these basic elements of the Arab cities, climatic influence seems to dominate the overall fabric of any small or large development.'

Talib, 1984

▲ *St Ettienne, France: Medium rise apartment blocks in an unrelieved carpark setting*

▲ *Runcorn New Town, Cheshire, UK: Five-storey Southgate housing scheme of the 1970s, 1500 units for 6000 residents by Stirling & Partners. Rigid, schematic organisation without any links with the surroundings. The scheme was subsequently demolished*

▶ *Isle of Dogs, London: Social housing in a banal environment with no redeeming community open space*

DYSFUNCTIONAL NEIGHBOURHOODS Mass housing schemes that fail to cultivate a sense of neighbourhood have proliferated in developed Western countries, with consequent social dysfunctioning. Many have been demolished and accepted as expensive housing experiments as they were no remedy for the afflictions of modern times, such as loneliness, depression and stress. Others remain as monuments to the failure to involve the end users in the planning process.

a population of no more than four to five hundred people, and major roads must be kept out.

Clusters

In a survey of one hundred and fifty people in Levittown, New York, it was found that all of them were engaged in some pattern of regular visiting with their neighbours (Gans 1968). This visiting pattern is significant in that it underlines the fact that people want be part of a neighbourhood cluster. The extent to which the opportunity to visit is conducted formally or informally in a neighbourhood would depend on cultural and socio-economic factors. On a typical block each home is at the centre of its own cluster, demonstrating that the social patterning continues even when the conventional block

In recent times interest has been expressed by various individuals and government agencies in learning more from the past experiences and achievements of man as builder of his own environment and in the preservation and restoration of historic/traditional architecture, from which there is a lot to learn.

It is said in Hadith (the sayings of Prophet Mahommed) that each person in a community should take care of seven neighbours around him. This is the basis of the concepts of community and neighbourhood (mohalia) in Islam, and the basis for Muslim settlement formations.

Talib (1984)

layout, or neighbourhood plan, is not specifically planned as cluster units and instead tends to promote anonymity.

To replace a grid-like array of houses on a street, clustering of a more personal nature gives people immediate and effective control over their common land. 'A cluster is a dynamic social structure, which takes physical shape, and is governed above all by the common land at its heart and by the fluidity of the relations between the individual families and this common land' (Alexander et al. 1977). Control over the common space reinforces the community and is wholly important to successful residential neighbourhoods. Further, Alexander states that 'the cluster of land and homes immediately around one's own home is of special importance... and it is the natural focus of neighbourly interaction'.

The urge to cluster emerges in the presence of certain supporting factors. On the basis of a community keeping in touch, and meeting internally for decision-making, there appears to be the following pattern, Alexander observes:

﹅ The clusters seem to work best if they have between them eight to twelve houses each.
﹅ More than twelve houses and the balance is strained.
﹅ In all cases common land which is shared by the cluster is an essential ingredient.
﹅ Ownership is essential for the clustering pattern to take hold, and shared ownership of the social space reinforces the common interest.

Alexander recommends that houses should therefore be arranged in broadly identifiable clusters of eight to twelve households around some common land and paths. Clusters should also be arranged so that anyone can walk through them without feeling like a trespasser.

In residential contexts clustering is a phenomenon observed in spatial patterning throughout history where there is no regimentation through formal planning. It is a spontaneous process which Rapoport (1977) states: 'tends to occur in cities based on perceived homogeneity, differing interpretations of environmental quality, lifestyles, symbol systems, and defences against overload and stress.'

Clustering in dense conurbations enables mutual help, assimilation and urbanisation and the preservation of certain institutions, and helps maintain familiar controls and cultural patterns.

It is conceivable that 'people who are already under great stress need the support of familiar and even "prosthetic" environments, as groups

▲ *Phuentsoling, Bhutan/India border: Grand entrance gateway in the heart of a border town, demarcating the point of entry and departure from one country into another. Apart from providing architectural opportunities, such features are unusual but effective in defining territory within urban space*

◀ *New York, USA: Chinatown, typically an enclave approached through a 'gateway' where the cultural identity of an ethnic community is conserved, creating a sense of belonging in an adoptive urban environment*

who have lowered competence, or are in a state of cultural docility, are more vulnerable' (Rapoport 1977). In Africa there is a long tradition of identifying territory with ethnic groups. In more recent examples, clustering patterns are also observable in squatter settlements (Mangin 1970).

Other urban commentators have shown that in dense city environments a division into quite distinct and separate areas on the basis of place and origin, age, occupation, house ownership, recency of arrival and tribal origin is discernible.

A feature not common in most modern town planning practice is the introduction of a main gate to a housing precinct, to heighten the distinctiveness of the area and give it distinguishable identity. Alexander et al. (1977) advocates that 'every boundary in the city which has important human meaning - the boundary of a building cluster, a neighbourhood, a precinct' be marked by 'great gateways where the major entering paths cross the boundary'.

Israeli Ministry of Housing: Neighbourhood 'gateway' model, cultivating social networking and a sense of belonging

Common land

'People will not feel comfortable in their houses unless a group of houses forms a cluster, with the public land between them jointly owned by all the householders' (Alexander et al. 1977).

Common land should be provided as a social necessity, first to 'make it possible for people to feel comfortable outside their buildings and their private territory' and second, 'common land acts as a meeting place for people'.

There should be enough common land to be useful and to accommodate children's games and small gatherings. Also, Alexander advocates that 'the amount of common land needed in a neighbourhood is in the order of twenty-five per cent of the land held privately'. The automobile should on no account be allowed to dominate this land.

Personal space

It is in the nature of animals, including humans, to exhibit tendencies towards the defence of personal space. In so doing the instinct is to choose distance to define personal domains. This hypothesis is based on the observations that the simplest form of situational personality is that associated with responses to intimate, personal, social and public transactions.

Some people never develop the public phase of their personalities and similarly, others have trouble with the intimate and personal zones which require tolerance of closeness with others. A four-part classification system is considered the framework for determining territorial distances (Hall 1972):

⋙   Intimate distance: At this distance, the presence of another person is unmistakable and may at times be overwhelming because of stepped-up sensory inputs. Researchers divide intimate distance into two phases: close and far (i.e. 15 to 45 cm);

⋙ Personal distance: This distance can be represented as a protective sphere that an organism maintains between itself and others. In the close phase (45 to 75 cm), physical contact is possible if so desired, but equally so separation. Keeping someone at 'arm's length' is one way of expressing the far phase (75 to 125 cm) of personal distance.

⋙ Social distance: The boundary line between the far phase of personal distance and the close phase of social distance marks the 'limit of domination'. Impersonal business occurs in the close phase (125 to 215 cm). In the far phase (215 to 365 cm) business is conducted in a more formal manner.

⋙ Public distance: At the distance of the close phase (365 to 800 cm) an alert subject can take evasive or defensive action. At the far phase distance (800 cms or more), much of the non-verbal part of communication shifts to gestures and body stance. A whole person can be seen as quite small, and perceived in a setting.

◀ Madrid, Spain: Tower block of apartments where extensive outdoor balconies strengthen the opportunity for personalisation of space, and enable greater personal maneouvrability within the urban situation

Proxemic behaviour, which is in essence what has been described above, is culturally conditioned, individual and arbitrary; however, it is important for planners to understand human sensitivity to the phenomenon of personal space, the need for privacy and the escape from situations which precipitate stressful contact.

OPTIMUM USER LEVELS

Sharing of facilities, such as the multifunctional utilisation of school and other institutional facilities, for example sports facilities, is a reasonable consideration in all urban planning. Significant enhancement of choices in the residential environment can be achieved by more integrated design and, by implication, fewer constraints on the use of land and facilities. Such strategies require consensus amongst administrators at the planning stage.

Sustainable density options

Goals of sustainable density could be achieved through:

    ❂ the integrated design of residential environments for the more productive use of designated space. Through careful design, greater proportions of streets can, for example, be integrated into the housing environment as community social space;

    ❂ local shopping and commercial facilities could equally, through more open-ended zoning practices, be integrated into the residential environment in order to obviate the need for setting aside designated zones for these facilities. The practice of including shopping at ground level with housing above would be a traditional application of this option and could bring significant benefits; also

    ❂ alternative housing options should be explored. Research conducted into residential densities in cities across the world indicates that there are distinct advantages through employing a mix of high-density/low rise residential and the courtyard house forms. Much favoured in the harsh climates of Africa and Asia, the courtyard house has met the needs of cultures, where socio-religious practices are quite different to those of the West. However, this house form has more recently received increasing attention in other contemporary contexts such as Alexander's housing in Lima, Peru; research at Cambridge conducted by Martin and Marsh (Colquhoun 1999); recent housing projects in parts of Manhattan and Los Angeles; and housing estates in the Netherlands and Sweden.

The courtyard house

As an alternative housing option, the courtyard house is conceptually an efficient and versatile planning form.

▶ *Old cities of Jeddah and Riyadh, Saudi Arabia: Comparative figure-ground footprints of two historic urban environments achieving remarkably high densities generally only two storeys high. Such compactness, yet liveability and response to climatic conditions, was achieved through the use of the courtyard house form (After Talib, 1984)*

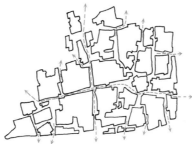

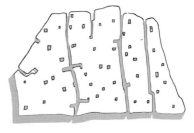

hot humid : air movement

hot dry : shade

▲ *Beni Isguen, M'zab, Algeria: The courtyard house satisfies the need for privacy in dense urban situations, particularly in hot, inhospitable climates, where survival demands that the shelter be internalised in shaded courts*

▶ *Temacine, near Touggourt, Algeria: Providing amenity, privacy, security and protection against harsh climatic conditions, a feature of the courtyard house is the walled flat roofs used extensively as outdoor family and sleeping areas, during the cooler hours*

DENSITY As a concept, density *per se* is not to blame for poor urban environments, as historical examples will demonstrate. The fault lies in the application where the communities' perceptions and socio-cultural needs are ignored.

Essentially amounting to the full perimeter development of a site without setbacks, as distinct from a building located centrally on the site, among the merits of the courtyard house are:

    ⬊ high densities can be achieved while still affording ready access to personal outdoor space; and

    ⬊ the spaces encapsulated within the built form lend themselves to being easily integrated into a tight urban fabric yet provide choices of community interaction, privacy, defensibility and surveillance of a neighbourhood by residents.

Small stands

Layouts should make provision for possible building additions in the long term to individual house units. An important planning principle is that, in a complex of small stands, the misuse of the stand's limited size should not negatively alter the quality or value of adjoining properties through overlooking or overshadowing.

The following principles should be observed with prototypical small stand layouts (Morkel 1988):

    The stand which is generally narrow on its street frontage and deep in its extent back from the street reduces the length of the service infrastructure along the street frontage corresponding to each stand. Financial and land resources for other capital works would thereby be liberated for amenity purposes.

    The road system should be designed to minimise through-traffic in residential areas, thereby allowing for a large reduction in the width of local access residential streets. Similarly, this would amount to the reduction in the amount of land and road infrastructure corresponding to each stand.

    The house should be placed close to the street to conserve the unbuilt-on area of the stand as a single area for private use, rather than a series of fragmented and unusable sidespaces. The house extending across the full width of the street frontage will provide a secure, private area to the rear of the site. In this way, the single frontage onto the public environment is reduced and maintenance minimised.

    Extensions to the rear of the house should be kept to the perimeter of the stand to ensure that the area of the private social space is maximised.

    Panhandle sites become a possibility with consequent efficiency in the layout of the service infrastructure.

With building frontages onto public spaces it is advantageous that 'the public edge of the building should house activities which benefit from interaction with the public realm, and can contribute to the life of the public space itself' (Bentley et al. 1985). To achieve this:

    Locate as many entrances as possible in such positions that comings and goings are directly visible from the public space.

    Encourage compatible uses within the buildings to spill out into the public area. This principle applies to uses on the ground and first storeys.

    Even if there are no public uses, most buildings contain activities which can contribute to the animation of the public space itself.

    It is still necessary to preserve the privacy of the indoor activity, so that the users will not feel the need to screen themselves totally from

◀ *Jerusalem, Israel: New neighbourhood, Ramot Alon, 1980s: An effective plan exploiting the hill-like topography of the site to offset any negative effects of high density*

DENSITY AND TOPOGRAPHY   Three 'historic' Mediterranean cities, showing varying levels of saturation in terms of density. Where the site topographic conditions permit oppressive effects of high density can be alleviated. Natural features, if conserved, can provide urban dwellers with essential outlets for recreation.

▲ *Athens, Greece: High density/medium-rise cityscape of unrelieved residential development 'wall to wall' between natural features*

◀ *Barcelona, Spain: View from Tibidabo towards the city's new waterfront, reclaimed as part of the 1992 Olympic Games plan*

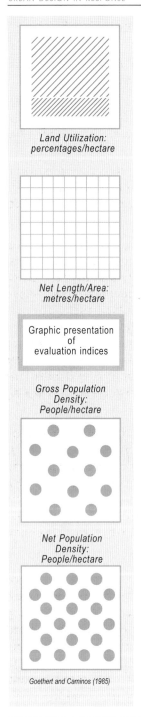

Land Utilization:
percentages/hectare

Net Length/Area:
metres/hectare

Graphic presentation
of
evaluation indices

Gross Population
Density:
People/hectare

Net Population
Density:
People/hectare

Goethert and Caminos (1985)

the public space. This privacy can be achieved by horizontal distance, a change in level and/or a combination of both.

⬊   The usefulness of the edge is important for people-watching and is greatly increased by the provision of places to sit.

With development of all settlements there are thresholds of tolerance regarding density. Although not exhaustive, as a rule of thumb, the test criteria conceived by Goethert and Caminos (1985) could be used as a guide.

Density test criteria

Practical experience indicates that at the early stages of a design, three simple tests should be applied critically to avoid the wasteful use of scarce land resources resulting in unnecessary expense and thus remaining a burden to the user and the public service agencies.

The test criteria are Land Utilization, Network Length/Area Index and Density, which provide the framework for evaluating early design and layout proposals.

The Land Utilization Index : The LUI is defined as a 'qualification of the land around a dwelling in relation to user, physical controls and responsibility'. In this context, four types of land are identified: public, semipublic, private and semiprivate. The LUI is derived from three separate scenarios:

⬊   the actual user, from the individual in a private lot to undefined groups in public streets;

⬊   the responsible agent, such as the public sector in streets and the individual user in a lot; and

⬊   the type and means of control, ranging from legal and social controls to physical barriers like fences.

To illustrate the application of the third parameter, for example, the addition of a fence increases control and may change the actual use of a piece of land to semipublic status from that of purely public.

The Network Length/Area Index: The NL/AI is defined as 'the ratio of the length of the network to the area(s) contained within, or tangent to it'. The Index is determined by measuring the total area served by a network, and the length of the network itself. Units are expressed in length per unit area, such as metres per hectare.

In addition to being an indication of access functions, this index provides a direct reference for utilities costs - street paving, water distribution networks, sewage disposal networks and electrical lines - and is also a reference for non-physical services, such as refuse collection. In general terms, the lower the value of the ratio the more cost effective the network, assuming that its basic service functions are still maintained.

Density: Generally defined as the ratio between the population of a given area and the area itself. It can be in terms of either:

   ⬚ gross density; or
   ⬚ nett density which refers to the population ratio with the residential land component only and does not include land set aside for other uses.

Density is often the most commonly accepted indicator and provides a reference for the amount of land needed for supporting facilities with regard to a given population and is also an indicator of the type of physical development.

In the application of these indices to the planning exercise, there must be some discreet definition or judgement of what constitutes 'appropriate' values for the three parameters. This would inevitably vary with the circumstances of the layout being planned. For example, site topography could relieve the perception of 'denseness' as can be seen on hilly terrain, as in the case of Jerusalem, Barcelona and Athens. The Geothert and Caminos system is a tool which when translated into simple graphics allows quick visual comparisons among several layout alternatives. The method enables planners to conduct initial studies with a view to optimising densities, so that land use efficiency becomes clearer at an earlier stage without involving heavy expenditure in terms of finance or time.

Whatever methodology is adopted to determine optimum density, an understanding of how the socio-cultural needs of urban communities transform into identifiable physical patterns is seminal to good urban planning: people-inspired historical settlements should be an inspiration for planners. Apart from the potential for effecting land-use efficiency, as a starting point for formal planning it is essential to recognise and accept the phenomenon of the social need/spatial form interdependency.

URBAN IMPRINTS ON NATURAL REGIMES

Broadly speaking the factors causing deviations of the urban climate from the prevailing regional macroclimate are: the changed surface qualities of pavements and buildings; the buildings themselves casting shadows; the buildings acting as barriers and channelling wind with localised increases in velocity through their mass; the absorption of heat which is slowly released at night; the daily energy seepage of heated buildings, output of airconditioning plants, heat output of the motor vehicle and electrical appliances, and heat loss from industry; and atmospheric pollution

Chicago, Illinois USA: Cityscape: The bulk of the buildings influences wind flows, while the orientation of the streets and the vertical walls of reflective glass add significantly to the urban climate. Contemporary urban planning and architecture delegate design solutions to energy-consuming technologies which are heat producing and heavily air polluting

arising from the waste products of production or transportation creating a higher volume of solid particles in the urban atmosphere. These contributory factors may assist in the formation of fog that, under favourable conditions, can produce rain.

The air temperature in a city can be 8° C higher than the surrounding countryside, and relative humidity reduced due to the quick runoff from hardened surfaces and absence of vegetation. Wind velocity can be reduced to less than half of that of the surrounding open country, whereas it can be more than doubled due to the funnelling effect between tall slab blocks, and along narrow streets. Eddies can be set up along leeward corners of obstructions (Koenigsberger et al. 1974).

Conserve ecological diversity

If Nature is 'the world untouched by man', then it follows that, with global population growth statistics in mind, the remaining pure natural regions should be safeguarded from human intrusion. On the other hand, if managed landscapes such as farming and forestry are regarded as part of the natural setting, the city and the inhabited countryside should also be considered as one unit. There is the view that 'sometimes it has been [seen as] the unity of the exploiter [city] and the exploited [countryside], but they have always been linked together socially, economically and politically' (Lynch 1981).

The integration of natural regimes is not just a matter of saving plants and animals, but of making their presence apparent and appreciated. 'The movements of sun and tides, the cycles of weeds and insects and men, can all be celebrated within the spatial network of the urban setting. The urban dweller can be liberated from the dichotomies of city and country, artifical and natural, man versus other living things, once the city can be accepted as being as natural as a farm' (Lynch 1981).

In contrast to the construct of City versus Nature, the integration of natural regimes into the city environment brings a balance to city life and thus a greater sense of well-being. Also, an integrated environmental management approach to city or building and context cultivates a greater awareness of the real interdependency of the urban and natural environments.

The United States Multiple Use/Sustained Yield Act of 1960, 'mandated the U.S. Forest Service to recognise both the diversity and ecosystemic characteristics of land..., and the need to regulate the resource yields of these lands in a way that could be sustained' (Steiner 1988).

The destruction of common property resources will remain a continuing problem for society, whereas pollution emanating from urban consumption may become the greater threat for the following reasons (Stauth 1983):

    ⚹ Pollution is an insidious phenomenon because it is often a gradual process.

◀ Bear Run, Pa., USA: Falling Water, 1936, the embodiment of Frank Lloyd Wright's ideal place for living fused into Nature. Consciously the architect conserved the natural regimes in the final statement of the concrete intent, so that they continue to function on a sustainable basis

⊠ The negative effects are not always so obvious, and the ultimate implications for social well-being are far from clear; and

⊠ It will probably prove to be a more intractable problem because dealing with it will require much greater sacrifices on the part of society.

Natural resources have a place in the urban environment. To be managed on a sustained yield basis adequate physical space for the integration of resource areas into the fabric of the urban environment should enjoy more than token commitment. Stressful modern urban life demands greater emphasis on the incorporation and enrichment of green space in the urban ecology.

Biogeographical principles

Maintaining biodiversity backed by practical application is central in the promotion of species-rich urban environments. Although urban growth tends to destroy wildlife habitats and to reduce the diversity of flora and fauna, the new buildings, open spaces and sources of food and waste in cities provide a great variety of ecological situations readily exploitable by particular types of plants and animals. An equilibrium develops within each of such urban habitats between the colonising plants and their physical and biological environment.

'The notion of corridors linking "habitat islands" together is perhaps one of the more practical uses of island biogeographic theory in urban areas.' This approach 'should allow for the development of open space networks which are ecologically resilient and diverse, and combine a low cost of maintenance with high, scientific, educational, aesthetic and recreational value' (Roberts 1985). The open space network, including the primary street system, the neighbourhood street and square and private social spaces, should all potentially contribute to the 'linking corridor' concept, strengthening the ecological base and encouraging ecological diversity rather than destroying it.

To promote species diversity, the application of biogeographical principles to urban open space certain criteria need to be satisfied (Roberts 1985):

⊠ A large habitat area is better than a small one for two reasons: the large area can hold more species at equilibrium, and it will have a lower extinction rate.

⊠ Several smaller areas adding up to the total of the single area are not biogeographically equivalent to it, since they tend to support a smaller number of species.

⊠ The equilibrium number of species in one of the smaller habitats can, however, be raised by increasing the immigration rate to it. This

◄ Örebro, Sweden: Older cities have the advantage of the healing power of time to merge the built environment with natural regimes. The restorative power of the natural environment should niether be under- , nor overestimated but instead be exploited in the modern urban situation

can be done by judicious juxtaposition of the several scattered reserves, and by providing corridors of stepping stones of natural habitat between them.

❇ Any habitat should be as near-circular as other factors permit, to minimise dispersal distances within the habitat. If the habitat area becomes narrowed or has dead-end peninsulas, local extinction rates are likely to be high due to the presence of small populations and peripheral disturbances, and dispersal is unlikely to keep pace with extinction.

In a pioneering article the following policy is advocated to achieve sustainable biodiverse environments (Brady et al. 1978):

❇ A combination of careful planning and benign neglect.

❇ The need for some abandonment of the 'well-entrenched manicure complex' to ensure that the natural diversity of regenerating nature is not entirely replaced by the uniform and technology-dependent landscape of established design tradition.

❇ The recognition that urban habitat islands and corridors are biogeographically valuable, as they provide 'reservoirs' and 'stepping-stones' for a variety of plants and animals.

Only by rethinking the approach to planning, and indeed management policy, can ecological viability and conservation of indigenous flora and fauna be achieved. By ignoring the linking of open space resources, biogeographical capabilities of the open space network become limited.

◀ *Nr Padua, Italy: Seasonal flowering of poppies extends the biogeographical principle to conserve species diversity in an area of intensive mono-agriculture*

Compared to the traditional park, woodland-like communities may be more expensive to establish initially, but these new natural areas may well prove cheaper in the long run, because they require less maintenance than the traditional mown grass and flower bed culture of the conventional park.

Offset geomorphic impacts

Prudent urban design would set out to compensate for the destruction of the ecological base, and minimise the alteration of the existing natural regimes. An important contributing factor in the equation is the alteration of the geomorphic base.

The city is a new landscape with new forms such as man-made cliffs, long narrow tracts of hardened surface, sometimes broken by the intervention of the original natural landscape. The nature of the land cover is a major factor in affecting climate, wind patterns, nutrient status and diversity of the 'intra-urban ecosystems', as city habitats and biotic communities might be described. Extremes in the characteristics of urban settings range from completely covered, built-up central business areas on the one hand to remnant relics of the rural landscape on the other, usually in the form of woodlands, copses, commons and urban heaths.

The hydrological changes associated with urban development cause exposure of the soil during the development of new construction sites promoting rapid erosion of soils and increased silt loading in streams up to as much as 100 times. Such conditions can influence the extent of floodplains (Douglas 1983). The extraction of groundwater by the standard practice of hard channelling of stormwater withholds water from the subsurface, which may create physical changes that induce subsidence and slope instability. In planning new urban environments, the possibility of precipitating mass ground movement must be met with solutions which include lessening of hard surfacing in the urban situation and incorporating the relict landforms as far as is practicable.

Legal controls, introduced in North Carolina, USA in 1973 to limit the effects of development activities on natural systems, require:

   ⎖ a sediment and erosion control plan for all urban development on areas greater than one acre;

   ⎖ re-establishment of cover on disturbed areas inside 30 days, if active construction is not proceeding;

   ⎖ retention of a buffer strip between the disturbed areas and streams or lakes; and

   ⎖ grading of cut and fill slopes to a stable angle, and application of vegetation or structural measures within 30 days of slope modification.

It is important to observe the objectives of ISO14001 which deals with the management and auditing of the effects of construction activities on natural systems (See Appendix II).

Coastal sites are particularly sensitive to change due to the dynamic and complex nature of their forms. Impacts of development affecting estuaries cannot be evaluated simplistically and require specialised study.

Apart from changes to the landform and surfacing in the built environment, it should be understood by designers and planners that changes to the environs occur when buildings are grouped together (Douglas 1983):

   ⎖ They influence the energy balances of one another and complicate the air movements and heat flows in the intervening spaces.

   ⎖ The bulk of two buildings of differing size adjacent to one another affects wind flows so strongly that the downward flow of air on the taller block creates higher wind speeds in two zones. Such effects can be avoided by carrying out appropriate analysis at the design stage, if necessary with windtunnel models, to determine an optimum spacing to minimise gusting.

   ⎖ Vertical walls tend to reflect solar radiation towards the ground rather than the sky. Re-radiation from the ground bounces back on to the walls of the adjacent buildings. Skyscrapers can absorb more than six times the heat absorbed by the featureless rural plain, but an area

Dallas, USA, 1990s: View from Dallas City Hall and Convention Center Plaza epitomises the urban desert of a typical North American downtown. There is little evidence of 'soft' landscaping to promote biodiversity or offset hydrological changes to the original landscape

of dispersed suburban housing would absorb only slightly more than the rural plain (Terjung 1973):

The orientation of the streets, the season of the year, the techniques and materials used in building construction may all affect the absorption of short-wave radiation.

The intensity, size and shape of any urban heat island varies with the topography of the city, land uses within the city, patterns of artificial heat generation and the weather. The inevitable changes to weather patterns in the region of urban development are well documented. Changes in the chemistry of the rain due to the emission of substances into the atmosphere accelerate geomorphic processes, as well as the deterioration of building materials. Chemical weathering of building materials will be interlinked with any change to the quality of air over urban areas.

The built environment is accompanied by a 'capillary rise of saline groundwater [which] may cause salt attack after the structure is completed' (Douglas 1983). Changes in the groundwater conditions under new urban development 'trigger off' changes to the hydrological subsurface profile, which in turn can alter soil chemical profiles. In planning new urban settings, it is therefore important to observe subsurface characteristics and to plan to allow a high degree of surface water penetration, employing measures which allow penetration through carefully conceived landscaping (Douglas 1983).

The city modifies the natural energy balance and air circulation through its multiple reflection and absorption patterns, its rough, uneven surface, its lack of water and vegetation over many tracts and additional sources of heat and dust provided by human activity. Intensive landscaping and 'greening' policies by both the public and the private sectors should be practised to conserve and sustain ecosystems, as well as successful social environments in urban settings.

To offset these negative manifestations of the built environment, every aspect should be considered in urban design. Legislative controls should be updated where they are deficient. Solutions to these problems require expertise and in-depth study, commencing with the identification of the geomorphic characteristics of the original natural site and new landforms envisaged for a new urban environments.

In conclusion, in all urban development projects, mitigative measures should inform the planning process with a view to conserving the natural regimes, planning for biogeographical sustainability and offsetting the effects arising inevitably from the alteration of the geomorphic properties of the original landscape.

Urban emissions and climate change

Aside from mitigation measures which reduce the effects from hardened non-reflective surfaces and energy consumption characterising the urban heat island, the modern city culture's dependence on transportation produces greenhouse gas emissions. Yet the scientific lobby is divided as to whether an imbalance in the global heat budget leading to global warming is the main cause of climatic change now being experienced:

The global climatic events of recent time bringing extensive floods to the coastline of many countries raises the question whether the floods in southern Africa, heavy rains in South America, and windstorms in Central Europe were caused by global warming. To answer this question, it is not possible in fact to prove or disprove that a given severe weather event occurred only because of a rapidly warming global climate.

Arguing from first principles it is a fact that a warmer atmosphere will hold more moisture and, therefore, have the capacity to deliver heavier rainfall. Also, warmer ocean temperatures potentially provide tropical cyclones with increased energy to make them more vigorous and the rainfall more intense. But in neither case can it be construed with certainty that particular rains were caused by global warming. Alternatively, does statistical evidence show that such intense rainfalls have been recorded before in a particular part of the world? In some situations, yes. But have such heavy rainfall events become more frequent? This analysis has been performed in some regions such as the United States, United Kingdom and Australia, but not everywhere. Evidence has been found for a trend towards more intense daily rainfall totals in recent years. It is possible that, even with the world 0.5 degree Centigrade hotter than today, climate scientists will still not be certain that any specific extreme weather event is caused by global warming.

If the question is approached from a different angle, however, there is something important to say about the relationship between global warming and extreme weather events. This needs saying now, and repeating each time the need for action to mitigate climate change, or to adapt to its consequences arises. It is known that global climate is warming and that the rate of warming has accelerated in recent decades. Following on the 1996 report by the United Nations intergovernmental panel on climate change, the balance of evidence reveals a detectable human influence on this warming.

A warming global climate will inevitably lead to changes in the behaviour of all weather systems - the systems that actually deliver weather to continents, extreme or not. A global climate warmed by human pollution of the atmosphere must yield different magnitudes and frequencies of a whole spectrum of local weather events. In a sense therefore, the weather experienced present day is the result of a semi-artificial climate; in a fundamental sense, it is different from the weather that would be experienced on a parallel planet which humans had not polluted. All weather events experienced from now on are to some indeterminable extent tainted by the human hand. There is no longer such a thing as a purely 'natural' weather event.

Massive risks are being run by altering the climate of our planet in ways not fully understood, let alone by making predictions with confidence. As with genetically-modified organisms, humanly-modified climates potentially bring exposure to risks that are largely unknown and unquantified. And the longer mankind continues to rely on a carbon-based energy economy, the greater these risks will be. It will take more than the 20% reduction in greenhouse gas emissions announced in March 2000 by the United Kingdom government to bring these risks under control.

Gambling with our climate may be acceptable to those of us living in affluent societies in the north, reckoning that we can adapt or buy our way out of climate trouble, but this gambling mentality is not one that would find many takers in the undeveloped countries where the suffering is real.

Hulme (2000)

◀ *Delhi, India, 2001: To mitigate against the heavy air pollution from vehicles, the state promotes the use of compressed natural gas (CNG) in transportation in a city with a population of 11 million largely dependent on motorised transport for mobility. The vehicles are either new or retrofitted to provide cleaner emissions and easily visible in their dstinctive livery*

SENSORY ATTRIBUTES

Nowhere do mathematics, science, philosophy and the natural senses permeate one another so intimately as in the understanding of the character of a piece of architecture and that of urban space.

Although that which presents itself as visually harmonious to one may not necessarily be perceived similarly by another, the character of architectural or urban space will inevitably depend on the assembled attributes of scale, proportion, form and colour. That indefinable combination of the elements which enclose space to create architecture will be determined by a style, or design language, involving all the intellectual signals and sensory responses.

PROPORTION AND SCALE

'Man is the measure of all things', according to Protagoras, the Greek philosopher of the fifth century BC. Although the art forms of the West and East are vastly different, they do reveal a commonality beyond the surface diversity in their preoccupation with the human condition and physical form. This can be substantiated by constructions of harmonious relationships in Hellenic sculpture, and the studies by Vitruvius, the Roman architect and writer of the first century, who demonstrated 'that the ancient Greeks even laid out their temples according to human proportions' (Doczi 1985).

Doczi has demonstrated that for centuries proportional harmonies have been fundamental to spatial philosophy in Japan. For example, in the Zen Monastery Temple garden, near Kyoto, which dates from the beginning of the fifteenth century, five groups of rocks are placed on a rectangular field of coarse, raked, white sand. This outdoor space is designed to be seen from the verandah of the monastery and from paved walkways around it. In his words 'The field of sand has proportions corresponding to two reciprocal golden rectangles… multiple constructions of the golden section show how the distances between the rocks within the field share proportional relationships corresponding to the root harmonies of music. Thus the rocks and field become one' (Doczi 1985).

Although subjectivity underlies the individual appreciation of good proportion and comfortable scale, it can also be shown that visual harmony of proportion has mathematical roots. The roots of proportion have been studied scientifically since the time of Vitruvius up to modern times, with the development of the 'Golden Section' concept at the turn of the twentieth century. Unity in the manifold diversities of Nature, brought about by the sharing of the same 'ideal' harmonious proportional manifestations, occurs too frequently to be ignored. A formula has been derived for the celebrated Golden Section, which is described as a 'uniquely reciprocal relationship between two unequal parts of a whole, in which the small part stands in the same proportion to the large part as the large part stands to the whole ... The complete reciprocity of this proportion strikes us as particularly harmonious and pleasing, a fact that has been proven by many scientific experiments.....'(Doczi, 1985)

Proportion and the Golden Section

In the fifth century BC, initiates of the mathematical and geometric mysteries of the philosopher Pythagoras communicated their fellowship with a secret sign.

On meeting a stranger, a Pythagorean would offer him an apple. If the stranger was also Pythogorean he would cut the apple laterally across its core to reveal pips laid out in the shape of a pentagram.

The pentagram was a sacred symbol of Pythagoreans, as it contained within it reference to the mathematical measurement known as the 'Golden Section' or phi ratio: 'There seems to be no doubt that the Greek architects and sculptors incorporated this ratio in their artifacts. Phidias, a famous Greek sculptor, made use of it. The proportions of the Parthenon illustrate the point.'

Indeed it was after Phidias that phi was named. Phi is to do with proportion - being the ideal ratio between two lengths that produces the most aesthetic effect on the eye when incorporated into the measurement of a work of art or architecture. A rectangle made of sides whose relationship to one another is based on the phi ratio will be more visibly pleasing than any other rectangle...

Quite why phi produces such an aesthetic effect is a mystery, but the Pythagoreans saw it as reflecting the harmonies of nature - for the same figure is found widely in the world in organic life. The spiralling of a snail's shell incorporates phi, as do the distances between leaves on branches. The proportions of the human body also relate to phi - for example, it is the ratio of the length of the body from the head to the navel and from the navel to the feet.

Thus the Pythagoreans claimed that 'all is number' and used geometry as a metaphor for higher concepts and metaphysical assertions. To them phi expressed beauty - not as a subjective opinion as in 'beauty is in the eye of the beholder', but as a quality intrinsic to the object itself. Beauty is in the beheld.

Starting from a square, using the midpoint on the baseline for the centre point A of a radius B, an arc drawn from the top corner of the square to intersect with the baseline C, the rectangle produced becomes proportioned in the Golden Section.

The significance is that the lesser portion 'a' is to the greater 'b' as the greater 'b' is to the whole 'a+b'.

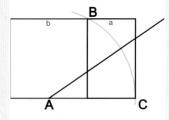

Hancock, Bauval and Grimsby (1998)

The phenomenon of the Golden Section is made all that more mysterious through its counterpart, the Fibonacci series named after its medieval discoverer, Leonardo "Fibonacci" de Pisa. By starting with 1 and adding the last two numbers to arrive at the next: 1,1,2,3,5,8,13,21,34 etc. the series is produced. By coupling any pair of the numbers in the series after 3, the Golden Section ratio of 1:6 is approximated. Like the Golden Section, besides bearing a curious relationship to many botanical forms the Fibonacci series exerted an influence on art and architecture.

Bergamini (1965)

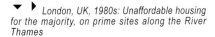 

London, UK, 1980s: Unaffordable housing for the majority, on prime sites along the River Thames

SELF-SERVING ATTRIBUTES Some latter day developments follow no precedent or architectural code but reflect the response of developers to the trendy demands of a burgeoning affluent class. The question arises whether such creations are architecturally sound showing little regard for design principles, site context or protocol.

A mathematical approximation of the Golden Section is a rectangle of approximately 5:8 proportions. It can be defined geometrically as a line that is divided such that the lesser portion 'a' is to the greater 'b' as the greater 'b' is to the whole 'a+b'. This can be expressed algebraically by the equation of two ratios: $a/b = b/a+b$.

Proportion and aesthetics

Subjectivity surrounding what constitutes an ideal proportion for a given application raises the issue of how to lay down rules or predict visual responses. Proportion in aesthetics is an imperative and generally understood by designers, even though its definition and application can be elusive in the actual design process.

It is, however, possible to develop quite simple proportioning systems. There would be two objectives, namely to create pleasing aesthetics through harmonious proportion and to create a sense of order among the elements in a visual construction. Euclid holds, according to Ching (1979), that 'a ratio refers to the quantitative comparison of two similar things, while proportion refers to the equality of ratios'. The relationships which are generated by the application of ratios tend to create visual order and can be sensed, accepted and even endow a given space

◀ ▲ *Pisa cathedral and tower, Italy: Architects and craftsmen of past architectural treasures generally acknowledged the value of good proportion to achieve aesthetically pleasing design. In some cases only simple proportional rules were applied ensuring a consistency to which the eye is unconsciously sensitive*

or facade with a specific identity. As has been indicated earlier, the Golden Section could be explored by those who design in architecture or in urban space as a useful maxim for visual harmony.

Human-related scale

Generally people have to rely on visual rather than tactile experience of space and their perceptions are largely based on familiarity or past subconscious associations. As in architecture, so also in urban open space, questions of scale centre mainly around two considerations, namely, the size of the space relative to the human body and the size of the building elements or mass enclosing or standing in that space.

Of the three dimensions of an open space, the vertical scale contributes more effectively to the sense of scale, as the human eye perceives a change in height more readily than a change in the plan dimension. Such ready appreciation of the vertical scale would not, however, be without visual reference to the other dimensions. For instance, a small change in height would not be appreciated in a space with a tight, enclosed ground plan as the visual foreshortening would influence the perception of any change. The scale of texture of the building elements as well as the colour also play a significant part in influencing visual relationships in the enclosure of space. 'A design, or part of a design, can be described as 'in scale' if it conforms with human norms, or as "large scale" or "small in scale" according to its departure from these norms' (Reekie 1972).

Reekie concludes that the question of scale arises not only in regard to the planning and design of the building, but also to the juxtaposition of buildings and other structures, the scales of which could be so dissimilar as to produce discordant and objectionable visual effects. The solution is not necessarily to prescribe a set standard for facades, but to require that a satisfactory relationship exists between them, specifically a scale common to all.

Movement affecting proportion and scale

On the matter of the effect of movement on scale and proportion, driving in a vehicle leaves little time for viewing and diminishes a person's capacity to absorb detail. Pedestrians have a better awareness of place than drivers or passengers in moving vehicles. Appropriate adjustments about proportion must take four factors into account (Bentley et al. 1985):

⧄ The range of distances from which the various parts of a space an be seen.
⧄ The speed of movement at which a space can be seen.
⧄ The length of time during which each view will be experienced.
⧄ The relative number of people likely to see the building from each different viewing position, whether from a travelling vehicle or on foot.

Similar adjustments in terms of architectural detail and scale need to be taken into account. Where the motor vehicle determines the speed of movement a different level of complexity of detail and scale other than the human scale is likely to be more appropriate to the context. Conversely, an environment that is visually comfortable from a motor vehicle could become monotonously boring on foot (Rapoport 1977).

As speed increases, concentration becomes specific and several other things happen: (Tunnard and Pushkarev, 1963):

⧄ The point of concentration (or focus) recedes from 185 metres at 40 km/h to 610 metres at 105 km/h. As a result elements in the environment must become larger in order to be noticed or appreciated at all. Also, while objects perpendicular to the road become prominent those parallel to it lose prominence.
⧄ Peripheral vision diminishes so that while at 40 km/h the horizontal angle is about 100 degrees, it reduces to less than 40 degrees at 80 km/h. One result is 'tunnel vision' which may induce hypnosis or sleep.

Side elements need to be quiet and subdued and perceived subconsciously in the blurred field of peripheral vision, with the main features on the axis of vision and the point of concentration periodically moved laterally to maintain attention.

⑃ Foreground detail begins to fade due to the rapid movement of close objects. The earliest point of clear view recedes from 9.5 metres at 65 kmh to 33 metres at 95 kmh. At the same time detail behind 430 metres cannot be seen as it is too small, so that the range is between 33 metres to 425 metres - and that is traversed in 15 seconds. Elaborate detail is thus both useless and unnecessary.

⑃ Space perception becomes impaired so that near objects are seen, get close and disappear very quickly. They thus tend to 'loom' which can become extremely stressful. Elements too close to the edge or overhead on traffic freeways, and sudden curves should be avoided.

Architectural elements along a fast trafficway should provide information at an intermediate rate by using a scale or texture discernible at a higher speed. Also, to achieve gradual transitions - sudden contrasts are visually disruptive and should be avoided.

COLOUR AND TEXTURE

Potentially colours in the built environment have an emotive effect on people. While such mental reactions are subjective and particular to the individual, there is evidence that, in general, 'certain colours are likely to produce certain feelings and this aspect should receive consideration in regard to external design as well as internal design' (Reekie 1972).

Considering the use of colour in the urban environment the goal at all times should be the enhancement or revitalisation of the aesthetics of the building or place. Toward that goal, there is, however, a great deal of scope as to the character or effect desired but, to this end, certain human responses to particular colours first need to be understood.

Reekie provides broad empirical observations of typical responses to colour :

⑃ Blue :   soothing effect if not too strong;
⑃ Green: similar in effect to blue;
⑃ Yellow: cheering and stimulating;
⑃ Red: exciting;
⑃ Purple: in small areas, rich and comforting;
⑃ Browns: restful and comforting; and
⑃ White: cheering and stimulating.

London, UK: The famous lights of Piccadilly in the heart of the metropolis. Visual stimulation through brightly illuminated commercial advertising creates a mood for night life at a heavily trafficked entertainment node

Barcelona, Spain: The annexe to the cathedral, Gotic centre, providing a backdrop for a tasteful banner display publicising an exhibition of cultural importance to the city

REVITALISATION THROUGH VISUAL STIMULI Architecture in old as well as new precincts in cities comes alive with contemporary effects such as lighting or colourful banners that draw attention to an important cultural venue or event or as a crowd-puller for entertaining events.

In appropriate situations, such as at the brightly lit Piccadilly Circus in London, even drab buildings can become the backdrop to a permanent or semi-permanent display of colourful lighting or advertisement that has the effect of attracting commercial activity at all hours. Contemporary examples of the use of well-designed advertising banner displays on historic buildings can temporarily 'update' the social space for a cultural event. Both these types (there are others) of opportunistic visual stimuli should be regarded as art forms which, in a sense, utilise an existing public setting in a semi-permanent or temporary manner appropriate to the place.

Writing about colour in architecture, Schumacher (1981) promotes the axiom that architectural forms should be simplified if colour effects are to be successful, and as a corollary that colour should be employed 'wherever the opportunity to create effects by means of formal articulation has been denied... '. John Ruskin first advanced the theory that 'form and colour were enemies and should therefore be set on essentially different paths... The highest intensity of colour, in his view, should never coincide with the highest complexity of form' (Schumacher 1981). These are guidelines but not absolutes, in view of changing cultural trends and norms of acceptability.

Colour theories, of which there are a number, assist in the understanding of the colour spectrum and towards successful employment of colour to excite various responses in the viewer. To venture into the realm of colour, with a view to the enhancement of environmental appreciation, presupposes a working knowledge of the nature of colour and chromatic terminology. There are many reference books on the subject, which deal with the response characteristics of colour in depth.

Colour terminology

Colour quality is the specific character of colour that arises from the attributes of hue (chromatic colours) degree of lightness (or value), purity (or saturation), intensity and emotional effect. Hue is that attribute of a colour by which it can be distinguished from another of the same lightness and purity. Often, based on the arrangement of the colours on a wheel analogous to a compass, a colour's hue is termed its 'direction'. Lightness refers to the degree of difference of the colour from black as the 'darkest', and white at the 'lightest' end of the spectrum. Colour purity (or saturation) is that attribute which determines the degree of difference between a certain tone and neutral grey. Colour intensity is the strength or power of a colour, where the saturated colours of the colour wheel are perceived to be the most intense. Both intensity and saturation are diminished by the addition to a colour of white, black or grey. This means that each colour reaches its highest point of intensity and saturation at a different degree of lightness, e.g. yellow at a higher degree of lightness than blue. Nor do all saturated colours affect the eye with equal strength; no saturated green, for example, can approach the intensity of saturated red.

Apart from the emotional value of a colour arising from the psychophysical effect it has on us, working with colour in buildings or in the urban landscape can exploit certain visual expressiveness resulting from the inherent properties unique to each colour (Schmuck 1968):

≫ Directional colour contrast : When two colours on opposite sides

▲ London, UK: Housing of the 1960s/70s in Marquess Road, sponsored by the Borough of Islington, displays much ingenuity in terms of central city high-density/medium-rise planning, but little success in the choice of colour and texture for the prevailing conditions, in particular the poor light of winter

COLOUR, CLIMATE AND LIGHT Ambient light intensity differs seasonally as well as from north to south, east to west throughout the world. Choice of colour plays an important part in architectural expression and is generally culture-specific. In colder climates colours appear drained of their hue, whereas in sunnier climates colours appear vibrant and intense. Ironically, in the northern climates where buildings often reflect a complexity of form and detail, cultural preference has leaned towards the conservative application of colour, whereas in sunnier climates bright, sometimes pure colour is applied without reserve.

▼ Jaipur, Rajahstan, India: The 'pink city', where in celebration of the visit of a British monarch, the maharajah decreed that the buildings be colourwashed in pink, a practice that survives up to today. The result is a highly distinctive cityscape, arising largely from the application of a single colour, well chosen to suit the use of red sandstone in numerous important historic buildings and the colourful culture of the region

▲ Arequipa, Peru: Santa Catalina convent where the unbridled use of pure primary colours has lifted the simple vernacular out of the ordinary

of the colour wheel (eg. blue and orange) largely determine the overall composition, this is known as a directional colour contrast.

\ Light-dark contast : If the central contrast in the composition is light-dark, the values of the colours used will come particularly into play and have a great influence on the overall effect. Here the hues play a secondary role, being merely an accessory to the light-dark contrast.

\ Pure and greyed hues contrast : If the composition is carried out largely in one range of value (or lightness), its effects will rest on the contrasts between pure and greyed hues.

\ Cold-warm colour contrast : If the colours belong to the accepted cold or warm part of the spectrum the predominance of one over the other will create the contrast; and

\ Single hue compositions : Variations of a single hue with accents picked out by contrasting degrees of lightness or and darkness.

Colour systems

Colour systems are an essential aid to the designer as they represent classifications devised with great care. Systems are set out to include as many variations of colour as possible in a sequence of colours neatly listed by hue, saturation, lightness and interval. Some go further such as that published by Schuitema, for example, which provides a number of suggested colour combinations, to assist the designer's decision. Colour systems are fine aids to composition as they bring order into the confusion of the colour range.

The system devised by Schuitema provides a number of suggested colour combinations that make the designer's decision that much easier. Other colour systems are:

\ Newton's Colour Wheel
\ Mayer's Colour Scheme
\ Lambert's Colour Pyramid
\ Runge's Colour Sphere
\ Benson's Colour Cube
\ Ostwald's Colour Norm Atlas

Modifying properties of texture

In urban design it is important that there should be textural harmony in a building or in a group of associated buildings. Ironically, a fragmented facade of visually rich building elements could conceivably be placed alongside a plain building, on the other hand, two facades dissimilar in the scale, proportion and colour of the facade elements could be discordant. Reekie (1972) states that 'Texture modifies colour. If two surfaces

◀ *Barcelona, Spain: Casa Battlo 1906, by Gaudi: The facade elements display an 'organicness'. Where the wall surface appears to be of leather, soft and supple, it glitters in numerous colours from the small round plates that project randomly like fishscales. The dreamy quality of softness and naturalness is continued inside the building*

▶ *Chicago, Illinois, USA: Glass tower, Chicago: The beguiling reflective quality of the surface, made possible by the highly developed glass technology of modern times*

▲ *Saa'na, North Yemen: The dark earthy colour is less reflective to the brilliant light and the texture provides partial shading to the surface of the building to offset solar gain*

TEXTURE AND COLOUR Decorative texture and appropriate colour application provides both aesthetic appeal and functional purpose: in wetter climates smooth texture will shed rain more efficiently - in drier, hot climates rough textures provide surface shading which reduces heat load. In the developed world, the thin reflective glass curtain wall has other economy spin-offs - the advantage gained of liberating additional floor space for rental income despite higher energy costs and polluting emissions into the atmosphere.

TEXTURAL RICHNESS The employment of colour and texture can be beguiling, but requires to be in tune with the architectural style to avoid the impression of being alien or added on. Strong textural effects can merge the architecture with its setting, lending a strong sense of rightness with the place.

◀ ▲ *Barcelona, Spain: Parc Guell and the Sagrada Familia: The gloriously sculptured and embellished architecture of Antoni Gaudi displaying endless diversity of colour and texture*

are both of the same hue and intensity, but are of different textures, they will not look alike. Texture can be considered as the impression through sight of what can be experienced by touch... the same words, e.g. rough, smooth, etc. are used to describe texture whether a surface is seen or felt.'

The decorative application of colour and texture is carried out with a definite aim in mind, whether aesthetic or functional. In such instances, colours and textures are used to articulate, distinguish and enliven surfaces and objects, and so enhance the aesthetic attributes of architecture. It is equally valid to employ texture to provide a uniform surface where imperfections would otherwise detract from the aesthetic appearance of a building. For example, a high gloss paint finish on old plaster would emphasise the imperfections, whereas a more textural paint would assist towards their concealment. An important contribution of texture other than that of purely aesthetic is that, if used selectively, texture can reduce reflectivity and therefore unwanted glare from the sun on horizontal as well as vertical surfaces. The vaulted architecture in the hot, arid regions of North Africa, for example, is often coarsely finished externally to provide partial shading from the sun.

Richness in design is not purely a visual matter: it has deeper sensory appreciation. In the design of social space, it is important to look at what promotes sensory stimulus. On emotive arousal some insights have been provided by research: 'Behavioural and neurological evidence has accumulated which suggests that the hedonic or rewarding value of a stimulus depends on how arousing or de-arousing it is. There appear to be two distinct mechanisms involved, one of which produces reward when stimulation is decreased after it has risen to the point of being unpleasant or painful, while the other comes into play when arousal is raised to a moderate extent' (Heath 1984).

To assist observation, patterns of stimulation are received, which intrinsically hold meaning (Gibson 1979). For example, where the gradient of a textured surface is visible to the observer, spatial depth can be evaluated better as the texture appears less coarse or rough as it stretches away, thereby influencing the eye of the beholder.

Notion of 'noticeable differences'

Rapoport (1977) offers that the notion of 'noticeable differences' is critical to design, and certain cues become noticeable through meaningful design - they become messages. People make instinctive choices, which relate to their senses and consciously or subconsciously will evaluate:

> ➤ Physical differences: (1) Vision: shape, profile, size, height, colour, materials, texture, details. (2) Space : size, shape, barriers, links, merging, transitions. (3) Light and shade : levels, temporal changes in light. (4) Greenery: man-made versus natural, type of planting. (5) Conformity versus variety. (6) Well-maintained versus neglected. (7) Scale and urban grain. 8) Road pattern. (9) Topography. (10) Location : prominence, at junctions.

◄ *Saqqara, Cairo, Egypt: Although entirely different in scale, the modelling of the profile of the gateway has a strong affinity with that of the Step pyramid of Unas. The corollary of the construct of 'noticeable difference' is that of 'noticeable similarity'*

⚈ Kinesthetics: (1) Changes of level, curves, speed of movement, the speed of movement and the human eye's capacity appreciate detail, (2) Different levels of complexity and scale, other than the human scale..

⚈ Sound: (1) Noisy versus quiet. (2) Man-made sounds, versus natural sounds. (3) Dead versus reverberant. (4) Temporal changes in sound.

⚈ Smells: (1) Man-made versus natural.

⚈ Air movement.

⚈ Tactile.

⚈ Social differences: (1) Activities : type and intensity, uniform or mixed, cars or pedestrians, movement or quietude. (2) Street use or non-use, front/back distinctions, private/public distinctions, introverted versus extroverted. (3) Hierarchy or symbolism.

⚈ Objects: Signs, advertisements, fences, decorations.

⚈ Temporal differences: Long term versus short term.

The deployment of the sensory aids in design enhances what the observer sees and, in the architect's palette, should be seen only as devices for refinement. Apart from the choice of proportion, scale, colour or textural refinements, the excellence of the final architecture rests on other more robust pillars, those of form and fitness for purpose. Significantly, colour and texture could play an important part in architecture which responds to the New Age milieu of resource, and particularly energy consciousness.

ARCHITECTURE IN RESPONSE

Much of what is currently presented under the banner of architecture and, curiously, rewarded and applauded by architects themselves, is preoccupied with excess - such as designs which are inappropriate to climate, such as glass curtainwall structures in hot, sundrenched climates, necessitating complete reliance on high-energy resources.

The activities of urban life take place in public and private spheres and the behavioural patterns are similar to both. The way in which public space is organised will determine the canvas for how architecture provides commodity, and a sense of comfortable utility for the user(s).

Architects have to reconcile the multidimensional requirements of the briefs for which they are commissioned. This poses a seemingly impossible challenge but none so great as that of commitment in all areas of ethical responsibility. Synoptically, an architectural brief requires sensitivity in the various spheres of accountability:

    ⬉ The manner in which a building addresses the site, the street or other social spaces, and provides amenity and utility to the urban dweller.
    ⬉ Protocol in terms of respect for what already exists architecturally, culturally and naturally.
    ⬉ Economic sustainability of a design so as not to place a future intergenerational burden on the individual or the community as a whole.
    ⬉ The responsible utilisation of natural resources.
    ⬉ Landscaping and upgrading the urban setting.
    ⬉ Protection of the biodiversity of the site and environs.
    ⬉ Pursuing architectural quality in the interests of a better urban environment as well as the cultural legacy of the past and needs of the times.

THE CONTEXTUAL EDGE

An attempt should be made to enhance the social interaction along the perimeters of urban space by giving attention to the design of inviting building frontages.

Buildings in the public realm that do not create the possibility of a connection with the world outside, and do not invite the public near will present an image of being aloof, private territorially and exclusive to those who are inside. Such buildings add nothing to the amenity of the urban environment.

In situations where there is no strong connection between the internal functions of the building and the public setting outside, this could be at the root of a performance problem, in terms of both the building itself and the public space.

Active building fronts

With building frontages onto public spaces it is advantageous that 'the public edge of the building should house activities which benefit from interaction with the public realm, and can contribute to the life of the public space itself' (Bentley et al. 1985). There are principles for optimising this relationship:

⟋ Locate as many entrances as possible in such positions that comings and goings are directly visible from the public space.

⟋ Encourage any compatible uses within the buildings to spill out into the public area. This principle applies to uses mainly on the ground and first storeys.

⟋ Even if there are no specific uses, most buildings contain activities which can contribute to the animation of the public space itself.

⟋ It is still necessary to preserve the privacy of the indoor activity, so

▲ *Shopping street, Cowes, Isle of Wight: Curved shopfronts on a curved street provide maximum showcasing of merchandise to the street and invite entry for closer inspection*

▼ *Stockholm, Sweden, 1950s: A universal downtown solution to a business/retail precinct - clinical and presenting an uninviting face to the public space*

◀ *San Fransciso, USA: Where no windows are possible onto the street, other ways of presenting a frontage can be devised*

BUILDING FRONTAGES   Aside from economic considerations, the way architecture addresses the public space is a commitment to ensuring the social vitality of the urban environment. Blank walls at street level become the 'kiss of death' for the economic sustainability of a street.

that the users will not feel the need to screen themselves totally from the public space. Privacy can be achieved by horizontal distance, a change in level and/or a combination of both.

⟍ The usefulness of the edge is important for people-watching and is greatly increased by the provision of places to sit.

Building edge design

In designing with deference to context, the building edge alone can be configured variously in profile and take the form of a spectrum of familiar elements within the architect's usual design repertoire. Good, socially focused buildings could draw on numerous familiar frontage profiles (Krier 1990) :

⟍ With projection on pedestrian level in the form of an arcade or a solid structure. This device creates a pleasing human scale aside from the real body of the building.

⟍ A free-standing low building placed in front of a higher one.

⟍ Halfway up the building the section is set back by half its depth; this allows for extensive floors on the lower level and apartments with access to balconies on the upper level.

⟍ Top floor set back reducing the height of the building visible to the eye.

⟍ Random terracing.

⟍ Sloping elevation with vertical lower and upper floors.

⟍ Sloping elevation with protruding ground floor.

⟍ Stepped section by floor.

⟍ Free standing ground floor.

⟍ Standard section with moat.

⟍ Building with ground floor arcades.

⟍ Building on pilotis.

⟍ Building on pilotis, with intermediate floor similarly supported.

⟍ Sloping ground in front of building.

⟍ Buildings atop very shallow inclines.

⟍ Building with arcade along the frontage above ground level and access to pedestrian level.

⟍ Building with balcony accessed from the public place.

⟍ Inverted stepped section.

⟍ Building with pitched projections.

⟍ Building with free-standing towers.

These design options illustrate the wealth of design choices for an appropriate response to context, without even consideration of stylistic or typological preference.

Architectural protocol

Good neighbourliness in architecture is as important as the social intercourse it should promote.

At the time of a widely practised indifference to past legacies, i.e. the decades of the 1950s-60s, architecture in the mould of modernism rode roughshod over traditional urban landscapes. A striking example was the tower block, the Torre Velasca, Milan, which ignored the general height conformity of the historic urbanscape of the city. Such practices were to the detriment of many old city environments. Evidence of similar unmannerly trends in established city contexts continues up to the present day. Such manifestations frequently rely on political intervention and are generally self-serving at the expense of the social interests. Where buildings would otherwise address the street, and sustain the performance of an urban environment, lack of protocol can permit the destruction of that interdependency.

On the other hand, the practice of architectural protocol has many faces. The saga of the long awaited British Library by architects St John Wilson and Partners of the 1990s was characterised by a protracted and heated debate. The originality of the design set out to enhance the distinctive vertical massing of its august Victorian neighbour, the St Pancras railway station, by expressing a 'no contest' approach. Typical of the present day media's selective vision, the issues of cost and delay in its completion featured more prominently than the real issue of the potentially controversial

◀ *Milan, Italy, Torre Valesca, 1950s: In sight of a fine Italian Gothic cathedral, the Duomo. Permitting the mean height of the centuries-old urban landscape to be exceeded, demonstrates a lack of protocol and urban design judgement*

◀ ▲ *London, UK: The contemporary British Library, the 'gentle giant' (Spring, 1997): Strong horizontal massing of the new succeeds as a foil to the equally strong verticality of the Victorian St Pancras railway station*

PROTOCOL Good neighbourliness in architecture is as important as the quality of the design. Both good and bad examples abound. Whereas acceptable approaches do not preclude contrast, overscaled neighbours can be construed as bad urban design or poor architectural manners.

horizontal massing and the library's facade expression. The architecture succeeded in being shortlisted for one of the highest awards but lost, whereupon it was later stated in Building Design (1998) that: 'the judges of the RIBA Stirling Prize should have embraced controversy and awarded the prize to the new British Library, rather than the American Air Museum [by Foster and Partners] '. By awarding the safe choice, the jurors bypassed a worthy attempt to elevate a novel form of architectural protocol, and arguably conservation, to its rightful place in architectural appreciation.

Contemporary into traditional settings

Through architecture all cities show the layers of time, some more visibly than others. Barcelona is particularly proud of its architectural tradition and its uncompromising patronage of contemporary work. As a city and centre of a proud regional culture, it holds some veritable lessons in how architecture can revitalise the jaded urban environment without destroying it. Meier's Barcelona Museum of Contemporary Art (1995) provides an appealingly friendly and finite architectural statement within the weft and warp of the older part of the city. It is neighbourly and affords a visual unity with the old while creating an architectural intervention that is cool and inviting in a climate which can be uncomfortably hot and humid.

With a burgeoning intake of student numbers at England's famous universities, Oxford and Cambridge, during the 1960s architects were for the first time challenged to introduce modern extensions into the ancient stone fabric of age-old architecture. Mainly due to the volume of soleless architectural

▲ Nîmes, France: Architect Norman Foster's Carré d'Art, showing responsibility to the context by paying a refined tribute to the 2000 year old Roman temple. The square was redesigned to link the two buildings and in the process, the temple was revitalised as an art gallery in partnership with the new building

▲ Brasenose College, Oxford, UK: Modern extension to traditional college architecture

▲ Milan, Italy: Without replication of the existing context, a modern intervention conserves the integrity and enhances the qualities of the neighbouring architecture

COALITION OF OLD AND NEW The sensitive integration of contemporary with historic buildings or precincts can often best be served by the less obvious conservation approach: sensitivity of scale and detail, conformity of building mass and height, colour and texture. Slavish emulation of the original is unlikely to satisfy contemporary cultural needs or perceptions, or revitalise the quality of an integrated whole.

◄ Barcelona, the Museum of Contemporary Art, 1995, by Richard Meier Architects, in an architecturally correct and neighbourly relationship with the historic Centre for Contemporary Culture of Barcelona on the left

With the knowledge of the soil and subsoil of human nature and its potentials, we shall raise our heads over the turmoil of daily production and command views over the earth which we shall have to keep green with life if we mean to survive - not cramped full with all the doubtful things of a too thoroughly commercialised technology. Tangible observation rather than abstract speculation will have to be the proper guide. And drifting will no longer do.

Neutra (1954)

products of the post-war reconstruction programme, this was a decade when Modernism in Britain was regarded with disdain. Partly in response to the shortage of resources during and after World War 2, 'New Brutalism' was characterised by exposed concrete, a risky departure from traditional brick or stone cladding. The contemporary residential extension within the grounds of the old merges with considerable success by complying with massing, scale and colour and by projecting its presence as lightly as possible,

Sense of place

From the micro-(individual building) to the macro-scale (a city) in development, the response of a development to the site is as important to the success of a piece of architectural or urban design as its style or its functionality.

The flat or rolling or precipitous topography or the vegetation of a site should be permitted to lend character to a development. Where the terrain is not flat, the modern compulsion is to flatten - a disturbing development, placing the site as well as the building rising on it discordantly out of context with its original setting. Thus, using the characteristics of the site to inform the urban designers' or architects' response to the character of the place has been ignored. Rome was founded on seven gentle hills, and that Eternal City derives character from its topography. Arguably, towns where design imagination has responded to the changing levels

Is talking about an abstractional view of the environment too impersonal?

It may be useful to review briefly some of the main themes where Fritz Steele (1981) in *The Sense of Place* relates the environment to people:

When people are unaware or unappreciative of the ways in which place experiences affect their lives, for better or for worse, the places tend not to have much conscious influence on the nature of experiences. People seem to be willing to overlook a poor setting (or accept 'inferior goods') in ways they would not if they were making decisions about an automobile or a new outfit, possibly because the costs of a poor setting are more subtle and less conspicuous than those of a malfunctioning car or a badly fitting suit. Yet the actual human cost to us of bad place experiences can be enormous when accumulated over a lifetime.

The relationship between people and the environment is transactional: people take something (positive or negative) from and give or do things to the environment; these acts might alter the environment and influence people.

I now believe that the concept of place should actually be psychological or interactional, not just physical. The environment is made up of a combination of physical and social features; sense of place is an experience created by the setting combined with what a persons brings to it. In other words, to some degree we create our own places, they do not exist independent of us.

There are however, certain settings that have such a strong spirit of place that they will tend to have a similar impact on many different people. The Grand Canyon, or the Left Bank of the Seine in Paris are excellent examples.

Settings obviously have an impact on people, both short term and long term, and there are some patterns to this impact.

People have an impact through how they care for, create new social forces, and design new physical features for settings. This can be positive or negative, short term or long term.

◀ *The city of Rome, Italy: 'Sense of place' does not only apply to cities, but also to towns, villages and individual pieces of architecture. Rome, founded on seven hills, provides potentially seven vantage points to escape the intensity of urban living and view the historic cityscape recreationally*

▼ *Positano, Italy: A coastal resort town responds to place through its merging of layout and architecture*

of a hilly terrain are likely to be more characterful environments. On the other hand, flat arid sites even without vegetation can provide unique settings for strong architectural forms that assert a powerful visual impact. The pyramids of Giza, Egypt, rising skyward on the vast relatively flat sands of the desert, come to mind.

Place experience is real, but often not realised in modern day architectural practice, where the demands of time and expedient responses to human needs usually foreclose on the desire to engage with the more spiritual qualities of the environment itself. Speed of mobility through the motor car, the fast food culture, the predigested media coverage across global boundaries determine a fastness of change that overshadows the instinct to develop a sense of place.

Other factors influencing the use of a site should include the optimised allocation of the land resource to the needs of habitation, agriculture

◀ *In the Gorge du Tarne, France: The town St-Enimie: Such natural settings are enchanting and visually seductive and have been enhanced rather than destroyed by the presence of settlement and the chosen architectural idiom*

SENSE OF PLACE   Older towns often demonstrate an intuitive 'sense of place', creating characterful, organic environments much sought after by modern day urban dwellers, who live and work in cities. Very often modern urban structures are devoid of amenity apart from the ubiquitous mall culture, which has little to do with place.

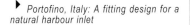 *Sperlonga, Italy: A fishing village becomes a tightly facetted sculpture of white walls on a rock promontory*

▶ *Portofino, Italy: A fitting design for a natural harbour inlet*

◀ *Giza, Cairo, Egypt: One of the Great Wonders of the World and a timeless phenomenon. The siting of the pyramids has been linked with celestial bodies - 'it was a very clever, very ambitious, very exact way to mark an epoch - to freeze a particular date (10 450 BC) into architecture if you like.. ' (Hancock 1996). From a modern perspective, the Egyptian architect Imotep's use of the pyramid form has the quality of inevitability and timelessness in the vast planal landscape of the desert*

and other aspects of community life. Typically, in older villages of Europe, the best tracts of arable soils were conserved for agriculure and the rocky outcrops set aside for buildings. In another situation a seafaring community might choo-se a vantage point above the ocean to site their living arrangements for better observation of changes in the weather, on which their catches depend, and the comings and goings of their fishing boats. Often such habitation, due to site limitations, is dense and multistorey, with public circulation along narrow walkways and even under buildings.

Arising from a pure symphony of response to the strong contextual pointers in the landscape, many older villages, towns and cities can be seen as models worthy of emulation by present designers of urban environments.

Perhaps one of the most unusal revelations regarding the optimum siting of man-made constructions is the more recent discovery that the 'celestial plan' of ancient Egypt can be shown to have determined the siting and alignments of key religious constructions.

'Archaeo-astronomers making use of the latest star-mapping computer programmes had recently demonstrated that the three world-famous pyramids on Egypt's Giza plateau formed an extact terrestrial diagram of the three belt stars in the constellation of Orion. Nor was this the limit of the celestial map the Ancient Egyptian priests had created in the sands on the west bank of the Nile. Included in their overall vision, ... there was a natural feature - the river Nile - which was exactly where it should be had it been designed to represent the Milky Way' (Bauval 1994).

◀ *Chenonceaux on the Loire, France: Spectacular use of a major waterway for defence while at the same time insinuating graceful living, political power and influence*

RESPONSE TO SITE River, hillside or hilltop sites all prompt appropriate architectural response, some using the site with deliberate purpose, whether for defence or to the glory of God or in memory of the fallen in battle.

◀ ▲ *Hilltop sites in France and Switzerland both exploiting the terrain to architectural advantage*

Chinese palaces of antiquity and modern multinational corporate headquarters in Asia share a guiding principle for the siting and design of their buildings - *feng shui*, the Chinese art of placement. The premise of *feng shui* has remained the same - the pursuit of the most harmonious and auspicious place to live and work. For thousands of years the Chinese have felt that their lives were magically linked to their environment. They believed that certain places were better and luckier, and more sacred than others, and that features of the environment - hills, streams, roads, walls and doors - all could affect a person. They concluded that if a person changed and balanced his surroundings, he could balance and improve his life. As Lin Yun, a *feng shui* practitioner in North America, explains, 'I adapt homes and offices to harmonize with the currents of ch'i', meaning man's energy and cosmic breath. 'The shapes of beds, the forms and heights of buildings, the directions of roads and corners all modify a person's destiny' (Rossbach 1987).

Conservation

Where architectural protocol and respect for the site are indispensable imperatives for the architect's brief, there are other important conservation issues of both the cultural (buildings, social space, historic sites) and natural

What are the options for the conservation of a building or an environment?

The term conservation means prevention against change or deterioration of a building's fabric and the maintenance of its authentic character. This implies that intervention from honest restoration to holding measures aimed at the stabilisation of a building could both be categorised as strategies for conservation. Applying maintenance measures only is appropriate where a building has particular aesthetic merit or has historical and cultural value, or is in a reasonable condition but where there are insufficient grounds or resources for the execution of rigorous conservation procedures. Preservation is the safest form of conservation as no historic evidence is thereby removed, but the value of the status quo is maintained.

Restoration

This term applies to situations where a building is expertly returned to a former state and existing components are restored and later additions of no historic value are removed. The approach is founded on respect for the physical and documentary evidence, and terminates where supposition starts. The process of restoration is only appropriate when sufficient information exists regarding the structure in its earlier appearance, and only if the restoration of the structure to that original condition will revive the cultural importance of the building itself.

The greatest mistake that restoration can bring about is to return a building to its original condition in such a way that is not relevant to its particular history. However, a building need not be restored to its earliest stage, especially if later evidence is of cultural importance or the important historical evolution of the building has to be removed in the process.

Reconstruction

To completely rebuild a building to the original form of an existing or demolished building. Reconstruction is appropriate when a museum wishes to reconstruct a historical era or streetscape. Reconstruction should not be confused with hypothetical reconstruction (virtual, derivative or imported environments).

Renewal/renovation

Renewal embodies the renovation of a building in keeping with its character. This approach is appropriate where a building has no intrinsic value, but is part of a harmonious group or streetscape.

Rehabilitation

To make a building usable for a specific purpose through renovation and changes while meaningful features, which contribute to its historical, architectural and cultural value, are maintained.

It is of the utmost importance that the conversion of such buildings only takes place where compatible usage is envisaged. In this way there is some guarantee that there is not a dramatic departure from the building's original cultural importance. Rehabilitation, a relatively new concept in conservation, has unfortunately given rise to redesigned aberrations that leave a poor legacy of the original.

Recycling

Changes and conversions of a building for uses other than the original purpose. It is preferrable to find new uses for historic buildings that contribute to a cityscape rather than to allow deterioration or replacement to take place. The trend of paying lip service to conservation by building contemporary buildings behind the mask of the old facade is token and architecturally dishonest.

CONSERVATION-WORTHINESS Efforts to preserve conservation-worthy or historically important environments, whether architectural and natural, have to be mandated by particular cultural and political values, local, regional, national and sometimes international.

◀ *Cape Town, South Africa: Recycling of the facade of an old theatre as an entrance portico to a contemporary building. The new not hiding behind the old is a reasonable gesture and in keeping with a conservation ethos*

▶ *Giza, Cairo, Egypt: View from the base of the Pyramid of Cheops showing the looming threat of mass housing advancing on the Giza plateau. Encroachment of development of this kind on a World Heritage Site indicates a serious lapse of social and political judgement*

environments. That the rights of community should override those of the individual is being universally and continually challenged, particularly in democracies where freedom of choice is statutorily enshrined. When the issue of rights is interpolated into the sphere of positive or negative development, there are no enforceable universal laws. In exceptional cases treaties between nations have been concluded to protect heritage environments, e.g. development in Antarctica, or World Heritage Sites. With no internationally recognised protection, the Giza plateau on the outskirts of modern Cairo has become particularly threatened through the encroachment of contemporary mass housing, currently at the critical threshold of destroying the integrity of a world famous cultural site. Even though the Giza pyramids are one of the Wonders of the World, in practice, such perceived status has been afforded scant protection against the pressures of insensitive or uncaring development.

Conservation, as a philosophy, carries with it the need for specialised understanding of what is at stake. For architects, slavish replication of past typologies should not be the required or prescribed option, and the modern tendency of 'keeping the original facade' to front a new development behind is at best token, patronisingly avoiding the true nature of conservation. It has been shown that with modern interventions that conform with height, mass, scale, proportion, colour, detailing, texture and general character, contemporary architectural design can be enhancing and revitalising to an historic environment - Foster's Carré d'Art (1993) building comes to mind. On the other hand, there are examples where only certain facade elements have been conserved and integrated into a contemporary piece of architecture without detracting from their historical function.

There are several categories to explore within the concept of conservation, from a purely 'holding' undertaking to full restoration, in fact both demanding the advocacy of expertise beyond standard building practice.

SUSTAINABLE DESIGN

Traditional designs in buildings in both hot and cold climates and before the advent of technologies for heating and cooling offer timeless precedents from which contemporary architects could well draw inspiration. It is significant that in the sphere of sustainable design, Middle Eastern countries are returning to traditional typologies to make architecture work. There are, however, also many examples, particularly in industrialised countries (although some still developing countries can boast some remarkable models of energy efficient architecture), where modern building design has liberated energy needs to similar levels of sustainability as their traditional counterparts.

Sustainability is multifaceted, and turning to the example of the Lloyd's Building, London, (Rogers Partnership 1990s) at first glance it would seem that its super-expensive external finish and detailing have not shown consideration for energy efficiency issues. The aesthetically seductive stainless steel of the exterior cladding providing the envelope to the building and its services have a more significant message to convey - a permanence, arguably as sustainable as clay brick technology. The building comprises long- and short-life elements. Its contribution to energy efficiency lies in the internal storing of energy in the internal structure and the triple glazing, providing a highly insulative external skin. Heat, generated by

▲ Lesotho, southern Africa: The African hut: High altitude conditions requiring careful orientation, building mass and insulative performance. Materials are derived from immediate regenerative local resources

▲ Lloyd's of London, UK: The capital intensive route to sustainability, based on the 'pay back principle' with a longer term approach to resource efficiency and financial return on capital invested through energy-conserving measures

SUSTAINABILITY Sustainability has many faces. Intergenerational, environmental and external costs are taken into account. Sustainability can mean the use of natural resources from regenerative sources, measures to limit energy costs, recycling, reuse, maintenance-free buildings, or an architectural design based on payback principles.

the sun is drawn out from within the window depth, and stored in basement tanks and recycled when required. The high capital investment has been justified on the grounds of the permanence of stainless steel and the recyclability of the materials used in this landmark high-tech building.

As has been demonstrated down through the ages of architectural form, it can be argued that 'fitness for purpose' is a useful measure for achieving sustainability in both architecture and urban design. Stated differently, timelessness is a yardstick for architecture of relevance, and this maxim could equally apply to the design of urban social space. There are many well-known examples where the vitality of a particular public space enjoys sustained use, even over centuries.

Although design linguistics or idiomatic design present an interesting exercise for the designer, architecture which is purposely stylistic might not serve more pressing issues of sustainability. In retrospect, the contemporary principles of 'fitness for purpose' and relevance have been around since the Vitruvian principle 'commoditie' was coined as his prescription for good architecture.

▲ ▶ *Schwartzwald, Germany: Typical evolved farmstead vernacular*

◀ *The Bhutanese farmhouse vernacular compares to its European counterpart in terms of fitness for purpose*

THE VERNACULAR AND FITNESS FOR PURPOSE Some regional vernaculars such as the chalet genre of Alpine Europe have achieved a timelessness and the wide regional application due to a capacity to house the farmer, the farm stock, fodder, implements and farm vehicles all under one roof. The architectural response to the extremes of climate was also developed to a fine art in terms of comfort and energy efficiency.

Arising from the highly developed environmental technologies of modern times, such as airconditioning, the concepts advanced for energy-inefficient design may sometimes find a basis in the pay back principle - the principle of redeeming the initial financial outlay over time from the operational cost savings. In the case of a building that is highly dependent on fossil fuel energy sources, there is potential for resource depletion to precede the life of that building. Often missing from the equation for sustainable design, is the eventual depletion of energy resources leading ultimately to the large scale obsolescence of entire central business environments, particularly in developed economies. In the foreseeable future, fossil fuels could be facing depletion thus shortening the useful life of the glass heat-absorbing skyscrapers of the latter half of the twentieth century which depend on such energy sources.

Vernacular architecture, mostly of pre-industrial times, invariably 'got it right', and was in many instances the result of constraints on resource availability, whether financial or naturally imposed. Historically, and without modern means, extraordinary enterprise produced architecture often of the most distinctive character and ingenuity in the creation of shelter with only limited means available. Examples can be found in both urban and rural situations. Functionality, shelter, security and status were expressed in vernacular styles, raising again the relevance of the aesthetic which can arise from 'fitness for purpose'.

After the start of the industrial age, whole communities collectively experienced the rigours of urbanisation and responded with modesty to their habitation needs. From prudent beginnings vernacular architecture evolved geographically, with marked characteristics related to regional influences.

The unfortunate common denominator of contemporary development policy is the economic 'bottom line', where expediency in the short term often overrides prudent deployment of resources with long-term vision. Ironically, practising an environmental philosophy in architectural design can reward the end user with significant short- and long-term economic benefits. It requires the will of the developer and designer to be committed to a responsible design ethos. As with vernacular architecture, a building that is in harmony with the local climate derives optimum indoor comfort with minimal dependence on energy-consuming artificial heating and cooling.

As a guide, designers should develop a code to determine the level of commitment to 'greenness' as distinct from 'greenwash'. In architecture

◀ *Cairo, Egypt: Contemporary city building*

▼ *Godalming, Surrey, UK: Office block, early 1990s*

DERIVATIVE ARCHITECTURE Styles which derive their design language from regional native origins. The desire to emulate the past could range from the availability of local building skills to preference for the regional aesthetic, to the proven climatic efficiency of the architecture or to the patriotic desire to maintain a cultural linking of the present with the past.

DESIGN IN RESPONSE TO NEED Some of the most distinctive vernacular designs were invariably in response to a particular need, such as for wind power to drive machinery or defence. Modern engineering structures are often the closest contemporary version of buildings designed for 'fitness for purpose', thereby adding meaning and relevance to the design.

▶ *Carcassone, France: Essentially a castle with the clear purpose of defence, despite the romantic idiom*

◀ *Holland: The windmill, a common sight in a low-lying country - functional structures designed to grind wheat, to power sawmills and drain land lying below sea level*

▶ *The Thames barrier, London: A modern day design for an essentially functional structure with a strong expression of its 'fitness for purpose'*

this approach, according to Vale and Vale (1996) can be founded on six principles:

    ≲ Respect the site: a building should touch the ground lightly.

    ≲ Work with the climate: design with natural energy sources in mind.

    ≲ Minimise the use of new resources : do not reconstruct anew where upgrading of existing structures is possible.

    ≲ Conserve energy: a building should be constructed so as to minimise the need for fossil fuels to run it.

    ≲ Respect the builder and the end user: recognise the importance of the health and safety of all people involved in the building process.

    ≲ Design holistically: embody all green principles in the production and the end product.

Respect for the site

Land characteristics are situation-specific, as are its natural attributes. The manner in which a programme is set up to transform a site and manage building operations is demonstrably the first measure of and architect's resource-mindedness. Traditional methods using human labour to prepare the site for a building have been replaced by massive, time- and labour-saving, earthmoving technology and explosive devices. Rather than permit the site to inform the design, commonly used modern mechanised methods have the capacity to recreate the characteristics of a site within hours to suit the design. In the process of remodelling the site, respect for the site in terms of its intrinsic characteristics, particularly in the case of 'green

RESPECTING THE SITE Without modern day earthmoving and site-making technology, cultures of the past relied on organisation of the site by manual means, and thus conceded more readily to site constraints. Conscious stewardship of good soils was also conducive to 'respect for the site' and ensured that buildings were compact, sometimes multistorey and located on terrain otherwise unable to support viable agriculture.

▲ *The village of Caramany, Rousillon district, France: Occupying the unarable rocky site, thereby liberating the best soils to cultivation*

▶ *Gorge du Tarne, France: A farm complex situated on the natural bank of the River Tarne*

◀ *Cornwall, UK: The Minack Theatre: A modern day version of the Greek amphitheatre that merges the sculptured rocky attributes of the precipitous terrain into an architectural wholeness - a model of design sensitivity celebrating the site*

field' sites, is bypassed. As with 'sense of place' described earlier, liberating the design from the physical and the resource attributes of the site removes the architecture from its context. The architectural product generally can be likened to a peacock on a heap of energy-spent destruction - and at significant environmental cost. The habitats of other species and culturally important sites in the wider context can equally be demeaned by the transformation of a single site.

Where development is about to take place, a 'Green Scorecard' (Chernushenko 1994) highlights the areas needing to be considered in the pre-design process:

- If not the developer, has an agency been identified to be accountable for environmental costs?
- Will any natural spaces or wilderness be developed?
- Will buildings be expanded into protected natural areas?
- Is an Environmental Impact Assessment needed and has it been prepared?
- What steps have been taken to protect natural spaces, habitats or species?
- What restorative or rehabilitative measures will be taken?
- Will any habitat or species be harmed or eliminated so that it cannot be remedied?
- Will any significant cultural site be affected?
- What steps have been taken to protect such cultural site(s)?
- Have energy and water conservation technologies, waste management measures and energy-efficient principles and building technology guided the design process in a meaningful way?
- What will the impact be on transportation levels and infrastructure?
- How will any anticipated demand increases be addressed?
- Has public transport been encouraged and infrastructure improved?
- What external environmental cost will there be to service the site with roads and other services?
- What steps have been taken to mitigate external social and environmental costs?
- What steps have been taken to ensure a positive legacy from the development, economically, socially and environmentally in terms of its sustainability?

These issues of 'greenness' would apply equally to infill development, where a 'newcomer' building should show respect for the architectural character of the context and for the preservation of important archaeological and natural imprints.

Working with the climate

Together with a site's geophysical and ecological characteristics, climate, viewed in the overall perspective of human settlement, is the single most important seasonal constant in our landscape. Socio-economic and political conditions, style preferences and aesthetic sensibility will evolve, but climate remains on a discernible cyclical course. Historical studies of settlement show that even the ancient civilisations recognised regional climatic adaptation as an essential principle in the creation of architecture.

Harnessing the potential offered by the climate can assert a dramatic effect on design and when fully exploited for the comfort of the occupants of a building, can make a profound difference to its energy demand. A climatically responsive building can enhance the occupants' sense of well-being, while enabling them to experience the external climate of the place - the diurnal and seasonal changes. In so doing the blandness of spending long working hours indoors in an otherwise artificial environment, invariably controlled throughout the year, is avoided.

An important factor in climate-conscious design is the position and angle of the solar arc in both winter and summer in all regions. Armed with

◀ Ghardaia, Algeria: Capital city of the hot, arid, M'zab region, population 38 000. Sited on a rise to capture every breeze, the busy hierarchical network of lanes provides a tight fabric within which the courtyard house shelters the occupants from the temperature fluctuations between day and night. The city is skirted by a greenbelt of palms sheltering dwellings and known as the summer town where historically the inhabitants would take up residence during the hottest summer months

▼ Nakhla, near El Oued, Algeria: Desert settlement in a hostile climate, where sandstorms necessitate an introverted architecture of durable construction

WORKING WITH CLIMATE Cities in hot, hostile desert climates of, for example, North Africa, must develop an effective pattern of shelter and shade in their construction. The architecture, such as the courtyard house, is generally introverted within high mud walls thereby reducing solar gain into the internal courts so that life can continue in reasonable comfort. After sunset a violent drop in temperature usually changes the function of the roof terrace from parasol to sleeping area.

data on the incidence of solar penetration seasonally, the optimum orientation of a building layout and detail design of sun control devices can be determined. Solar charts to refine orientation and solar control elements should be seen as an indispensable design aid to the architect.

It is useful to compare graphically the variations of solar radiation intensities on horizontal and vertical surfaces for different orientations. The following observations emerge for two contrasting locations, one at the equator and the other at 33 degrees latitude south from the equator:

⟍ In both locations, especially at the equator, the horizontal surface receives the greater intensity.

⟍ East and west facing walls receive high intensities in the equatorial location and similarly at the higher latitudes.

⟍ In the equatorial location, north and south walls receive the least intensity and only for short periods of the year.

⟍ At high northern or southern latitudes, the wall facing the equator receives the highest intensity in winter, when the sun's arc is lower, but very little in the summer.

The conclusion can now be drawn that in the equatorial location, if solar heat gain is to be avoided, the main windows should face north and south. At the higher latitudes, an orientation away from the equator would receive the least sunshine, but here it may be desirable to have some solar heat gain in the winter, when the sun's arc is low - so an orientation towards the equator may be preferrable. In both locations only minor openings of unimportant rooms should be placed on the east and west side. Solar heat gain on the west side can be particularly troublesome as its maximum intensity coincides with the hottest part of the day. The proviso is that these conditions are valid in situations where all other factors are equal (Koenigsberger et al. 1974).

Taking three contrasting climate types, the Mediterranean climate with winter rainfall, a distinctly hot and dry but minimal summer rainfall region, and that of hot and humid regions - differing approaches would be required not only towards architectural design but also to the layout and orientation of entire developments. Mediterranean climates are usually coastal, the summers being hot and dry with cooler nights. Winters, with high rainfall, are cold but milder than inland regions, while coastal winds predominate in summer. Layout and design of buildings would favour:

⟍ Urban layouts, traditionally compact, provide protection for external spaces from coastal winds.

⟍ Orientation should be with the longest sides facing north and south.

RESPONSE TO CLIMATE Before the advent of airconditioning, the climate of different parts of the planet would reflect strongly in the architecture of a region - geography thus influencing the vernacular. Building design in the northern climes would favour the introduction of large window areas and less shade, whereas that of the hot, dry Middle Eastern regions would favour the opposite.

▲ *Cheshire, UK: Little Moreton Hall, the Tudor approach to climate, affording maximum solar benefit during a moderate summer and cold winter months with extensive fenestration. A feature is the linear ambulatory in the upper storey enabling indoor exercise amongst other activities during long winters*

▶ *Cairo, Egypt, Ibu Tulun (Old) Mosque: Deep, densely shaded courtyards in a hot arid climate to shelter the masses while at worship or during meditation*

⟍ Solar gain in winter is desirable.

⟍ Thermal mass concentrated in the external and internal walls and floor, is advantageous in summer to stabilise temperatures indoors.

⟍ Roofs can be lightweight but well insulated.

⟍ Openings should facilitate ventilation. Hinged shutters over window openings are efficient.

⟍ Openings should be protected in summer and exposed to sun in winter. This can be achieved through having deep reveals to the openings and without roof overhangs.

⟍ Outdoor living spaces should be protected in summer and exposed to sun in winter. This can be achieved by the typically favoured device of a pergola and deciduous creepers, such as the vine species.

It is important to note that in winter, unless the building fabric is properly insulated, cold rainy conditions can produce condensation on inner surfaces of the walls and ceiling. In masonry walls this condition can be avoided using cavity wall construction.

By comparison, in distinctly hot, dry regions the summer rainy season is accompanied by strong solar radiation with little cloud cover. Temperature swings can reach 18° C and light reflected off the ground produces glare. Layout and design of buildings would favour:

    ⟋ Buildings arranged around courtyards with small openings on the outer walls, and larger into the courtyard.

    ⟋ Buildings compact and grouped together for mutual shading.

    ⟋ External surfaces largely reduced with larger dimensions facing north and south.

    ⟋ All surfaces white or light coloured to reflect heat.

    ⟋ Shading on walls, roof and outdoor areas, with vegetation if necessary.

    ⟋ Roofs, walls and floors should have mass (thermal capacity) to utilise the large temperature variation.

    ⟋ Night ventilation is desirable to remove stored heat.

    ⟋ Openings should be closed and shaded during the day.

Contrasting with the previous two climate types, zones characterised by high temperatures and high humidity with daily temperature fluctuations of less than 5° C demand (Holm and Viljoen 1996):

    ⟋ Free-standing buildings to allow air movement through generous openings in north and south walls.

    ⟋ Narrow plan shapes with single rows of rooms for cross ventilation.

    ⟋ Good ventilation to remove excess humidity and provide thermal comfort.

    ⟋ Totally shaded walls and external openings using broad eaves and deep verandahs.

    ⟋ Lightweight construction with shaded walls.

    ⟋ East and west facing walls preferrably without windows or openings.

    ⟋ Ventilated roof space to counter the effect of high solar radiation.

Checklist for energy-conserving design

Through practical, energy-conscious design a building should be constructed so as to minimise the need for fossil fuels to heat or cool the interior. In this way the potentially win-win situation is in keeping with sound, economically sustainable development.

A generic checklist to highlight areas for the application of energy-conscious design would cover (Holm and Viljoen 1996):

    ⟋ The use and cost of energy in buildings on a long-term basis.

    ⟋ The climatic characteristics in terms of solar radiation, temperature, humidity and wind.

◀ Nakhla, near El Oued, Algeria: Heavily textured barrel vaulting and domes contribute significantly to the partial shading of that already provided by the curved roof forms

▼ Yemeni village: Domes employed for structural as well as thermal reasons. The spherical form affords progressive diurnal shading to moderate heat gain to the interior

LESSENING SOLAR GAIN The architecture of authentic cultures in desert locations evolved through accepting the climatic severity as a challenge. The curved form of the dome and the vault have the advantage of being partially in shade most of the day, which lessens solar heat gain. The use of a heavy texture on the vault surface adds significantly to shading of the surface and therefore cools the structure further.

≶ Thermal comfort of the occupants.

≶ Architectural guidelines for effective solar design.

≶ Planning and siting of buildings.

≶ The building envelope: Mass, glazing, daylighting, insulation, ventilation and systems.

≶ User control mechanisms.

≶ The incorporation of renewable fuels into building design.

A checklist has the effect of prompting a closer look at the potential for passive design measures or the employment of alternative environmental technologies.

Heat in large buildings accumulates mainly from internal sources, such as the heat from people or the building mass that can be exploited to advantage. By storing excess daytime heat and using it to warm the building during the night a system can be evolved that radically reduces energy consumption during the day. By storing heat during nocturnal off-peak hours, a significant cost saving can be effected.

EASTGATE, HARARE, ZIMBABWE (PEARCE PARTNERSHIP)
A TERMITARY FOR WORKING IN

In 1991, architects Pearce Partnership and engineers Ove Arup, were commissioned to design the largest mixed-use development in Zimbabwe. It was to be appropriate to the economy, the market, the climate and the technology of the developing country and hence to be of local materials, have small offices that would be naturally comfortable, and the building was to be maintenance-free. Acknowledging the challenge, the client body agreed to pay the mechanical engineers the same fee as through the building were fully airconditioned. Could the professional team design a building that would be comfortable for its users by drawing only on the passive effects of the structural fabric, and not resort to artificial cooling?

We were inspired by a videofilm by David Attenborough on the termitary which had to use the immediate environment and the dynamic forces of the biosphere to create a comfortable internal environment for its occupants. The metaphor led us to ask questions like: if the termites themselves are the control system, the source of heating as well as the constructors, in what ways are we different from them? The termites maintain a controlled range of 30-31°C while the external temperature could be 40°C plus. They used the thermal mass of the ground; underground water for evaporative cooling; and the diurnal range for convection power. Besides the ants are hard working; continuously altering air passages and forming mud gills.

'We were not looking purely at structural fabric but at creating an organism - a living system or an ecosystem. We soon realised that humans do not work like termites, and to have only the structural fabric as a tempering device would not suffice. So we had to use a machine, but part-time and simplified, to work in conjunction with the structure (Pearce 1999).

The towering mound built by *Macrotermes bellicosus* is really a giant ventilation chimney through which hot air from the nest can escape. Beneath the tower is a cave about three metres in diameter housing the nursery galleries, the queen's cell, and the fungus gardens. Below the main cave are cavities, ten metres or more deep, from which the termites obtain water. At the top of the main cave is a hole, which the termites can make bigger or smaller by adding or removing soil particles. This varies the speed of warm moist air passing up and out through the cave and chimneys, and controls the temperature to within one degree.

The interior architecture of many termite species is even more astounding. The distribution of the various chambers according to their different purposes is evidence of a definite building plan. But the functioning of a large termitary requires not only the systematic layout of the chambers, but convenient space for the royal cell, the quarters for the different age groups, the fungus gardens, and the associated network of communications.

When a mound of *Macrotermes bellicosus* formerly *natalensis* has reached a height of three to four metres, it contains more than two million termites. They live, they work and they breathe. Their oxygen consumption, which has been measured, is considerable. Without ventilation they would all be suffocated within the twelve hours. How is the termitary ventilated? Its solid surface shows no signs of windows.

Studies of termitaries of this species on the Ivory Coast of Africa show that these insects have established a strange and ingenious ventilation system. A cross-section through the mound shows the nest proper, which is almost round, with its royal cell in the centre (1), and its many chambers and passages. There is a larger space, the 'cellar' (2), while the central structure rests on conical supports and is further anchored by lateral struts. Another air space above it (3) reaches a long way into the nest proper like a chimney. On the outside of the mound, ridges and buttresses run from top to bottom (4). These are clearly shown on the horizontal cross-section. Channels as thick as an arm

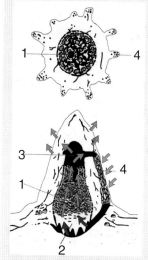

radiate from the upper air space into the ridges, where they divide into small ducts. These come together again to form channels as wide as the first leading into the cellar. The ventilation system of the termitary is completely automatic as termites do not flap their wings to ventilate the mound

The air in the fungus chambers is heated by the fermentation processes taking place there. Like any tightly packed group of breathing animals, the termites themselves cause a rise in temperature. This hot air rises and is forced by the pressure of the continuous stream of hot air into the duct system of the ridges. The exterior and interior walls of these ridges are so porous that they enable a gas exchange to take place. Carbon dioxide escapes and oxygen penetrates from the outside. The ridges with their system of ducts might be called the lungs of the colony. As has been experimentally confirmed, the air is cooled during its passage through the ridges; this cooler, regenerated air now flows into the cellar by way of the lower system of wide ducts. From there it returns to the nest via the surrounding air space, replacing the rising warm air *(Mound 1990; Skaife 1979; von Frisch 1974).*

At Eastgate, the architects were not looking purely at structural fabric but at creating an organism - living system or ecosystem. Their starting point was that humans are not like termites, and to have only the structure as the tempering device would not suffice. So mechanical means was necessary, but only part-time to simplify the system and to work in conjunction with the structure.

Through a system of ducts in the vertical and horizontal components of the structure, fresh air enters and stale air leaves the interior, on much the same basis as a termitary's performance. Immediately above first floor, behind an open cross-grilled string course, a service storey containing air intake fans provide forced air to the offices above. Vertical supply and exhaust ducts were placed in the centre of the rentable floors because external ducts would impact on window area. These ducts absorb 2,35% of the floor area, much the same as a conventional air conditioning system. The ducts supply a hollow floor under the offices (the equivalent of Roman hypocausts) and the cooled air enters the offices via grilles below the windows. Stale air is exhausted from the offices through the high-level bulkheads parallel to the core and then moves horizontally to vertical extract shafts. Eventually the slow moving mass of stale air is discharged from the building at roof level through a cresting of chimneys (Pearce 1999).

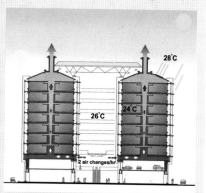

Shading of the walls by cantilevered sunscreens assists in regulating the interior comfort levels, by allowing the temperature of the reinforced concrete structure alternatively to cool the offices during the day and to heat them during cool nights. Optimum performance is achieved by supplying air at two air changes per hour during the day and seven during the night. These changes are adjusted for seasonal variations so that the ambient temperature in the offices is maintained between 21 and 25°C.

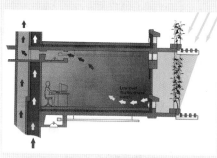

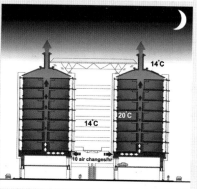

With acknowledgement to Pearce Partnership for photo images and graphics

To focus briefly on the example of a developed country such as the USA where consumption of energy is a major national (in fact global) issue, the argument in favour of energy-efficient buildings is conclusive. The energy required for heating of buildings constructed in the 1970s, prior to the oil embargo, can arguably be reduced through energy-efficient design by 85%. Significantly, the major costs of energy-efficient office building design need be no greater than an inefficient one. The solution lies in the employment of environmentally correct principles:

⚘ Reduction in artificial lighting needs by supplementing with natural light. Daylighting can reduce lighting bills by up to 15 % in commercial buildings.

⚘ Provide smaller double glazed fenestration.

⚘ Provide efficient insulation of the interior from the exterior.

⚘ Install automated lighting and thermostatic controls. Systems operated by photocells and controlled by microprocessors will activate dimmers in proportion to the amount of daylight present and provide even lighting throughout the building.

We humans may be proud of our inventions, but can we discern greater merit in our capabilities than in those of the master builders who unconsciously follow their instincts? The evolutionary roots of human behaviour reach far back into the behaviour patterns of animals. Those who are fascinated by these connections need only consider one such puzzle - the architecture of animals, to find a lesson even for the professional designer. The sum total of unsolved mysteries in nature will always remain immeasurably greater than the sum of our discoveries. Termites are architects for time eternity and termitaries can be likened to naturally airconditioned cities. The biggest and most complex of insect societies are built by termites. The nests of some species like the West African *Macrotermes bellicosus* may house up to many more termites than the human population of an entire country. They are extraordinarily complex buildings with full airconditioning,

Is high-rise not the antithesis of conservation architecture?

Ken Yeang is an inventive and prolific architect working in the rapidly developing economy of south-east Asial. Richards (1994) writes of Yeang's committed 'bio-climatic' design method which he has applied to his energy efficient architecture:

At the heart of the principles are the first and dominant concerns of energy reduction and buildings as open systems - interactive inside and outside in response to seasons. In essence, the fundamental propositions are very simple, but the overall, global effect of their consequences represents an optimistic and progressive vanguard of potential that is crucial to the effort towards a sustainable future world.

Underpinning Ken Yeang's work agenda is his personal methodology of Research Development and Design (RD+D). Implicit in this is his insistence on building his research and constantly improving his architectural production, a commitment which is rare amongst architects who have to achieve their commissions for a profit-driven clientele. What is in evidence here is an architect who is systematically at work on the whole built environment.

the design principles of which inspired the concept for the Eastgate building, Harare (Pearce Partnership 1991) seen on the previous pages.

Further consideration of human exploration into 'ecological architecture' - architecture which serves the user in his or her urban habitat - calls to mind the work of Ken Yeang, Malaysian architect whose demonstration of ecological architecture is based on a compelling philosophy:

'Here lies a likely trumpcard for affirming theoretical respectability: the design of energy-efficient enclosures has the potential to transform architectural

◀ *Stockholm, Sweden: A tower block of the 1950s with a fully glazed external skin necessitating total dependence on mechanical airconditioning*

▼ *Kuala Lumpur, 1992: Menara Mesiniaga, (IBM) Tower: Ken Yeang's design for a tower block showing environmental accountability on behalf of the architect and his client. Recovery rate of the initial additional capital outlay for energy-conscious design will accelerate over time when linked to escalating global fuel costs*

HIGH-RISE AND ENERGY Energy consciousness in the design of tower blocks is more difficult to achieve, yet shown by creative architects to be possible. Two high-rise buildings forty years apart in time show the design distinctions between an era when energy consciousness held no brief for the architect, compared with the need for environmental responsibility of recent time. Accountability for the depletion of the energy resources of the planet has become a design imperative for all involved in the development environment.

▶ *Garston, Watford, UK: The BRE building built to demonstrate performance specifications for the Energy Efficient Office of the Future (EoF). The five distinctive ventilation shafts running up the facade form part of the energy-saving natural ventilation and cooling system, and point to a new genre of architectural aesthetic*

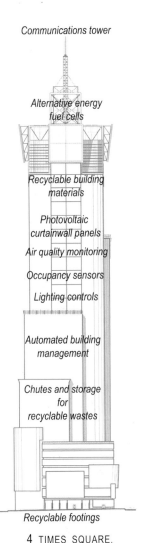

Communications tower

Alternative energy fuel cells

Recyclable building materials

Photovoltaic curtainwall panels

Air quality monitoring

Occupancy sensors

Lighting controls

Automated building management

Chutes and storage for recyclable wastes

Recyclable footings

4 TIMES SQUARE, New York USA, 2000

design from being an uncertain, seemingly whimsical craft, into a confident science. The theory of the design of a tall building might then be one that derives from energy conservation' (Yeang 1994).

Breaking ground for energy-conscious ethos in the design for the skyscraper is the millennium project 4 Times Square, New York (architects Fox & Fowle, USA) completed in the year 2000. Described as 'environmentally friendly' (Turner 2000) it exhibits a commitment to 'green' issues in the design. Through the incorporation of 'photovoltaic panels in the curtain wall cladding, the building generates 5% of its own electricity requirements' and also makes use of fuel cell technology using 'clean-burning natural gas in a chemical process'. The airconditioning system 'allows an instantaneous 100% air flushing of any floor at any time... to take noxious air from interior spaces directly to the roof'. In this way the possibility of the likely advent of 'sick building syndrome' is diminished. Whereas sceptics might concede that this project is an attempt to bring 'green' thinking into the design process, a significant reduction in the energy demands of glass enclosed, force conditioned super towers to any significant level with current technologies still remains unachievable. More advanced technologies, yet to be developed or invented might change this scenario. The building is in other respects a socially responsive workplace, and indeed appropriate to context through its sense of location at the commercial hub of a major city.

Prudent investment in energy-efficient technologies might have to achieve a pay back time of less than 5 years, to achieve viability. However, the individual consumer and the needs of big business and industry would logically need to have differing yardsticks. The external and social costs of providing a major new supply utility and the attendant infrastructure to meet the escalating energy demand could, for example, present a 10 year payback period attractive in national terms. Repricing of energy to include all externalities (the real cost) is therefore an essential part of the overall strategy for attitudinal changes in energy consumption.

Commencing with governments who commission major building projects where substantial environmental and economic gains could be made,

▲ New Mexico, USA: Tiered houses of the Taos Pueblo, founded c.1250, proving sustainability in terms of durability

▲ Taos, New Mexico, USA: Church of Spanish colonial architecture. Resource efficient, ecologically based design in vernacular architecture, this mud architecture complies with the principles of energy efficient building, as well as sustainable construction methods

RESOURCE EFFICIENCY In Third World countries, environmentally correct architecture is concerned with labour intensivity as much as the economy of resource consumption. The efficiency of mud structures has been significantly proven in cities where, either single or multistorey, they satisfy the criteria of a high levels of sustainability. Historically, indigenous building technologies have served societies well throughout the world, generally showing remarkable ingenuity and use of renewable resources.

▶ San'a, North Yemen: Multistorey mud structures are commonplace

◀ Ouarglua near El Oued, S. Algeria: Single storey with efficient barrel roof vaulting in response to the absence of timber supplies

or who could provide subsidies or tax incentives, the environmental technologies industry could receive an important boost, with inevitable spin-off into the private sector.

SUSTAINABLE CONSTRUCTION

Current issues in sustainable construction have occupied many conference agendas, particularly in the First World even to the extent of bringing 'together people of like mind and with similar interests to exchange information and assess progress in the new discipline that might be called "sustainable construction" or "green construction"' (Hill and Bowen, 1995).

Apart from financial cost factors, the capacity of the human to shape the environment anywhere on the planet requires huge environmental accountability. Some commentators estimate that one-tenth of the global economy is dedicated to constructing, operating and equipping homes and offices. Such a demand would account for roughly 40% (Roodman and Lenssen 1994) of the materials flow entering the world economy for buildings, with much of the remainder being consumed for road and bridge building and vehicles.

Compliance with the 'green code' set out in ISO14001 regarding the potential impacts and controls of construction activity, the training of personnel, accountability, conservation and mitigation measures is essential for environmental correctness on the construction site (See Appendix II).

Considering the proposition that sustainable construction means 'creating a healthy built environment using resource efficient, ecologically based principles' six initiatives of importance emerge (Kibert 1994):

- Minimise resource consumption - conserve and reduce use of resources.
- Maximise resource reuse - avoid and reduce waste.
- Use renewable or recyclable resources.
- Protect the natural environment.
- Restore environments degraded by past activities.

Straw bale construction

The majority of people around the world live in houses that are poorly constructed and uncomfortable much of the year. Maintaining adequate comfort levels in those structures often results in high and unaffordable utility bills, and damaging environmental practices such as the over cutting of timber.

Building with baled materials could dramatically improve housing conditions in a variety of climates and conditions. Anywhere that wheat, barley, oats or rice, or other straws are available, bale building can make economic and environmental sense. Wherever the goal is to provide ecologically sound, sustainable structures that are inexpensive to build and maintain, that are energy efficient and compatible with renewable energy sources, and can be owner-built to further reduce costs, bale buildings can be an ideal solution.

Steen et al. (1994)

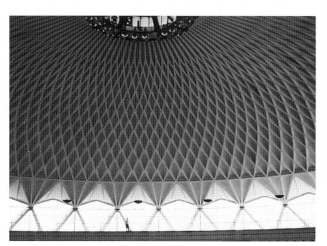

▲ St Etienne, France: Formula One Hotel of prefabricated concrete room cells, assembled on site. Architecturally precasting can deliver efficiency but usually at the expense of design sensitivity

▲ Rome, Italy: Palazzetto della Sport - exhibiting Nervi's ferro-cement construction method of efficiency and elegance

STRUCTURAL EFFICIENCY AND ENVIRONMENTAL COSTS
All concrete construction relies heavily on the earth's resources, the exploitation of which involves major capital and drastic interventions into natural deposits and extreme disturbance of the original topography. The marginal and external costs of production should determine whether the plasticity and precasting advantages of concrete effectively reduce dependence on other raw materials and their attendant environmental costs.

▶ Church, Maputo, LM: Folded concrete construction can be efficient in materials use due to the inherent strength of the folds in the shell construction

＼＼ Create a healthy, non-toxic environment.

＼＼ Pursue quality in creating the built environment.

In the developing world it is important to include further principles relating to 'people skills development' through the promotion of 'labour intensive methods, skills, training and capacity building of local people' (Hill and Bowen 1994).

Sustainability in construction relates not only to the extraction and production of raw materials, but also to efficiency in terms of the design execution of the structure. A significant contribution to this area of sustainability is the work of Pier Luigi Nervi whose work came to prominence in the 1950s using what came to be termed *ferro cemento* construction.

Striking in resource efficiency, the ultimate design elegance achieved with ferro-cement made it a suitable method for many of the stadium structures for the Rome Olympic Games of 1960 where the technique

▲ *Giza, Egypt: Ramses Wissa Wassef's Arts Centre, 1974, using sustainable construction techniques, and local materials, derived through energy efficient methods. The project received the Agha Khan's Award of Excellence for architecture*

▶ *Alberobello, Apulia, Italy: The trulli, with domical corbelled roofs of local stone*

SUSTAINABLE CONSTRUCTION The use of ecologically acceptable materials determines corresponding building technologies and historically has resulted in strong vernacular aesthetics. Modern day building methods and materials sourced from non-sustainable sources tend to be ecologically incorrect and energy inefficient. The designer becomes the consumer and thus becomes accountable for the stewardship of scarce resources.

was used extensively for the large span roof construction of the sports facilities.

'Conditions at the time led Nervi to work on a new type of construction which he calls ferro-cement. It is based on the principle of a very thin (sometimes 25 mm), highly reinforced slab obtained by forcing a very good quality cement mortar of cement and sand through several layers of steel mesh and small diameter bars, joined together over a mould, also shaped in ferro-cement.

Mortar was forced either by hand or by vibration between the mesh and the results were extremely successful, because of the exceptional flexibility, economy, strength and freedom from cracking of slabs so obtained.

The edges of the moulded panels are so shaped that when placed side by side they form channels of 100 mm between, which are then filled in with insitu concrete. Main ribs support the moulded panels and are cast in situ. The pattern of ribs is designed along the isostatic lines of the principal bending moments, a design which makes possible strict adherence to the lines of statics, and therefore makes the most efficient use of materials. Structures of 60 by 180 metres have been successfully erected using ferro-cement technology. It has even been used in the construction of ships of tonnage not exceeding 500 tons' (Thomas 1958). Inexplicably since the 1960s there has not been wide application of this construction method.

Minimise resource consumption

Conservation supports the principles of sustainability, whereas the unholistic exploitation of natural resources runs counter to such a goal, usually for reasons of short-term economic advantage. Past ages never considered resource depletion. With the threatening prospect for all of eventual depletion of the global resources, only energy-efficient buildings and construction methods utilising heating, cooling and lighting technologies that minimise the use of non-renewable energy sources should become the norm. Considering the processes of production, from extraction of raw materials to the final product, energy in various forms is embodied in building materials generally. Ways of minimising energy costs in building materials are best served by the use of local materials as well as by designing for minimise

▲ *Loire Valley, France: The seductive aesthetic of Château Chambord built by Louis XIV as a hunting lodge is the antithesis of resource efficiency in terms of design, construction and energy consumption*

waste and limiting the unnecessary use of packaging materials arriving on a building site. The life cycle potential for reuse of materials and building elements at the outset of a project should always be considered and assessed.

Water is a natural resource found in varying levels of abundance or shortage throughout the world. However, planning for sustainability is the ongoing cost of consumption irrespective of the current global availability of water. Seen from the viewpoint of limiting external environmental and social costs, it would be correct to limit the consumption of water through: rooftop rainwater harvesting for outdoor irrigation; water efficiency in buildings through the use of conserving fittings such as low-flow showerheads, tap aerators, dual flushing toilet mechanisms and in external landscaping the use of indigenous, low water dependent plant species.

Pearson (1989) in *The Natural House Book*, checklists the following criteria for the limiting resource consumption by raising issues as to whether the materials intended for use are:

⧵ renewable and abundant;

⧵ low impact on the environment at source;

⧵ non-polluting, emitting no harmful vapours, particles or toxins during either manufacture or use;

Cob architecture

Cob buildings are constructed of straw and earth, or 'cob' as this ancient method of building is known. 500 year old cob buildings can still be found in Wales, where the concept possibly originated.

Affordability and sustainability are key attributes of this form of construction, which involves low technology methods.

All cob structures require a stone foundation, or equivalent, usually 45 cms thick and rising 45 cms above the ground. Multi-layers of cob are then packed onto this base and carefully kneaded to bond using thumbs and palms or specially shaped pieces of wood. Cob mixes are a blend of clay, earth and sand. Depending on the type of soil, a good cob mix only needs a clay content of 20 per cent. Water is added according to pliability, not too firm and not runny. The straw is then added, preferably wheat, which is more fibrous than oats straw.

The best way to mix the ingredients is to use one wheelbarrow full on a tarpaulin and tread heavily after the water is added to the sand and clay.

This method is continued after adding the straw and is ready once the straw is coated with earth and the clumps have a plastic consistency.

Floors can be laid in cob in two layers, the first structural and 150 cms thick and the final finishing layer of 2 cms. The floor surface final finishing can be four coats of boiled linseed oil and beeswax for waterproofing. The result is a pleasing shiny dark-brown, which can be offset by giving a lighter honey colour to the walls, using an application of a boiled mix of cake flour and water, to which can be added some kaolin and finely sifted building clay.

Cremer and Schùrmann (1998)

⧄ energy efficient, using low energy in production, transportation and use;

⧄ durable, long-lived and easy to maintain and repair, and be convincingly tested in their application;

⧄ equitable and produced via socially correct means, e.g. good working conditions, fair wages, equal opportunity; and

⧄ low waste and capable of being reused and recycled, thereby saving the vast amounts of energy spent on processing raw materials. Recycled steel, for example, saves more than 70% of the energy used in manufacturing new steel from primary ore.

Timber products such as cork, linoleum and composite boards each have their particular levels of environmental acceptability. Cork, sourced from the outer bark of the cork oak, can be formed into sheet material for use on floors and walls, where it requires only sealing. The cork oak regenerates the outer bark on stripping and so cork is 'farmed' sustainably. Linoleum is made from powdered cork, linseed oil, wood resin and wood flour, mixed with chalk and pressed onto a backing of hessian (burlap) or jute. Cork has all the advantages of durability and meets the environmental criteria for minimising resource consumption. A paste derived from wood should be used in lieu of synthetic adhesives.

Composite boards are made from waste timber and vegetable matter but due to the heavy demand, most often fresh timber is sourced from hard-pressed forests. Fibreboards, plywoods, blockboards and particle boards are produced with the use of toxic glues containing formaldehyde, phenols and adhesives. Such toxinic elements prejudice their use; however, some manufacturers in developed countries are producing 'formaldehyde-free, or 'low emission' products which do not present a health problem.

Maximise resource reuse and recycling

The avoidance and reduction of waste is another sphere of commitment to sustainability. For example, the refurbishment or reuse of existing buildings wherever this can be achieved. Where demolition is necessary building elements such as doors and windows, wooden floors, staircases, and structural steel, or any other material which has reuse potential should be salvaged. For this purpose a forward plan is essential to avoid damage during a wrecking operation.

Recycling differs from reuse in as much as the element can be reduced to raw material and used in new products, such as bricks crushed for gravel paving, concrete crushed for new aggregate, with the obvious saving of energy costs normally needed for stone and landfilling in the

Paris, France: The D'Orsy Museum, originally a railway station, 'recycled' to become an exhibition gallery for the work of famous sculptors, such as Balzac, Rodin et al. In the developed world the reuse of original fine historical structures for contemporary functions has become a trend and is to be welcomed

conventional situation. A global case study shows that timber resources are being used up at an alarming rate, threatening sustainability at the source. The reuse and recycling of old timber has significant potential and in this way in most cases meets environmental performance criteria comfortably.

LANDSCAPING THE ENVIRONMENT

Where good urban design can be a canvas for good architecture, so too good landscaping is an essential element in the refinement of the whole. Over the centuries approaches to landscaping have evolved, on the one hand into highly mannered art forms and, on the other, that of benign neglect. There are many variations in between. After the austere Age of Classicism, there was a move to break out of the course of strictly applied rules. Romanticism in landscaping preached the freedom of feelings

---

Frank Lloyd Wright on architecture and culture

We will never have a culture of our own until we have an architecture of our own. An architecture of our own does not mean something that is ours by the way of our own taste. It is something that we have knowledge concerning. We will have it only when we know what constitutes a good building and when we know that a good building is not one that hurts the landscape, but is one that makes the landscape more beautiful than it was before that building was built.

for the subject, and became manifest most clearly in the gardens of the time. The era of the symmetrical, neatly trimmed and structural French garden was followed by the blossoming of the English landscape garden. Natural herbage was the maxim. Soon gardens that grew wild were all the rage - rather they were planted to look as if they were wild.

Contemporary tendencies are towards free-form layouts. All projects have their own characteristics, where the landscaping approach would either be subservient in prominence to the architectural statement itself, or be on an equal footing. Apart from effecting a balance in approach, landscape architects have to respond to briefs which can range from the individual residential plot to complete urban settings, thereby presenting significantly different levels of scale, style of expression and character.

As highways, parks and beaches become more crowded, beautiful places and quiet retreats where the urban dweller can relax and enjoy nature become more important to community health. Some cultivated landscapes become renowned internationally not only for their beauty but also for their acquired cultural importance. A case in point is Giverny, France, the garden at the studio of the painter Claude-Oscar Monet. Picture-perfect in its own right the garden has become the mecca of millions

◀ *The formal garden in the spring stretching away before the house and the studio, with a backdrop of trees of diverse form and character*

▼ *The waterlily pond, subject of the artist's greatest masterpieces, and leading to massive paintings in which the rhythm and colour of nature's harmonies, as revealed on the surface of the pond, give an overwhelming impression of tranquillity and peace*

INSPIRATION FOR THE MASTER   Giverny, France: The garden of Claude-Oscar Monet which inspired much of his work and his fame as one of the most outstanding artists amongst the Impressionists.

▲ Sweden: A church forecourt where the textural relationship between the ubiquitous birch trees and the brickwork creates a harmonious setting for the contrasting entrance structure

▲ Stockholm, Sweden: Architect Asplund's Woodland crematorium (1939). The striking use of the landscaped 'hill of remembrance' with weeping mulberry trees, conveys a sense of peace and acceptance for mourners

SIMBIOTIC ARTS Architecture and landscaping are separate disciplines but interrelated for the success of the whole. They share the same ability to raise the spirit and are capable of rising to a level of completeness not possible in any other way. The need for an environmental ethos is common to both as well as design principles such as water conservation, orientation and sustainability.

▶ Versailles, France: The grand vistas onto the Palace lined with lateral forests to enhance the perspective, while being duplicated in the mirror-like pond. The effect prompts an overwhelming sense of status and stature

of visitors from around the globe. The formal colourful garden in front of the house and the informality of the lily pond, filled by diverting water from the River Epte, are 'living paintings', and provided the true secrets of the artist's own famous canvases.

Such examples of 'tranquillity and peace' become more difficult to realise in a world where, with escalating exploitation, natural resources are being strained to the limit. Particularly in arid regions, and in view of continuing resource destruction, environmental responsibility requires serious commitment to the promotion of biodiversity, involving, for example, the use of indigenous, native plantlife as material for landscaping. All regions around the world have their own, often endemic, species that have successfully adapted to climate and should become the starting point for landscaping projects particularly in arid regions.

◀ *Barcelona, Spain: The public beach, a bland stretch of sand much enhanced by an oasis-like stand of palms, a botanical form introduced from across the Mediterranean*

LANDSCAPING AND ARCHITECTURE Through deliberate statements of stark contrast, evocative shape, affinity with nature, the whole becomes greater than just the interdependency of two elements - architecture with landscaping.

▲ *Jerusalem, Israel: Yad Lebanim: Striking memorial to the Israeli children who died in wars from 1948 onwards. A lone pine, contrasting with the stark geometry of the architecture, stands as a sentinel to the fallen*

▼ *Granada, Spain: The Alhambra terrace landscaped as a perambulatory to provide shade and the sound of water as a relief from the hot climate*

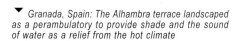

▼ *Parc Guell, Barcelona: Antoni Gaudi's accomplished fusion of natural with architectural forms*

▶ *Bhutan: Wealthy in indigenous forests of hardwoods, the state from time to time disseminates public information regarding Acts and Rules governing the forest resources and management on a sustainable basis. Not only can overexploitation deplete this valuable resource, but plant life hosted by the forest biosphere, such as ferns and lichen, is sensitive to atmospheric changes induced by air pollution*

PROTECT THE NATURAL ENVIRONMENT

Towards better stewardship of the planet's resources in this New Age the restoration of environments degraded through past activities should be considered a non-negotiable imperative for all cultures. All development has the potential for bringing about a negative two-pronged change to the natural environment, namely, the potential destruction arising from development of an actual site itself, and extraction of materials for construction purposes affecting external or remote natural resources (such as the felling of hardwood forests even on other continents). In addition potential impacts to the site itself, which are impossible to avoid during the act of construction, together with negative off-site impacts should be taken into account. In short, mitigation measures should accompany all on-site interventions and off-site impacts to minimise potential 'external costs', financial and environmental, of any significance.

Externalities are often conveniently overlooked by the developer and usually not given sufficient importance by the approval authority. The natural environment should not be viewed in isolation, but seen in context with social and cultural issues that are potentially real yet go unaddressed where the impacts, either positive or negative, are more difficult to compute.

Conserve site biodiversity

The designer and the patron developer are accountable for transforming the environment through development projects that inevitably will disturb the established biological diversity.

> I think harmony with nature is only possible if we abandon the idea of superiority over the natural world.
>
> *Mollison (1997)*

An informed understanding of potential impacts should be dealt with on a methodical basis. It is therefore more constructive at the commencement of a project to develop a checklist than a 'green scorecard'. By defining environmental issues at the outset potential impacts should not fall through the net.

For a preliminary impact assessment a methodological approach could be of assistance using, for example, the matrix procedure developed by Dr Luna Leopold et al. United States Geological Survey, in 1971. Developing two data sets, one related to environmental elements, and the other to project actions, as the coordinates of a matrix , it is possible to expand the scope and usefulness of checklists. Crossed with a diagonal line, each cell is able to receive two numerical or colour coded scores: firstly the magnitude, and then the importance of the impact. By considering each of the envisaged project actions in the context of each site-specific environmental element, and by marking the cells of the matrix above (magnitude) and below (importance) a diagonal line, the completed matrix simulates a near graphic depiction through numbers, symbols or shadings of all cells with above average impacts and their importance. The matrix could be expanded to include ratings for risk or uncertainty (Fuggle and Rabie 1983).

Utilising such tools as an initial scoping framework in the conduct of their practices, architects and urban designers could be afforded the basic means to become environmental generalists. A methodology as described, would at least ensure that further specialist expertise needed to complete a thorough investigation of likely impacts is identified at the outset to precede proper environmental impact assessments, from which mitigating measures may be developed. In this way architects can, with commitment, contribute toward the protection of the biosphere with equanimity, while satisfying the development goals of their clients.

Permaculture - living design

Permaculture, coined as a concept and as a term by Bill Mollison (1974), focuses on the development of a 'design system for creating sustainable human environments'. The word itself is a contraction not only of 'permanent agriculture, but also of permanent culture, as culture cannot survive long without a sustainable agricultural base and land use ethic'.

In a world where there are competing ends for the use of natural resources, and particularly energy forms, the aim of permaculture is to create productive systems which are ecologically sound and ecologically viable, provide for their own needs and do not exploit or pollute, therefore ensuring sustainability in the long term. Using the inherent qualities of plants and animals combined with the natural characteristics of landscapes and structures, life-supporting systems for city and country can be produced. In practical terms, for human settlements in both arid and tropical climates, permaculture embraces many spheres such as energy-efficient site analysis, planning and design; home placement and design; growing food in the city; tree crops and pastures; using greenhouses and shadehouses to effect; orchards and food gardens; and influencing microclimate around the house and garden.

Combining the wisdom contained in traditional farming systems and modern scientific and technological knowledge, permaculture can create a cultivated ecology designed to produce more human and animal food than is generally found in nature. Permaculture would harness internal natural energy, which is in flux and relatively harmless, and by using resources that are abundant, ensure that life on earth is not destroyed in the process.

Modern crop agriculture is totally dependent on external energies based on the practice of widescale annual and highly commercialised agricultural enterprise where land is regarded as a commodity involving a shift from low to high energy systems. The land is exploited and its own natural reserves destroyed by high intensity farming methods that demand external energy sources from the First World (ironically mainly provided by the Third World in the form of fuels, fertilisers, protein and labour), where the true cost is not computable in real terms. In permaculture the emphasis is located away from the huge, the mass produced and the mechanised. It is within the ethic of permaculture, even dense urban environments, that humans are able to regain their humanity, retrieve their self-sufficiency and self-respect. It has great implications for the economic, social, political and technological aspects of human endeavour. Permaculture will provide an avenue for the urban dweller to remain in touch with the natural world so often banished from 'make do' urban environments of these times.

HOLISM IN ARCHITECTURAL DESIGN

Judged on the basis of its aesthetic standard and fitness for purpose, the human habitat can become a place where either social goodwill is promoted, or alternatively where community life becomes dysfunctional. These characteristics are contingent upon issues that constitute holistic architectural design and thus sustainability.

THE END USER AND THE DESIGN PROCESS The aesthetic of a commercial building reflecting the involvement of the end users in the design process on social and technical considerations, as well as the respect for the scale of the environs, comprising a residential scale.

◄ *Amsterdam, Holland: The ING Bank building (1986/97)*

The principles of sustainability explored earlier cannot be resolved in an isolated or compartmentalised way. Kibert (1994) concludes that the 'Construction industry must inevitably change its historic methods of operating with little regard for environmental impacts to a new mode that make environmental concerns a centrepiece of its efforts.'

Due to wavering human resolve, the fund of available knowledge and wisdom does not guarantee that environmentally responsive policies will

Holistic design involves the users in the planning of a building

Tom Alberts, architect of the ING building, Amsterdam (1986), states:

Nature is the source of inspiration of my work. The beauty of nature is linked with organic architecture. For me every building has something unique, something natural that arises from working with its users. The interplay of form, colour and natural materials forms a harmonious whole in which people occupy a central place. And that is how this very special building came into being. It also met the requirements of functionality, flexibility and low operating costs. To achieve this, there has been been close cooperation between all those concerned from the start. Not only the client and the architect, but also the contractor, design engineer, technical adviser, landscape architect and artistic coordinator have made continuous and innovative contributions. In this way we have designed an ecologically sound building that is nevertheless rational, prefabricated and strongly industrialised. By adopting this method a building has been created that is completely different from any designed before. Architecture for the future.

always be followed. Instead, due to other priorities (most often economic) after initial commitment to an environmental ethos at the design stage, tokenism and compromise are frequently the eventual outcome. Aside from environmental issues, architecture of true quality is concerned as much with being aesthetically and functionally appropriate for human habitation as being the outcome of a commitment to 'green criteria' during the design process.

Although not definitive but a useful guide, 'holism' in architectural design would need to be a comprehensive amalgam of three essential parameters: end user involvement in the design process; technological advance aimed at sustainability and the conservation of natural resources; and, sound architectural principles in terms of aesthetics and construction efficiency. In all categories few examples of contemporary architecture can be described as achieving merit, whereas some elements of holism are to be found in individual buildings of the past decade. The illustrated examples presented here score highly in various overlapping areas of holism.

End-user and the design process

A worthy case study which includes the social aspect in the design of the workplace is the later headquarters of the ING Bank in a suburb of Amsterdam by Dutch architects Alberts and Van Huut 1983. The need to have a view to the outside and the careful choice of environmentally friendly non-toxic natural materials were only some of the decisions negotiated democratically with the users.

The development demonstrates that, although the one kilometre long building of 50 000 square metres of office space for 2 000 workers, plus a further 28 000 square metres of basement parking is set down on a site in a modest suburb, the impact is not perceived to be negative.

The architects have articulated the building into ten linked units of a scale appropriate to the more domestic-scaled context, thereby countering the potential for prolonged discord in an established neighbourhood.

Green principles and technological advance

Apart from consultative planning with the occupants, the ING Bank building in Amsterdam is derived from other important 'green' principles. In this instance Vale and Vale (1996) note that features of the green design include: the use of traditional Dutch brick that lends human scale to an office development that is the size of a small town; durable natural materials such as marble for the floors; each of the circulation towers has a different form, but all have prominent stairways to encourage walking up rather

◀ *Eastgate: Harare, Zimbabwe*

▶ *BRE building: Garston, Watford, UK*

than using the elevator; and roof glazing to the access towers allows light to filter down to the internal street, but large areas of roof glazing collect solar energy to preheat the ventilation air of the building. In this way it has been possible to maintain an internal temperature of 21°C while externally the air temperature is 7° C. without supplementary heating from the central boiler plant being activated.

Apart from the obvious environmental merits of this environmentally correct building, the resulting architectural aesthetic is low key and honest. The overall design is sustainable and a model for all who seek the confidence to venture away from conventional office building design and airconditioned working environments.

The Eastgate building in Harare, ('a termitary for working in', see earlier story pps. 160-01) deserves recognition as a serious product expressing commitment to passive environmental principles. In the process, an aesthetic of singular originality is achieved.

Similarly, the need to build a new office building at BRE's Garston site (see later story) was an opportunity to put new ideas on environmental technologies to the test. The brief to the architects (Feilden Clegg of Bath) called for 'the use of natural ventilation, maximum use of daylighting, maximum use of the building's mass to moderate temperate, and controls that would let the building meet its environmental targets but keep its occupants happy'.

Sound aesthetic principles

There are few complete examples that reflect real solutions to the entire spectrum of holistic imperatives, but numerous projects have successfully demonstrated commitment in various departments. As has been explored in earlier pages of this chapter, the final product's architectural worth should be assessed on how a piece of architecture addresses the contextual edge, enhances the cultural experience and derives its energy needs. A seminal issue in the design puzzle is the manner in which the aesthetic responds to 'place'.

Foster & Partner's integration of the new with the old in Nîmes, is a *tour de force,* with the sensitive design for the Carré d'Art building (1984-93),

ARCHITECTURAL INTEGRITY REFLECTING SOUND AESTHETIC PRINCIPLES Through concern for the urban design dimension, the newcomer is exemplary in the manner in which it has breathed life into its neighbour, the 2000 year old Roman temple, now used as an art gallery.

◀ *Nîmes, France: Norman Foster's Carré d'Art (1987-93)*

that could have resulted in a negative invasion of the space of an ancient Roman temple. The result has been widely acknowledged as a demonstration of good neighbourliness, aesthetic refinement and distinction. More significantly it is the strong revitalising influence of the elegant newcomer executed in modern materials, in this case, aluminium and glass, on the pachydermlike exterior of the ancient stone temple. The result is a visually palpable triumph for the judicious employment of a contemporary design idiom.

Returning to holism in architecture, all systems, social, economic, cultural and ecological, are interconnected and interdependent and if architecture has responded positively to these influences, a design will emerge that upholds what is best in architecture.

ORGANIC DESIGN IN ARCHITECTURE

Organic design will be largely distinguishable by its legible expression of 'fitness for purpose'. When considering organic design in architecture there is a tendency to imagine that the scope of the discussion starts with mud structures and ends with vernacular typologies. But, the evolutionary development in architecture suggests that organicism has modern counterparts, and does not have to be traditional even though the vernaculars of earlier authentic cultures often appear to have a greater claim to the definition. There is a regrettable yet understandable trend that those who have the ability and means to influence what is created in the name of responsive architecture and urban planning seek to 'drop out' and move away from

> Organic simplicity might everywhere be seen producing significant character in the ruthless but harmonious order I was taught to call nature. I was more than familiar with it on the farm. All around me, I, or anyone for that matter, might see beauty in growing things and, by a little painstaking, learn how they grew to be beautiful. None was ever insignificant.
>
> *Lloyd Wright*

Spirit of man in architecture

In all buildings that man has built out of the earth and upon the earth, his spirit, the pattern of him, rose great and small. It lived in his buildings. It still shows there. But common to all these workmanlike endeavours in buildings, great or small, another spirit lived. Let us call this spirit, common to all buildings, the great spirit, architecture.

So modern architecture rejects the major axis and the minor axis of classic architecture. It rejects all grandomania, every building that would stand military fashion heels together, eyes front, something on the right hand and something on the left hand. Architecture already favours the reflex, the natural easy attitude, the occult symmetry of grace and rhythm affirming the ease, grace, and naturalness of natural life.

Modern architecture, let us now say ORGANIC architecture - is natural architecture - the architecture of nature, for nature.

Frank Lloyd Wright

New York, USA: Frank Lloyd Wright's Guggenheim (1946-59) - 'rejecting Classical architecture in favour of architecture of nature, for nature'

◀ , Barcelona: Casa Milà (La Pedrera - 'The Quarry', 1910): Pure art forms evolved from natural forms which are sublimated in the continuing, changing waves, bulges and niches. The overall impression is of something that is essentially 'natural'

▼ The Espai Gaudi attic of La Pedrera - its slender brick rib vaulting characterises other works by Gaudi - the often whimsical sculptor shows himself here to be a precise engineer

ORGANICISM IN DESIGN It is in the use of natural forms that distinguishes Antoni Gaudi's work from Art Nouveau artists. The ornamental strain in Art Nouveau is based on natural forms, but remains purely ornamental, where Gaudi employed natural forms for structure. Daring structural elements and arch forms were developed using upside-down models with strings from which small sacks of sand were suspended to simulate structural forces and loading. He took the eucalyptus tree as his example, so that it is no surprise that the network of columns in the main nave of the Sagrada Familia resembles a forest executed in stone (Zerbst 1993).

poor city environments rather than mastermind improvement in their own urban landscape. Their weekend escapes to the south of France, the Greek islands, to the cabin in the outback or to the smaller towns of authentic cultures and vernacular communities tend to indicate a dissatisfaction with their failed home environments. Locations where refuge is sought from poor city environments are invariably those which have qualities to which humans naturally respond - the human scale, the human dimension, prudent environmental values, and societies where the experience of self-identity can be relived. Is this exodus because the architecture in more outlying situations is invariably vernacular with roots in organic honesty?

The breakdown of quality in modern city environments cannot be restored by weekend escapes into the past. The evolving needs of humankind is a dynamic process, and a return to design forms to which moderns are likely to respond positively must become an imperative if a popular solution is to be found. Arguably organic design in architecture affords greater potential to correct past wrongs through a heightened aesthetic appreciation and spiritual experience. The paradigm shift in cultural life in the New Age requires new directions in architecture.

Today, designers have become empowered through the electronic revolution to bring the complexities of a contemporary form of organic architecture into being, evident in some landmark projects, such as Gehry's Guggenheim in Bilbao. Gehry has engaged with digital technology and co-pioneered the application of 'fractal geometry' in design, developed from studies of the scientifically based chaos theory in nature. So far in large public commissions, such as museums and libraries, the new aesthetic, and the non-linear forms which it is able to achieve, has been widely acclaimed. This contemporary form of organic design could become the catalyst towards reversing the impoverishment and decay of urban environments. The widespread flight away by affluent urban cultures to greener pastures could then become a shortlived trend in the history books.

Fractal geometry

Nature presents itself as a complex web of relationships between various parts of a unified whole - the iterating and energetic geometry of fractals at different scales, where components must be defined through interrelationships between one another and the dynamics of the whole system. The study of wholeness is akin to the study of chaos as represented by fractals, and holds exciting possibilities for new organic design forms.

Science and fractal geometry

Scientists felt emotional parallels between their new mathematical aesthetic and changes in the arts in the second half of the century. They felt that they were drawing some inner enthusiasm from the culture at large. To Mandelbrot the epitome of the Euclidean sensibility outside mathematics was the architecture of the Bauhaus. It might just as well have been the style of painting of Josef Albers: spare, orderly, linear, reductionist, geometrical. *Geometrical* - the word means what it has meant for thousands of years. Buildings that are called geometrical are composed of simple shapes, straight lines and circles, describable with just a few numbers. The vogue for geometrical architecture and painting came and went. Architects no longer care to build blockish skyscrapers like the Seagram Building in New York, once much hailed and copied. To Mandelbrot and his followers the reason is clear. Simple shapes are inhuman. They fail to resonate with the way nature organises itself or with the way human perception sees the world...

Gert Eilenberger, a German physicist, states: 'Our feeling for beauty is inspired by the harmonious arrangement of order and disorder as it occurs in natural objects - in clouds, trees, mountain ranges or snow crystals. They shapes of all these are dynamical processes jelled into physical form, and particular combinations of order and disorder are typical for them.'

Gleick, 1997

On a wintry afternoon in 1975, aware of the parallel currents emerging in physics, preparing his first major work for publication in book form, Mandelbrot decided he needed a name for his shapes, his dimensions, and his geometry. His son was home from school, and Mandelbrot found himself thumbing through the boy's Latin dictionary. He came across the adjective fractus, from the verb frangere, to break. The resonance of the main English cognates - fraction and fracture - seemed appropriate. Mandelbrot created the word (noun and adjective, English and French) fractal.

Gleick (1997)

This source book up to now has dealt more with the prosaic level in urban and architectural design, using typologies which are largely scalable or measurable. In the New Age the urgent need is a movement towards spiritually, physically and mentally satisfying urban life - stimulated through the dynamics of a productive environment, rather than being locked into an escalating consumer-oriented mode. The maxim 'think globally, act locally' begins to suggest a first step in the way forward. Through nature - and a greater understanding of the instrinsic design cues which emerge - architecture could be inspired to explore new directions of responsiveness and sustainability.

In nature certain phenomena appear chaotic with no apparent structure or pattern, thereby eluding conventional linear mathematics. That is no longer the situation and the apparent chaos has become legible graphically through a clearer understanding of the nature of fractals and with it 'non-linear' geometry. The discovery of this phenomenon in the 1960s is that of Mandelbrot and described in The Fractal Geometry of Nature (1977). The possibilities presented by applying the principles of the 'order' underlying apparent chaos found in natural forms to architectural design are breathtaking in scope, affording new directions into more natural expressions of the built form. This can be expressed in self-similarity and scale of the parts and the whole that are hallmarks of fractal geometry.

Mandelbrot argued that in order to appreciate how the points, lines, planes and solids of the real world fill space, the Euclidian idea of distance (and measure) should be abandoned. He first contemplated what are now called 'linear fractals' that indicate the lines in the figures stay straight as the iterations proceed. He also discovered that by using 'non-linear' equations the feedback of iteration that produces a fractal can bend straight lines into curves and swirls, and make the self-similarity at different scales deformed and unpredictable. The non-linear version exists in a purely mathematical form. The third type of fractal introduces a random element to the iteration and allows fractal artists to model the natural roughness or irregularity of waves, clouds, mountains, and so the fractal dimension of any complex, apparently chaotic feature, such as the branching patterns of a tree, can now be determined (Briggs, 1992).

Trees can be plotted fractally in both two and three dimensions. Wherever self-similarity is generated across scales by a repetition of a simple branching, then tree like structures emerge, graphic examples being rivers with visible inflow channels, or the routing of nerves and blood flow in the human body. On an urban scale the structure of many ancient cities is generally

Fractal geometry and ethnic art meet

Traditional arts and crafts meet the unlikely world of higher mathematics in the work of Dr Chonat Getz of the Department of Mathematics at the University of the Witwatersrand, Johannesburg, South Africa. Her latest research using the geometric patterns of colourful copper wire baskets (izimbenge) woven by the local Zulu people, offers new hope to those who want to understand more about maths and computer programming, but are afraid or too intimidated to ask.

Fractal geometry at the third and fourth year university levels is not easy. Having battled to find concrete and user-friendly ways to convey complex forms of mathematics, Getz, in 1998, suddenly saw new possibilities in her long-standing love of traditional arts and crafts. Instead of studying spirals and other shapes in the abstract, the relevance of rooting them in the world around in the traditional weaving and beadwork became obvious. Using the computer, the patterns could be analysed mathematically, and in that way mathematics could be integrated with the rest of human experience instead of putting it into a separate compartment - and demonstrate tangibly how mathematics is core to everything we experience.

Traditional patterns providing a basis for understanding mathematical symmety

In Hillbrow, a vibrant centre city environment in the heart of Johannesburg, people take apart multi-coloured PVC-covered copper wire and spend many hours recycling the strands into the most exquisite baskets - often into traditional patterns that unconsciously incorporate complicated mathematical concepts of symmetry. The use of traditional cultures as a source for instruction at all levels, is becoming increasingly popular around the world. South African handicrafts are well-known, such as everyday objects like cloths, pots, bowls, woodwork, wall murals, beadwork and baskets. Because these artifacts are familiar, beautiful and well-loved, they can help to get rid of some of the fear that surrounds the dreaded unfamiliarity of mathematics.

Seen in this context, woven *izimbenge* an be instructive not only in the complex mathematics of symmetry

tree-like with radial street systems converging on and growing around the historic centre, alikened to fractal carpets (van Niekerk 1999).

Exploring human response to natural chaos, in *Fractals - The Patterns of Chaos* (1992), Briggs observed :

'Most people find the haphazard profusions of nature so intensely pleasing, even spiritually profound, that it seems common sense to say that there is an invigorating, even mystical order to the variable shapes of waves as they break, swallows on a summer evening, and the weather. Yet for centuries scientists have dismissed such order. For a long time their attitude

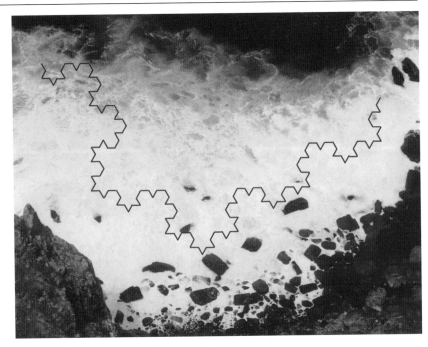

▶ *The generation sequence of a classical fractal (linear fractal) called the Koch island made by adding a triangle to the middle of every straight line at each iteration. A linear representation of a typical coastal configuration showing a 'self-similarity' at all scales*

made sense. The traditional task of science has been to simplify nature, expose its underlying logic as a means of control. But complex natural phenomena such as the weather cannot be stripped down, cleaned off and studied under a glass in a laboratory. An individual tree is a result of a vast, shifting set of unique circumstances, a kaleidoscope of influences such as gravity, magnetic fields, soil composition, wind, sun angles, insect hordes, human harvesting, and other trees. An individual tree is a dynamical system, whose state changes over time. Systems such as these are multifaceted, complex and interdependent.'

In the New Age there is widespread belief that there is something in the development of life that cannot be explained in physical terms alone. When considering the ambiguity and intractability of the late twentieth Century city, experience suggests that the myriad of social and physical complexities of urban life are perceived as mainly negative. Until recently, the phenomenon of fractals has not been sourced as a touchstone for the conscious generation of architectural form, and to a large extent has remained unexplored as a basis for aesthetic expression. The possibilities have yet to be proved conclusively relevant in architectural design, although in its short history of limited application, the proponents of this non-linear mathematical basis for design have achieved significant acclaim from users of their architectural creations.

The Barnsley fern is a another excellent illustration of the fractal phenomenon. It has been generated using a special mathematical technique that takes the geometry of a real fern and computes how its branches transform into one another at different scales. What appear to be random dots on a page in fact reflect a mathematical structuring. In this way more levels of detail can be generated *ad infinitum.*

Briggs (1992)

The issue remains as to whether the application of fractal geometry holds the potential to bring about an architectural renaissance through its associations with natural principles.

Fractal geometry and architectural design

Expressions of fractal geometry in architecture are essentially organic in character amounting to a continuity or a continuous linking through iterative cues and cognitive association. To experience organic form is to appreciate the distinctive interconnections over multiple scales. Jencks (1997) points out that virtually all who refer to organic architecture, including Gropius and Wright, insisted on work that shows fractal self-similarity, or 'unity with variety'. Similarly, composers use thematic phrasing iteratively in music so that the entire composition is consistent with the parts and vice versa.

Even an earlier work, the Paris Opera House by Garnier (1861-74), is described by Mandelbrot as 'having no scale because it has every scale', which links strongly and lucidly with the principles of fractal self-similarity. As one walks down Rue de l'Opera, the closer one gets, the more of the building's self-similar detail comes into view. This seemingly odd comparison of this baroque Beaux Arts building to objects in nature highlights the fact that although works of art may often look very different from 'realistic' objects, the deep intent of many artists is to create forms that exhibit something of the inner structure of life to be found in natural forms. As a basis for comparison, Mandelbrot concluded that 'it is fruitful to call Mies van der Rohe's buildings "scalebound" - a term a physicist would use to describe a flawless crystal and the solar system - and to call the Paris Opera House a "scaling" building - the term scaling being applicable

Measuring the repetitive morphology of nature

Most of mankind's giant leaps forward in space discovery have followed advances in weapons technology. It should therefore come as no surprise that the computer-processing technique best adapted to testing signs of artificiality in the Cydonia images is one that was originally developed for military purposes... Put simply, nature tends to repeat herself in specific areas in terms of the morphology of natural features. An example is the fronds of a fern - each of which is a scale model of the larger, whole fern. - or cracks in rock, which resemble great mountain crevices, only on a smaller scale. The basic patterns which make up natural structures are called 'fractals', which are repeated in a range of different scales. Because of this quality of natural objects being self-similar, a computer can be used to detect the repetition of the basic morphological fractal, and to distinguish this from an object that does not correspond to the fractal pattern.

Militarily this technique can be used to detect man-made objects and installations camouflaged in any terrain. First the computer calculates the 'normal' fractal model for the locality, then it analyses the entire region and highlights any part of that terrain which does not seem to fit the fractal model. If these objects are non-fractal to any great degree then they are judged alien to the specific locality - i.e. they are in all probability man-made. It has been calculated that fractal analysis correctly identifies artificial objects with roughly 80 per cent accuracy.

Gleick (1997)

The Opera House, Paris, France, by Charles Garnier, a Beaux Arts paragon, with its sculptures, gargoyles, its quoins and jamb stones, its cartouches decorated with scrollwork, its cornices topped with cheneaux and lined with dentils. In keeping with his fractal philosophy, Mandelbrot states that 'art that satisfies lacks scale' and the Paris Opera House has no scale because it has every scale

to typical views of the Alps and the visual characteristics of many other objects in Nature.'

It would be constructive to examine more contemporary examples, where fractal geometry has inspired the design form.

Perhaps the most prominent and critiqued of all modern examples of the expression of fractal geometry in architecture is Gehry's Bilbao Guggenheim Museum in Spain. Jencks (1997) on architecture emergent in the 1990s comments as follows:

'No architect has yet reached this organic state of flexibility - Frank Gehry at the new Guggenheim Museum in Bilboa, has been approaching this fluidity; he has pushed the grammar he first developed at the Vitra Museum in more supple directions. Smooth, continuous forms in steel and limestone flow towards a center point to erupt in a flower of petals. He has related the Museum to three city scales: that of the bridge, that of the roof tops whose heights are acknowledged by the atrium and lower forms; and

Patterns of uncertain opportunity

Perceptions change almost hourly as artistic and scientific investigators peer through the windows of fractals and chaos to discover meaningful patterns of uncertainty everywhere. The surfaces of some viruses are known to be fractal. Fractal rhythms and distinct fractal signatures have been found in dopamine and serotonin receptors in the brain, and in enzymes. Fractal geometry is being used to describe the percolation of oil through rock formations. Composers are creating fractal music; programmers are studying the effect of chaos on computer networks; chemists are applying fractals to the creation of polymers and ceramic materials; economists are locating a strange attractor underneath the fluctuations of the Standard Index.

Briggs (1992)

the Bilbao River, an important historic waterway, which is taken into the scheme, both literally through the large windows and the viscous, silvery forms. To connect the Museum to the city, Gehry has used limestone which relates to the sandstone of the adjacent structures.'

Gehry, like others, has spoken of the way in which new computer software, designed for other technologies such as aeronautics, can be utilised in the architectural design process. Fractal geometry is applied through programmed formulae in the software and then manipulated to create the resultant form. The design grammar is emergent from randomly testing shape and spatial organisation - like fractal-shape geometry. Instead of forcing conventional geometry onto natural landform, the dynamic positioning of architectural form in context with its site using an iterative design syntax of fractal geometry (form) and inherent organic landform (site) will present design possibilities in a meaningful way. A prerequisite is that both architect and urban designer are oriented toward the new non-linear science, such as Gehry and others have demonstrated in their use of organism-as-metaphor (van Niekerk 1999). The response to Gehry's masterly resolution in a single project has been unprecedented in modern times, locally and internationally, evoking as it does a rather closer mystical bonding of the experience of man with artifact.

Coming from a Deconstructivist background, the extension to the Berlin Museum with the Jewish Museum Department by Daniel Libeskind is transitional into the metaphor of fractal geometry. The building form (see earlier plan page 52) evokes emotional dislocation and disorientation that Jews experienced as they were forced to flee to other parts of the world. Fractal geometry can be seen discerned in the way the openings on the vast aluminium cladding reflect the form of the plan and section.

Can architects afford to ignore the relevance of this non-linear form in the light of the evident success of such design approaches? Jencks (1997) poses the question: 'The most profound question is: Why does it matter? Is the new Non-linear Architecture somehow superior, closer to nature and our understanding of the cosmos, than Old Modernism? Is it more sensuous, functional and livable? Is it closer to aesthetic codes built into perception? Has it supplanted the traditions of Form from which it has grown - Post-Modern and Deconstructivist Architecture? The answer to these questions, which implicitly justify a change, must be "yes", but it is too early to tell - there are several more motives at work in this runaway paradigm - its plural goals and styles are irreducible - so Non-linear Architecture will prosper until the Millennium, fed by the new science of complexity

NATURAL 'CHAOS' AND ORGANICISM IN DESIGN With the opportunity of new forms and space achievable through the application of fractal principles as a generator, a new vista for architecture and urban design could emerge. Architects from passed epochs have sourced architectural forms intuitively from nature. With contemporary electronic aids, the spirit of fractals, the grammar and syntax of nature, could show the way.

▲ ▶ *Bilbao, Spain: The Guggenheim Museum, a major work by Frank Gehry (1990s) that pushes the boundaries beyond conventional architectural design through the application of fractal form to aesthetic principles. Owing to their mathematical complexity, the sinuous stone, glass and titanium curves were designed with the aid of computers. The 'fishscale' titanium panels give the surface greater tactility and beauty*

- whatever way it goes this new approach will challenge both the Newtonian and traditional architecture that have gone before.'

Gehry's Bilboa building, however, raises a number of issues regarding the extensive use of titanium for cladding, a non-renewable resource that is normally extracted from coastal dune sites in mining operations that impact radically on viable seaboard ecosystems. Conservation lobbies in various quarters of the globe have been picking up the cudgels regarding the ramifications of such mining where claims that post-mining mitigation can restore the ecosystems destroyed in the process remain unsupported scientifically. The next chapter highlights the complex problem of quantifying ecological sensitivities or social, environmental and energy costs of such activities even in economic terms.

Returning to architectural issues, form and aesthetics will always be the result of social and cultural processes. Information technology is part of a cultural process of contemporary development and is rapidly manifesting itself, pushing the creative boundaries further and further. For the designer equipped with a knowledge and understanding of fractal geometry, the possibilities could be ground-breaking for New Age architectural expression. The prospect of environments better designed according to a theory which has distinct resonance with nature, could transcend the pedestrian mediocrity of present day built environments - and even remedy past legacies particularly those of impoverished urban environments. It is a reasonable thesis that states that buildings conceived in the womb of fractal design theory give back to, rather then take away from, their urban context, thus showing a profound analogy with the ethos of productive rather than consumer urban environments.

On Environmental Economics

This branch of economics, otherwise resource economics, is perhaps the key to bridging the current huge divide between the expediency of big business enterprise on the one hand and the more conservationist vision on the other.

PROFIT THROUGH CONSERVATION

Both big business and the conservation lobby need not, should not, take the shortsighted view that providing profitably for the needs of mankind and managing the earth's resources are not mutually inclusive. On the contrary, it has been shown that, for example, 'less waste more profit' can have enormous appeal for the manufacturer and appease the concerns of the environmentalist at the same time.

The idea of 'sustainable development' is central to many debates about future economic progress, from local to global, and definitions of the concept abound. Yet in all the writings there is a common thread which identifies it as a system devised for ensuring that social and environmental goals are sustained through prudent human and natural resource management, while providing for short- and long-term horizons. Sustainability through good stewardship of the earth's resources will provide for the needs of the least advantaged in society (intragenerational equity) and on fair treatment of future generations (intergenerational equity).

Aiming to fill the information gap, and perhaps for a better understanding of the complexity, various commentators have attempted to identify the pivotal issues that constitute sustainability. The research executed by a team led by Dan Esty of Yale University, with support from Columbia University and the World Economic Forum (WEF), has developed an Environmental Sustainability Index that could become a useful platform for policy-makers (see box page 196).

In all countries the state also has a role to play in promoting sustainable development, for example through permitting tax credits as an incentive

---

Cities: prodigious producers of waste

Disposing of vast quantities of waste is a major problem complicated by mixing different materials together. The waste collection process in most cities still does not separate out materials. Kitchen wastes, plastics, paper, aluminium, batteries, and oils are thrown into the same dump, each type of waste releasing its own breakdown products as it rots. To make things worse, many cities co-dispose household and factory waste, the theory being that household waste soaks up any toxins in the factory waste. This toxic cocktail is a costly legacy for generations to come. In addition, pollution of groundwater is a problem wherever rubbish is dumped, and dumps give off methane, an explosive and highly potent greenhouse gas. Even if waste tips are sealed at great expense, the complex mixture they contain will take decades to decompose.

Girardet (1992)

Curitiba - Brazil: Urban planning model for cities

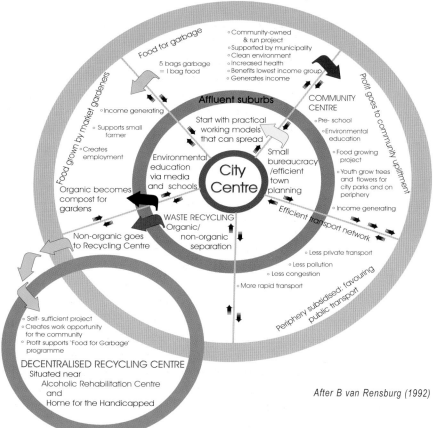

After B van Rensburg (1992)

for environmentally correct buildings. In the first year of the new millennium, New York State has introduced a pioneering scheme offering tax credits with supporting legislation to encourage 'green' design in one of the world's densest urban environments.

Planning for a sustainable environment has clearly guided policy in cities such as Curitiba in Brazil with its population of 1.6 million. This city has emerged as a role model for sustainable cities by using resource economics in a creatively practical way. Curitiba was once a city with sectors of poorly serviced shanty towns where garbage remained uncollected and in festering piles and raw sewage contaminated the rivers. An imaginative, yet simple scheme, which drew on the participation of the shanty dwellers, involved the collection of waste in exchange for social benefits. The key that unlocked the solution was a scheme devised by the mayor, architect Jaime Lerner, whereby transport tokens were offered to adults and food and books to children in exchange for bags of rubbish, delivered to local depots. Apart from the cleaner environment, the shanty dwellers have the opportunity to market their crafts and produce in non-corporate shopping centres, also initiated by the mayor. The localised economic fillip benefits all who can now in addition obtain food, rent, education and healthcare for their labours. The positive performance of the scheme on a metropolitan scale is a genuine success story, by all accounts to be emulated for sustainability in existing and new urban environments worldwide.

Policies which encourage and indeed ensure sustainability are clearly relevant to our burgeoning urbanisation challenge in the developing world. The application of useful economic principles such as the 'user pays' can lever us into greater accountability and at the same time educate us in the benefits derived from sustainability.

The making of materials for buildings out of the earth requires extraction, refining, fabrication and delivery. All are energy-consuming. The Vale and Vale have rated 'greenness' based on the energy intensiveness of

Sustainability Index

How can sustainability be measured so that economic gain and environmental costs could be reconciled?

On detailed assessment dozens of variables can influence the environmental health of economies. Often environmentalists have to rely on a paucity in reliable data, which has led economists to doubt the veracity of claims which should guide their economic policy. A significant research project at Yale University in the USA sorted sixty-seven wide ranging variables from which an Environmental Sustainability Index (ESI) was developed. The variables were distilled into twenty-two core indicators for the purposes of ranking the sustainability index of a number of countries from the developed to the undeveloped worlds.

The variables ranged from eco-efficient methods, to population stress factors, to the receptiveness of the private sector on issues of sustainability. In turn, they found that the indicators clump together naturally into five broad areas:

1. Environmental systems: An assessment of the state of health of biodiversity and other measures of environmental well-being, and whether they are improving rather than deteriorating, causes aside.

2. Reducing environmental stresses: The lowest threshold at which environmental systems might be harmed through human impact.

3. Reducing human vulnerability: A measurement of the extent to which environmental disruptions could have a negative effect on people's basic needs (such as health and nutrition).

4. Social and institutional capacity: The capacity of a country's institutions and social patterns of skills needed to cope with negative environmental challenges or events.

5. Global stewardship: An evaluation of a country's performance in cooperation on international, national, regional and local levels, relating to environmental challenges such as global warming, ozone depletion and acid rain.

Although not claiming to be definitive, regarding the linkages between economic and environmental issues, the chief virtue of this index is that it begins the process of shifting environmental debates on to firmer foundations, underpinned by data and a greater degree of analytical rigour.

Esty and Chertow (1997)

Jaime Lerner, Mayor of Curitiba observes : 'There is no endeavour more noble than the attempt to achieve a collective dream. When a city accepts as a mandate its quality of life; when it respects the people who live in it; when it respects the environment; when it prepares for future generations, the people share the responsibility for that mandate, and this shared cause is the only way to achieve that collective dream.'

Meadows (1995)

building materials, noting that the energy content of a material is demonstrably connected to its closeness to the earth. The more a building material has to be refined the more energy it contains. In this context it is interesting to note that low energy materials are sand and gravel, and the highest energy consuming material by far is aluminium.

It is no longer sufficient to consider only the energy intensity of the production of a building material. There is a growing lobby of interests who consider the long term performance (intergenerational) of the building fabric. The eventual reuse of its elements once its first purpose has been fulfilled is an important factor in environmental correctness.

The significant success of the consumer industry towards curbing the use of additives and preservatives and promoting healthy foods as a better alternative, as an example, should similarly become the touchstone for consumer pressure on the building industry to favour materials on the basis of their sustainability. Producers will respond to market pressure and consumers in increasing numbers should be exercising choice in a number of areas concerned with environmental degradation.

Nearly a quarter of a century ago, the West German government launched a scheme under which environmentally safe materials could display the 'Blue Angel' symbol. Introduced in 1977, the use of the symbol was initially exploited even in cases where there had been a reduction of only 20% of harmful materials in products, such as formaldehyde (Pearson, 1989). To prevent this, private laboratories now conduct independent tests to uphold the conditions that require strict compliance for the use of the symbol.

Blueprint for a green economy

On the consumer front the real price of energy and water, and the management of unwanted waste and pollution have actually never been borne by the user, and essentially places the global situation in arrears. This fact, coupled with the cost to those caught in the spiral of urban poverty, implies a looming socio-economic problem of gargantuan proportions. These areas of economic myopia are all areas ripe for change.

The most assured and most obvious starting point for improving the lot of the urban dweller would be one where affordability and sustainability were non-negotiable conditions for all urban development. This could be achieved through democratising environmental economic participation, where the individual and the community become 'empowered through knowledge' and indeed have a firmer basis to assert pressure for better urban environments on those charged with commissioning development.

In a *Blueprint for a Green Economy* (1989), Pearce et al. link sustainable development and public understanding with the science of environmental economics:

⟍ A basic aspect of environmental economics concerns our understanding of the ways in which economics and their transacting environments interact.

⟍ Fundamental to an understanding of sustainable development is the fact that the economy is not separate from the environment in which we live. There is an interdependence both because the way we manage the economy impacts on the environment, and because environmental quality impacts on the performance of the economy.

⟍ One of the central themes of environmental economics, and also central to a sustainable development mindset, is the need to place proper values on the services provided by natural environments... many of these services are provided 'free'. They have zero price simply because no market place exists in which their true value can be revealed through the acts of buying and selling. Examples might be a fine view, the water purification and storm protection functions of coastal wetlands, or the biological diversity within a tropical forest... Very simply, the cheaper it is the more will be demanded. The danger is that this greater level of demand will be unrelated to the capacity of the relevant natural environment - or its resources - to meet the demand. The destruction of the Amazon rain forest is sustainable only as long as the forest remains, a case where economic expediency has ignored the real cost to the entire planet should the Amazon disappear from exploitation.

⟍ The important principle is that resources and the environment serve economic functions and have positive economic value.

⟍ The proper price for products and services is one that reflects the wider social costs of production and distribution to the point of consumption.

Sustainability in the context of traditional societies

In the past traditional societies had few adverse impacts on the sustaining natural environment. Many primitive cultures evolved unconscious but effective controls on exploitation of their resource base through taboos, myths and rituals... man was seen as part of a great system whose importance transcended that of their individual lives, and myths stressed harmony and restraint to maintain nature's unity...

New technology and other influences have led to greater pressure on resources and this has often resulted in serious environmental problems. Command economies are generally concerned with improving social well-being by increasing throughput, and therefore greater emphasis is placed on transforming natural goods into capital and consumer goods.

Today's consumers are biased toward short-term, direct benefits but government agencies are responsible for providing long-term, general benefits in the interests of both present and future generations.

Stauth (1983)

◀ A common sight in Spain: Traditional windmills on the horizon evoke an understanding of the potential for alternative technology using the forces and energy of natural elements

▶ Nakhla, near el Oued, Algeria: A manually operated well providing water in a parched landscape to serve the needs of an isolated settlement

◀ Yemen: Housing with the 'rowshans' or 'mashrabiyas' which were developed in response to the hot, humid climates. These latticed projections provide cross-ventilation, and privacy, another function being to provide evaporatively cooled drinking water contained in earthenware jars

TRADITIONAL FORMS OF ALTERNATIVE TECHNOLOGY Spain, Yemen and Algeria: Traditional alternative technologies expressed in vernacular architectural forms. Windpower, water resources and airconditioning in hot, arid regions, all evolved from intelligent and resourceful measures, which served whole cities on a sustainable basis.

﹨ The theory of marginal social cost pricing is just as applicable to natural resource use and any natural resource should be priced to reflect the marginal cost of extraction or harvesting and the marginal external cost of any damage done by the distribution or use of the resource.

◀ *Houston, Texas, USA: Glass-enclosed skyscrapers, inner city parking garages served by multilane freeways that facilitate the use of the private motor vehicle typify modern urban culture dependent on fossil fuels to provide viable living and working environments*

INTERGENERATIONAL CRISIS With the expected depletion of natural oil resources needed to sustain such environments and with little potential for engaging with other energy sources, the potential for obsolescence will become a major liability for future generations. This globally important paradigm shift has yet to respond to 'development that meets the needs of the present without compromising the ability of future generations to meet their own needs'.
Brundtland Report (1987)

'Ecological economists' (resource economists) are claimed by some writers to be the first real ecologists. Bramwell in *Ecology of the 20th Century - A History* (1989) concludes:

⚒ Certainly the call to conserve scarce resources is today perhaps the strongest green argument. Economists have begun to look at the problem not only of allocation of resources but also of intergenerational allocation of resources.

⚒ The universe is now seen as a closed system: nothing came in, nothing came out... If finite energy resources were not conserved, the result would be waste and loss; eventually famine and disaster.

The internationally recognised endorsement of a company's responsible environmental management in manufacturing is the ISO14001 Certification. Visser (1998) questions credibility of big business as regards genuine commitment:

⚒ The days of superficial environmental 'greenwash' are over and Environmental Performance Improvement (EPI) has become as much a risk management and operational efficiency issue as a social responsibility item. As a result, the likelihood that environmental issues will affect the bottom line, positively or negatively, is high and increasing steadily.

⚒ But there still seems to be a gap between big business's environmental management initiatives and public perception of these, according to a survey... Findings showed the population blamed environmental destruction in the country first and foremost on companies, ahead of consumers, urban growth, governmental and agricultural practices.

Environmental (resource/ecological) economics can provide the platform for devising the most optimum opportunity cost scenario in development programmes and become a tool in demonstrating evidence of big business's commitment to responsible management initiatives.

Apart from the more judicious use of natural resources and the avoidance of waste, social costs should feature more adequately in the determination of the most optimum development scenario. Unfortunately, the focus in the industrialised world has been on the security of supply at the lowest possible cost. For example, the opportunity cost equation of the water and coal used in a coal-fired power station invariably omits some essential elements: the health and ecological cost of the pollution resulting from the use of coal instead of another type of fuel. It is imperative that in all environmental planning, all alternatives including the so-called 'do-nothing' scenario is evaluated as one of the serious options.

in 1983, the World Commission on Environment and Development was tasked by the General Assembly of the United Nations to formulate 'a global agenda for change'. It was a call for action and the outcome highlighted areas of concern that affected all nations and indeed mankind itself. On energy it identified the primary non-renewable sources of energy: natural gas, oil, coal, peat and conventional nuclear power. Renewable resources included wood, plants, dung, falling water, geothermal sources,

---

The deep ecology platform

Deep ecology is concerned with environmental ethics which recognises the moral standing of wholes, not the individual parts, and forms the basis of today's moralistic ethics. The platform from which deep ecology derives its meaning is:

1. The flourishing of human and non-human life on earth has intrinsic value. The value of non-human life forms is independent of the usefulness these may have for narrow human purpose.

2. Richness and diversity of life-forms are values in themselves and contribute to the flourishing of human and non-human life on earth.

3. Humans have no right to reduce this richness and diversity except to satisfy vital needs.

4. Present human interference with the non-human world is excessive, and the situation is rapidly worsening.

5. The flourishing of human life and cultures is compatible with a substantial decrease of the human population. The flourishing of non-human life requires such a decrease.

6. Significant change of life conditions for the better requires change in policies. These affect basic economic, technological and ideological structures.

7. The ideological change is mainly that of appreciating *life quality* (dwelling in situations of intrinsic value) rather than adhering to a high standard of living. There will be a profound awareness of the difference between big and great.

8. Those who subscribe to the foregoing points have an obligation directly or indirectly to participate in the attempt to implement the necessary changes.

Naess (1989)

and solar, tidal, wind and wave energy, as well as human and animal muscle power. Nuclear reactors that produce their own fuel ('breeders') and eventually fusion reactors are also in this category.

In their book *Green Architecture: Design for a Sustainable Future* (Vale and Vale 1996) the authors consider resources and materials and comment as follows:

'The built environment is no more than a remodelling of the immediate surface of the planet... whether iron and glass, or more modern aluminium and plastic, all materials are still won, or more precisely, wrenched, from the earth... The spoil is usually left in piles round the mine to form a physical and chemical hazard... almost every phase of the process can produce land changes and environmental contamination... Land is frequently not reclaimed after mineral extraction.

All contribute to the future global energy mix, but each has its own economic, health and environmental costs, benefits and risks - factors which interact strongly with governmental and global priorities. An energy strategy inevitably involves choosing an environmental strategy.'

The Commission examined the uncertainties of a high energy future which are generally disturbing and give rise to several reservations. Four stand out:

> ⬊ The serious probability of climate change generated by the 'greenhouse' effect of gases emitted to the atmosphere, the most important of which is carbon dioxide (CO_2) produced from the combustion of fossil fuels.
> ⬊ Urban-industrial air pollution caused by atmospheric pollutants from the combustion of fossil fuels.
> ⬊ Acidification of the environment from the same causes.
> ⬊ The risks of nuclear reactor accidents, the problems of waste disposal and dismantling of reactors after their service life is over, and the dangers of proliferation associated with the use of nuclear energy.

Coupled with these concerns is that of the growing scarcity of fuelwood in developing countries. If trends continue it was estimated that by the year 2000 around 2,4 billion people would be living in areas where wood is extremely scarce.

There is no such thing as a simple energy choice - they all involve trade-offs. Given the potential seriousness of future options, the Commission believes that energy efficiency should be the cutting edge of national energy policies for sustainable development.

► *London, UK: Lloyds Bank : Richard Rogers Partnership : Status, architectural expression and state of the art technology are expressed in the bold visual evidence of climate control technology*

▼ *Dubai, Emirates: Badgirs or windtraps: This form of traditional resource-efficient climate moderating device, evolved over centuries, is indispensably part of the architectural language of the place*

DIVERGENT SUSTAINABILITY OPTIONS Differing technologies for climate control can be widely separated in time, culture and available resources. In the developed world, sustainability of the adopted method is ever confidently supported by economic resources and high energy consumption, whereas to moderate seasonal extremes, the vernacular technologies employ architectural devices aimed at using the climate. In construction as well, the First World is potentially polluting and resource demanding, where the building methods of traditional societies cause few adverse impacts on the natural environment.

► *Lesotho, Southern Africa: Hut structures using natural elements, stone and thatch, used essentially to moderate climatic extremes in high altitude situations. The thickening of the walls around the entrances which invariably face the solar path, provides additional mass aimed at solar heat gain for comfort in the interior*

Poorer urban societies have difficulty in obtaining the basic necessities of life and tend to be as unconcerned about resource depletion as are more affluent societies, but for different reasons. This observation tends to be true in most cases. Historically, on the other hand, although they held socialist and egalitarian views, the disciples of nineteenth century energy economics never made it into socialist textbooks, probably because the humanitarian impulse was primarily to improve the lot of the poor, not through science characterised by bourgeousie socialism.

In environmental economics, two general classes of environmental problem are recognised: pollution and resource destruction. If this is the case, why do designers not ensure that their endeavours do not aggravate the problems, let alone neglect to investigate possible solutions for them?

Pollution, which is the unnatural concentration of materials in the environment, and is essentially the residual of human activity, adversely affects the next user of some environmental resource, and even the resource itself, and therefore man's well-being. Resource destruction is the removal or dispersion of natural concentrations of materials that impairs some ecological process or depletes some environmental resource otherwise capable of yielding benefits in perpetuity.

Resource destruction and pollution problems both result from the reallocation of resources through economic activity, of which there are three, namely, land (encompassing all natural systems in the biosphere), labour and capital. Economics is the science of allocating scarce resources among competing ends. Most often the externalities (social or environmental costs borne by society at large rather than the user of a resource) are

Architecture and the new technologies

The creation of an architecture which incorporates the new technologies entails breaking away from the platonic idea of a static world, expressed by the perfect finite object to which nothing can be added or taken away, a concept which has dominated architecture from the very beginning. Instead of Schelling's description of architecture as frozen music, we are looking for an architecture more like some modern music, jazz or poetry, where improvisation plays a part, an indeterminate architecture containing both permanence and transformation.

The best buildings of the future, for example, will interact dynamically with the climate in order better to meet the user's needs and make optimum use of energy. More like robots than temples, these apparitions with their chameleon-like surfaces insist that we rethink yet again the art of building. Architecture will no longer be a question of mass and volume but of lightweight structures whose superimposed transparent layers will create form so that constructions will be effectively dematerialised.

To date - and here I include early Modernism - architectural concepts have been founded on linear, static and hierarchical and mechanical order. Today we know that design based on linear reasoning must be superseded by an open-ended architecture of overlapping systems. This systems approach allows us to appreciate the world as an indivisible whole. We are, in architecture as in other fields, approaching a holistic ecological view of the globe and how we live on it.

Rogers (1996)

▼ ▼ *Harare, Zimbabwe: Eastgate: Novel forms of aesthetic are derived from passive energy-reducing design measures*

▶ ▲ *Garston, Watford, UK: The BRE Building: The design reflects the challenge of integrating structure and services to inform the aesthetic*

DESIGN MODELS FOR PASSIVE ENERGY Two modern day buildings aimed at providing passive energy sources. Situated in two different climate zones, the BRE and Eastgate buildings have different performance demands to meet from their respective systems. Invariably warming of air is utilized to drive the ventilation systems through convection. Low-speed fans assist the flow. Hollow structural floor slabs and vertical shafts are employed to provide for the circulation of air into and out of the interior.In the case of the BRE building, cooling of the air is achieved by circulating cold water from a seventy metre deep underground well through the slab.In northern climes, gentle underfloor heating can supplement solar heating during the winter months. In the southern hemisphere shading of the external walls is a necessary measure to control heat gain. Advanced reflector technology diffuses lighting upwards and reflects the rest downwards to provide good lighting levels at working level. Other advanced lighting technology such as high output/low wattage fittings significantly reduce energy demand.

Managing demand requires inducements and incentives and central to any attempt to manage demand is a realistic tariff structure across a sliding scale on the basis of 'the more you use the higher the tariff'.

In order to have the best effect, the 'punitive' tariffs should be offset by ways that make it easier for people to save water. 'Giving' them water-saving devices (they ultimately pay for them through their tariffs of course) is certainly one option.

We must show users the opportunity costs of their use. Find facts that touch the water conservation 'buttons', be it in terms of infant mortalities, degraded estuaries, dying kudus, destitute farmers, an old woman buckling under the burden of a bucket of water, or whatever it takes... Spell out the link between saving water when bathing and the saving of electricity....

Preston and Davis (1993)

ignored in input and output evaluation. Nature has limits and humanity's desires are without limits, which presents a problem needing a solution. Using environmental economics to evaluate the real opportunity cost of resource consumption weighed against the cost of providing energy-efficient architecture could be a useful tool to ensure sustainability of a natural resource.

The observations presented above uncover some aspects of the problem but also leave unanswered the issue of accountability and the cultivation of a value system which addresses the seriousness of a 'do-nothing scenario'.

Energy efficiency and water conserving strategies are not the only environmental challenges. Bearing in mind that biodiversity is a non-renewable resource, cities have the opportunity of a implementing a closed system whereby waste generated by producers and consumers can be well managed and contained within the absorptive capacity of renewable local sinks to break down biogradable wastes. A common example is the use of waste as fuel for space heating in city residential, commercial and industrial enterprises. Economies of scale can be achieved through providing heating installations for entire districts.

Proper waste handling facilities can enable the economic recovery of materials from the waste stream for reuse or recycling - witness the success of Curitiba's programme of waste management.

APPLICATION OF ECONOMIC PRINCIPLES

The first step in conserving natural resources is to reduce demand. However, the first step towards commitment to the reduction in demand is creating awareness of the need to do so.

There are signs that in the more developed countries attitudes are evolving, even at the level of personal accountability, regarding resource conservation and management through education and understanding the economic benefits. Together with changes of habit in the more responsible consumption of resources, appropriate technology is at the core of the solution toward resource conservation. But, the most effective mechanism for checking the culture of rampant consumerism lies in the application of economic principles.

The user-pays principle

It could be constructive to conduct a research programme aimed at educating the consumer into the social costs of their use of resources, such as water and electricity. A captive user would, for example, be a

◀ *A pollution solution? Light taxi vehicles in Delhi designed for and fuelled by compressed natural gas (CNG) aimed at reducing CO_2 emissions and harmful particulates into the city atmosphere. The benefits of CNG technology should be weighed against the environmental cost, i.e. resource depletion and capacity of the supply infrastructure to keep pace with the growth in usage*

visitor to a nature reserve or resort. In a hypothetical situation, apart from the tariff for accommodation, visitors could have the choice of being charged for their use of resources on the traditional cost basis, a formula based on the conventional supply of water and electricity services. Alternatively, they could have the option of being supplied through metered energy and water resource-saving devices that have been installed in the units (e.g. compact fluorescent low wattage light bulbs; aerated low-flow shower heads and basin taps; water displacement bags/dual-flush mechanisms for cisterns; a tiered bin to promote recycling of waste). Charged on a 'user-pays' basis, not only is the latter more efficient economically, but the educational value as to awareness of the actual social and environmental cost has been shown to be significant where such measures have been implemented.

In large urban situations, a punitive but fair device for implementing the user-pays principle would be an escalating scale for services where consumers would pay a higher tariff for a greater use of resources.

User-pays measures have the potential to significantly influence the pattern of use of key resources through economic inducement. To further correct

Ecological accounting

In Denmark, environmental accounting, in the form of environmental status reports, environmental labelling, life cycle assessments is being disseminated widely and practised in municipalities and elsewhere in the construction enterprises and housing areas.

'The concept of economic accounting has been joined by the concept of "environmental accounting". An ecological statement of accounts is prepared like it economic counterpart, only the view point and the scale are different. Ecological accounting is about input and output, not about debit and credit, about resource and energy flows, rather than money flows. As such, ecological accounting involves material rather than financial records.

Ecological accounting is environmental accounting based on environmental values derived from the key figures of an input-output record. This is also true of environmental accounting fo cities and housing, urban neighbourhoods and residential areas.'

Jensen (1999)

> Recycling waste can enhance the resource efficiency of cities, bringing them economic as well as environmental benefits.
>
> Our throwaway society, left to its own devices, could end up discarding its own future. Yet it is quite feasible to replace throwaway consumption with 'total recycling', turning a linear process into a circular one.
>
> *Girardet (1992)*

consumer attitudes to water conservation, energy conservation, recycling and pollution control the project should be extended through a follow-up test of the 'take-home' effect of these measures. This would involve measuring the changes in resource utilisation in respondents' own homes by way of a follow-up survey. In the commercial sphere, a similar system would provide the opportunity to assess the reactions of commerce to the application of the user-pay basis.

The payback principle

A hypothetical case using solar heating apparatus compared with that of conventional water heating sources could provide the basis for illustrating the 'payback' principle. The analysis is dependent on the going price of electrically heated cylinders and the investment yield on the capital difference between the cost of the conventional as compared with the solar installation. Other factors which influence the outcome would be the percentage escalation of electrical energy cost from present value, and the lower maintenance cost of the solar installation over the payback period. However, in most circumstances these factors should not alter the result significantly.

Whereas each situation comprises project specific parameters, an outline of the essential components for calculating the payback period for a hot water installation using solar panels is as follows:

⊠ Requirements in terms of heating demand monthly for an energy resource.

⊠ Capital costs (inclusive of any value added tax) for the installation of environmental technology for hot water installations.

⊠ Operating costs monthly (inclusive of VAT):

Capital gain through conserved energy

Energy conservation has already made more energy available to the US economy than any other single source. Yet there is room for larger gains. In 1985, the USA spent $440 billion on energy, which amounts to $5000 per household or 11 per cent of the GNP. If all cost-effective conservation measures were taken and the USA became as energy efficient as, say, Japan, the country would consume half as much energy as it does today, thereby saving $220 billion per year. The annual cost of achieving this goal would be only about $50 billion per year.

Moreover, it is calculated that to slow the growth of demand for new energy capacity, conservation could liberate 10 per cent of USA industrial investment capital for other uses. Already the rate of capital investment in new power plants has fallen sharply owing to energy conservation. In 1982 utilities spent $50 billion. By 1991 it is forecast to fall to $17 billion. The electric industry predicts that investment will eventually rebound to $45 billion, but if conservation measures are adopted by 1990, the need for new capacity can be delayed and attenuated.

Given that it pays to save energy, how should consumers and society choose among conservation options? The individual consumer normally considers 'simple pay-back time' or the time that must elapse for an annual saving from conserved energy to repay initial investment.

Rosenfeld and Hafemeister (1986)

▲ ▶ *Jerusalem, Israel & Copenhagen, Denmark: New neighbourhoods: The placing of solar heating panels on the roofs of new apartment blocks - showing the right energy conservation ethos and a blatant acceptance of technical installations attached to the otherwise thoughtful residential architecture*

(a) Actual cost exclusive to hot water installations.

(b) Projected cost assuming conventional energy supply were used.

Utilising the above data, the payback period (assuming that electrical energy cost inflation equals capital investment return rate) would be equal to the length of time in months/years before the energy saving (using conserving measures) equalled or exceeded in value the additional capital cost of installing solar heating apparatus over conventional heating devices.

Taking into account that planning and implementation of major upgrading projects for metropolitan utilities, such as for water and electricity, takes at least a decade, a 'payback' approach to planning would assist in the decisions regarding policy. A longer-term vision should become mandatory for all projects in urban situations, where demand for services is incrementally outstripping existing infrastructure and requiring further large capital investment. The reliance on the conventional supply of energy through the urban grid is fast becoming the luxury option.

Although there are many arguments in favour of boosting energy efficiency in buildings, improvements are not proceeding as fast as would be expected. This is despite the fact that in the USA, for example, significant gains have been demonstrated through more efficient energy use. In the USA the 125 million household refrigerators in use today require the electricity from 30 standard 1000 megawatt power plants. If the se appliances were as inefficient as the average 1975 model, they would require 50 power plants. Reasons for the failure of an energy efficient ethos amongst

▶ *Urk, Holland: Modern form of windpower, a common sight in Holland, employed to drain the low country. Urk was originally an island but is now part of the reclaimed polder of Flevoland*

▼ *Arnhem, Holland: The traditional technology of the windmill is not only housed in a building, it is the architecture itself. A non-polluting source of energy its versatility can be applied in a variety of manufacturing operations, in this case paper*

POLLUTION-FREE ENERGY Forms of the contemporary and the traditional. Since 1995, the world's wind-generating capacity has increased nearly fivefold. Apart from windpower, in thirty years from now, millions of American homes and businesses may get their electricity from small on-site generators that create no pollution and need no powerlines. A fuel cell is an electrochemical device that combines hydogen fuel and oxygen from the air to produce electricity, heat and water. Fuel cells operate without combustion, so they are virtually pollution free and since the fuel is converted directly into electricity a fuel cell can operate at much higher efficiencies than the internal combustion engine. Now used to run spacecraft, fuel cell technology could well revolutionise the way homeowners get their power, especially in remote areas.

UTC Fuel Cells (2002)

consumers can be traced to a number of market failures (Rosenfeld & Hafemeister 1986):

　　⟍ The most important one stems from the different time horizons the various principal authorities consider when making decisions. Investments in energy supply are made by utilities and other large companies that raise billions of dollars (USA) for huge projects and expect to pay off their investors over a decade or two;

　　⟍ In contrast, most homeowners will not invest in efficiency if the payback time is 2.5 years, even though this represents a hefty 40 per cent (non-taxable) return on investment;

　　⟍ Large institutions such as governments, universities and corporations seldom consider paybacks longer than three years thereby rejecting a 30 per cent return on their own or taxpayers' money; and

　　⟍ Consumers do not perceive cost effectiveness now to be related to the higher prices the utility will charge when it is forced to build a new plant.

Economics can demonstrate the benefits of using alternative environmental technologies, but the application of such measures requires more - the commitment by consumers to a culture of resource conservation. As the going price of installing does not always favour or encourage the consumer to invest in alternative rather than conventional technologies for energy and water, some form of economic advantage through, for example, tax relief on property for consumers who invest in energy conservation measures is likely to be an effective starting point.

ALTERNATIVE TECHNOLOGIES

The use of renewable fuels for electric power generation and space heating include solar radiation, wind, water and wood. Considering the demand on global energy resources, passive energy-reducing design measures are no longer an option but a priority. A comprehensive system would include innovative passive measures for heating and cooling, the application of alternative technologies generally and the use of electronic controls for management and optimum reduction of energy costs. There is a wealth of technical literature on the subject of alternative technologies. A shortlisting is presented in Appendix I.

The interconnectedness between energy conservation and economic development should be seen as symbiotic. It is useful to take the example of a developed country such as the USA where consumption of energy is a major national issue, but is also having global implications due to sheer volume.

Given that in developing countries high percentages of households are without electricity supply, it is imperative that national (and even international) resources be directed to eliminating the backlog. To achieve this a reduction in energy demand in areas which already benefit from the energy infrastructure will release capital for investment in areas where no such infrastructure exists. A significant side benefit is that the alternative to traditional fuels such as coal and wood, local pollution levels will be reduced, and, accordingly, people's health will improve .

It pays to save energy but how should consumers and society choose from among conservation options? The individual consumer normally considers 'simple pay back time', i.e. the time that needs to elapse for an annual saving from a realisable return on conserved energy to repay initial capital cost of installing environmental technologies.

THE TIMELESS WAY

The imprint of history shows that from earliest times there have been social inequalities in living conditions. This is generally congruent with the widening gap between the 'haves' and the 'have-nots' as the affluent, through economic and political strength, have gained greater access to resources.

New Age thinking must emphasise the common denominator applicable to all cultures at all socio-economic levels: the need for societal accountability for better built environments and the sustainable exploitation of natural resources.

The timeless masterpieces in urban design and architecture of the past were achieved with comparatively less means and destruction than today. The human spirit and craft skills, virtually all that were available to less technological cultures, fuelled the drive often to heights of sheer creative excellence. Even today, through the incremental growth in tourism and intensive marketing of the past, such traditional urban environments can stimulate and sustain national economies. The touring masses journey at great expense to all corners of the globe to experience qualities perhaps lacking in their own modern urban environments. Such is the power of proven sustainability - a good product, of whatever age, that becomes an indispensable component of national income.

The vernacular typologies, those architectures which express with honesty the constraints of economy, of resource and energy scarcity, the site, the climate and the socio-cultural needs of earlier times, were constructed out of the fundamental need not only to survive, but also to attend to the multifacetted needs of the urban dweller. At the other end of the scale, public architectural achievements of past epochs have reached unimaginable heights of grandeur and technological skill, often dedicated to the glory of God or to the whim of indulgent monarchic lifestyles. With few of the either contemporary engineering skills or commonplace synthetic materials of today, a good example is that of the ancient Egyptians and Greeks, who left behind the persuasive power of their durable and monumental architectonic structures. In terms of stature, arguably these sustainable constructions of the past have not been emulated in either twentieth century Modernism or its trendy successor, Post-Modernism. They were also achieved without adverse employment of natural resources, on which contemporary architecture is so utterly dependent yet has not even begun to conserve.

Though the Greek period, celebrating great heights of mathematical design and skill edified in the Parthenon, was a hard act to follow, the subsequent Roman legacy showed a remarkable capability with architectural feats worthy of the best engineers and architects of today. Where most of the greatest architectural legacies of the past had their place in the monumental expression of power, religion and durability, today the imperative for the architect and urban designer is a distinctly different set of paradigms. Modern factors such as the democratic right of individual choice and social equality provide the sovereign individual, in the developed world, with rights hitherto unknown. However, such privilege has been shown to have its cost as evidenced by the overexploited resource base of our planet Earth. Ironically, through perpetrating our misguided plundering of natural resources in the name of progress while scorning the inevitable catastrophe, we are presenting our architecture rather as a symbol of our habitat destruction than our means of shelter and protection.

At the start of the new millennium, architects, urban designers and developers have a choice: either to accept the reckless, consumer nature of architecture as we know it or to rewrite the order book. This inevitably means a quantum shift towards community-driven and resource-conserving built environments, along with the issue of urgency. The contemporary syndrome of non-accountability for the pitifully impoverished living environments which influence the quality of our current daily experience requires instead a deliberate change of direction in all spheres of development.

Governments lean towards expediency to entrench political value structures for power and therefore, without an assertive popular constituency, they cannot be relied upon to initiate the political means for change. It is up to the user, all those involved with demands on resources, to set to right the priorities for good architecture and a sustainable future. It lies in the orbit of urban designers, architects and developers to work in unison with environmental scientists and resource economists.

In this age of intemperance the only route through which change can be effected depends on how much we care about the devastating effects of human urban stress, and indeed our attitude towards to consumer-induced modification to the climate, resource depletion and the continued health of the biosphere. At this auspicious juncture in time, widely acknowledged as the start of a New Age, it is in our hands to determine the future of life on Earth.

ALTERNATIVE TECHNOLOGIES: NUTS AND BOLTS

It pays to save energy but how should consumers and society choose from among conservation options? The individual consumer normally considers 'simple pay back time', i.e. the time that needs to elapse for an annual saving from a realisable return on conserved energy to repay initial capital cost of installing environmental, or what are often called alternative, technologies.

Methods of heating

Heat is a form of energy which is transferred from a body with a higher temperature to a body with a lower temperature. This transfer takes place whether through conduction, convection or radiation. Conduction is the transfer of heat through solid bodies; convection is the transfer of heat through air; and radiation is the transfer of heat through space.

The effectiveness and efficiency of long-wave heating equipment is influenced by the volume to be heated as well as the insulation of walls, roofs and floors. The kilowatt ratings required can vary from 35 watts/m³ in insulated areas to 170 watts/m³ in uninsulated areas. When using medium-wave heating equipment, the floor area will determine the required kilowatt ratings. Requirements can vary from 150 watts/m² in the insulated area where there are no draughts to 250 watts/m² in an uninsulated, draughty area. The floor area will also determine the kilowatt requirements when short-wave heating is used. Requirements vary from 100 watts/m² in non-draughty areas to 350 watts/m² in a draughty outdoor environment.

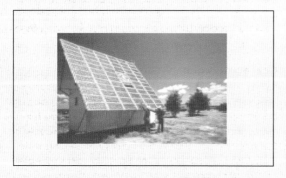

▲ *A typical array of photovoltaic cells forming the powerhouse of a large system*

Equipment that transfers heat through radiation is ideally suited for open air environments such as loading bays, hangars and areas requiring localised heating. Electrical infra-red (IR) space heating meets a wide range of needs, and is safe, economical, comfortable, reliable, clean and healthy as no products of combustion are released, ensuring minimum wasted heat.

Power generation by photovoltaic systems

Using photovoltaic (PV) systems permits electrical energy to be generated directly from the sun (Holm and Viljoen, 1996). The heart of these systems are the PV modules which convert solar radiation from a part of the spectrum into electricity. Features are:

☐ These systems are capable of providing reliable energy - particularly for relatively small loads.

☐ The photovoltaic modules are made of silicon wafers (involving a complex manufacturing process) sandwiched between plastic or glass.

☐ The modules generate direct current electricity at low voltages (between 12 and 14 volts).

☐ PV modules are rated according to how much power is produced (known as peak watts) and are varying size ranges generally from less than 10 to 100 watts.

☐ Energy which is not used immediately may be stored in a battery. The voltage to the battery is controlled by regulators.

☐ Batteries which are used in PV systems generally range from lead acid batteries (operating at 12 volts) to large glass cells (operating at 1.5 to 2 volts) that can be linked to provide 12 volts delivery.

To optimise on efficiency the module positioning is important and factors which must be considered are:

☐ Correct orientation to take full advantage of the solar conditions of the area.

☐ Wind shear conditions on the assembly due to the substantial surface area typically associated with the panels.

☐ Positioning to minimise cable length to the battery.

☐ The tilt angle should be approximately equal to the latitude of the site plus 10 degrees. This may however be refined to suit the circumstances.

To accommodate a PV system the fixing of a large assembly must consider the following:

☐ The total mass which is typically significant enough to require strengthening of the support structure such as that of a roof.

❏ Modules should be mounted out of reach to avoid vandalism and theft. Small installations can be mounted on a pole.

Solar panels in design

Under certain conditions solar water heaters (SWH) can be effective for provision of hot water.

Prior to selecting a system the following should be considered:

❏ Water availability and quality. If the water supply is from a borehole, then the quality of water in terms of dissolved solids and particles needs to be determined as these can clog the systems and reduce its effective life.

❏ The climatic conditions can influence the choice to use solar water heating. Low winter night temperatures normally would preclude the use of direct systems where freezing up of pipes can rupture the system.

Solar water heaters come in a variety of shapes and sizes. They may be categorised according to the type of collector (the part which collects the sun's heat):

❏ Flat plate - direct: These are systems in which the solar radiation heats water flowing in tubes or channels within a flat configuration.

❏ Flat plate - heat exchange: In these systems solar radiation heats a fluid (such as glycol) which passes through a heat exchanger wherein the water is heated. These systems can be used in difficult climates.

❏ Cylindrical and other: A variety of other systems are used, such as large diameter tubes in which water is both heated and stored.

In most solar hot water systems the heated water is stored. This may be in a conventional geyser or a close coupled unit, where the collector is adjacent to the geyser. Electrical elements may be added to the geyser to provide a back-up under prolonged adverse weather conditions.

While planning and installing a solar heater, the following need to be considered:

❏ Positioning and orientation: The position of the SWH in relation to the geyser, bathroom, kitchen, to minimise long runs of piping wherein heat can be lost (pipe runs should be lagged for efficiency). In direct systems, for heated water to rise convectionally, the geyser is positioned directly above the collector to inhibit the system from cycling cold water through the geyser on cold nights. The collector needs to be oriented due north or south, dependent on the hemispherical location.

❏ Vertical angle calculation: The angle at which the collector is tilted influences the operation - particularly during winter. The tilt angle should be approximately equal to the latitude of the site, plus 10 degrees.

❏ Mass consideration: Solar water heaters can be heavy when full. This has implications for the type of roof on which they are to be mounted. Close-coupled units have a concentrated mass and roof design must be able to support such installations.

Wind turbines and hybrids in design

Small and medium size turbines may be incorporated into domestic and institutional buildings in the developing areas. Wind regimes that can provide sustainable outputs invariably exist in coastal regions. Only small wind turbines are capable of being mounted on the roof or wall of a dwelling or small building. Turbines of over 250 watts need to be mounted on separate structures.

Features of wind turbine installations:

❏ Wind turbines can be noisy.

❏ Mounting of small turbines on stub supports can be effected directly to the wall of a building. Otherwise pole mounting is typical.

❏ The safety aspect must be considered as blades can be shed.

❏ The length of cabling to a battery or series of batteries should be as short as possible.

To complete the energy efficient plan, lighting for buildings that rely on renewable fuels should be selected for low energy demand/high output. To achieve this fluorescent lighting is generally used which could be either conventional straight or coiled tube.

Conserving water measures

Buildings, during construction and occupation, consume an enormous amount of water, the actual amount being dependent on its use or function. Despite the myth that the Earth has an abundance of water, many people in the world do not have a source of pure drinking water. Rivers are the main source of the world's drinking water, and many are polluted, some not showing visible evidence of real pollution. Although this might seem outside the realm of the consumer to solve, the pollution of rivers is inextricably tied up with air pollution caused by the burning of fossil fuels for energy. Urban planners and architects alike have a role to play to ensure that, on the one hand transportation in terms of trip distances is reduced to a minimum to urban facilities such as out-of-town shopping centres, and on the other hand that energy-conserving measures are planned into all buildings designed by them.

It is sobering to examine how water is consumed in the typical domestic situation in a Western country. The highest demand for water is for water closet flushing cisterns which are accountable for 32% of the total usage (higher in the USA), personal hygiene for 28%, laundering for 9%, washing up for 9%, drinking and cooking for 3%, irrigation and car washing for 6% and losses for 13%. Less than half of these uses need water of drinking quality yet, in most cases, drinking water quality is supplied for all uses.

Waste and pollution measures

To a large extent the maxim 'out of sight, out of mind' applies to the perception of waste as a byproduct of human consumption. The preferred method by far in most cities for the disposal of huge volumes of urban waste is 'bury' or 'burn and bury'. The unfortunate aspect of this practice is the production of what is known as 'landfill gas'. Depending on how this potential energy resource is utilised, landfill gas can have spinoff advantages from which entire neighbourhoods can benefit. Generally the problem with establishing good waste management policy is due to the likely obsolescence of existing expensive infrastructural installations and the lack of will to move away from established conventional methods.

Pollution from incineration devised to reduce volume at landfill sites is polluting in terms of groundwater resources as well as the atmosphere. Traditionally waste is dealt with at the end of the stream rather than at the beginning where it belongs, and where it can be separated by the consumer into recycled products or an energy source stream on a manageable scale. The entire issue of intelligent waste management is thus fraught with problems of a social, political and economic kind, or very often those associated with a lack of entrepeneurial initiative and vision on behalf of the responsible authority.

The most efficient policy for waste streaming would be separation at source to reduce volume. The consumer therefore becomes a participant, thereby reducing costs of collection and sorting of waste products with greatly increased potential for reuse, recycling or reduction. In the process the individual is thus being made accountable for the waste products of personal consumption, and aware of the collective responsibility to manage the urban waste stream efficiently. In a Western culture, statistics indicate that in a large city on average vegetable and perishable waste accounts for 35% by weight of the total, screenings below 2cms for 12.31%, paper for 31.12%, metals for 5.34%, textiles for 1.70%, glass for 9.31%, plastics for 2.97%, the remainder for 1.79% (Vale and Vale 1996).

In the absence of a metropolitan or district strategy regarding a reduction, recycling, re-use waste management policy, it still is incumbent on the individual to apply an acceptable waste ethos in the domestic situation. To this end a properly allocated rodent-proofed roofed space is essential to deal with household refuse, both dry and organic. Standards vary; however, a space half the size of a single motor garage with water point, raking floor and drainage would suffice in the domestic situation. Most metropolitan areas have a network of either commercial or local authority glass, paper, cardboard and metal containers removed to centralised recycling depots on a regular basis.

Rather than burning waste to heat buildings, industrial and commercial wastes, other than toxic which requires specialised disposal methods, can have other cost efficient applications. For example, a whole industry has developed around the use of small wood particles in chipboards and the like. A customised strategy for storage, collection and transportation of such recyclable waste products would have to be devised to suit each circumstance.

Economic subsidies from all levels of government could provide the necessary incentives for the introduction of alternative technologies in new and existing situations. All that is required is the political will to implement programmes and measures to lead urban communities into greater environmental accountability.

What is ISO14001?

ISO14001 is published by ISO, the International Organisation for Standardisation and is an International Standard for Environmental Management Systems. The aim is to assist organisations to comply with environmental law and manage the environmental impacts and risks of their activities.

ISO14001 applies to all types and sizes of organisation in the world in diverse geographical, cultural and social conditions, leading to registration for compliance.

Management principles contained in ISO14001 assist in the following ways:
• Reduction of risk to the environment of all forms of operations and products.
• Formulation of environmental policy and objectives.
• Training and organisation of people.
• Measurement of performance.
• Planning for emergencies.
• Life cycle assessment
• Environmental auditing

With pressure from governments and leading organisations, the management principles contained in ISO14001 will begin to gain wider global acceptance and application. A revision of ISO14001 in the year 2001-2002 aims to increase its application to small businesses and provide a link into principles of sustainability.

Computer software for the implementation of ISO14001 can be sourced from the World Wide Web and implemented to cover an entire organisation or specific operating units or activities.

Using indicative specifications for environmental management in a typical situation where construction activities are being carried out, the adjoining checklist is presented as a guide and adapted to suit actual circumstances.

Environmental specifications for application to construction activities

Environmental Awareness
☐ The Contractor shall ensure that all his staff and subcontractors and their staff attend the Environmental Awareness workshop that will be conducted by the Environmental Consultant before the start of construction.

Principal Agent's Brief
☐ Ensure that the environmental performance is monitored by a designated environmental professional/consultant.
☐ Ensure that a summary of the environmental performance with regard to the environmental specifications, is submitted to the Environmental Consultant as part of a monthly report on the project.
☐ Ensure that the Contractor implements the recommendations made by the Environmental Consultant.

The Environmental Consultant's Brief
☐ Monitor and evaluate compliance with the specifications.
☐ Issue regular reports to the Principal Agent in regard to any contraventions of the environmental specifications.
☐ Agree remedial action and the timeframe for implementation with the Principal Agent.
☐ Brief the Contractor's staff about the environmental specifications.
☐ Provide professional advice to the Principal Agent in respect of implementing the environmental specifications.
☐ Attend site meetings on a when-required basis, and monitor the performance in terms of the environmental specifications.
☐ Provide recommendations for improving the performance of the Contractor in respect of the environmental specifications.
☐ Ensure these recommendations are implemented.
☐ Advise the Principal Agent where adequate standards in terms of the environmental specifications are not being achieved and what remedial action is required.
☐ Be responsible for producing a comprehensive report at the end of the project, in which the environmental performance of the construction phase is recorded.

Site Establishment and Management Layout Plans
☐ The Contractor is responsible for providing layout plans of the construction site which indicate the following demarcated areas. The plan must be approved by the Principal Agent in consultation with the Environmental Consultant before site establishment is commenced:
• Planned access and circulation routes.
• Topsoil and subsoil stockpiles.
• Working areas.
• Contractor's camp.
• Storage areas.
• Waste collection facilities.
• Ablution facilities.
• Stormwater control measures.
• Buffer zones.
• Significant features (e.g. cultural and natural) not to be disturbed.
☐ Access routes and haul roads must be demarcated and vehicle movement to be confined to these roads.
☐ Excavated areas must be cordoned off and well marked to ensure public safety.

217

□ Construction activities to be restricted according to that designated on the aforementioned plan.
□ Materials: topsoil, building materials, waste etc. must be stored in areas in accordance with the aforementioned plan.
□ Site preparation and clearing is to be restricted to the areas designated on the layout plan.
□ Physical measures to prevent degradation of soil and water to be marked on the aforementioned plan.

Topsoil
□ The Contractor to ensure that the topsoil and subsoil are stockpiled as directed by the Principal Agent and the Environmental Consultant.
□ Topsoil to be stripped from the areas indicated below as a first step in establishing the site:
• Roads;
• Storage areas including those designate for stockpiling of topsoil;
• Areas designated for the storage of spoil; and
• Areas which could be polluted by any aspect of construction activity.
• Topsoil to be stripped to a depth as directed by the Engineer.
• The Contractor to ensure that topsoil and subsoil are not mixed during stripping, excavation, stockpiling, reinstatement and rehabilitation of the site.
• Topsoil/subsoil to be protected from wind and rain erosion.
• Both topsoil and subsoil stockpiles shall be kept clear of weeds. The use of chemicals to control weeds not to be permitted.

Rivers, Streams, Wetlands and other Water Bodies
□ Provision of buffer zones to be made by the Contractor between construction activities and any natural water bodies, rivers or streams in accordance with the layout plan.
□ Natural water sources not to be used for the purposes of washing of clothes or vehicles or bathing by site staff.
□ Natural water sources not to be used for construction activities such as for the mixing of cement or washing of equipment unless agreed by the Environmental Consultant and the relevant authority.
□ The Contractor shall not in any way modify or damage the banks of streams, rivers or natural water bodies.
□ Litter and silt traps to be provided by the Contractor as determined by the Environmental Consultant.

Stormwater Control
□ Natural runoff to be diverted around the site workings to prevent its pollution and routed to the nearest runoff course.
□ Stormwater control measures to be implemented in accordance with the requirements of the Environmental Consultant. These may include cross and side drains on access and haul roads.
□ Where stormwater retention ponds are included in the development plans for the site, these should be constructed in the initial construction phase for stormwater control purposes.
□ Where stormwater has accumulated in workings and needs to be pumped out, it should be disposed of in a manner to be approved by the Environmental Consultant. This means that the Contractor is to be responsible for having water tested in accordance with the Environmental Consultant's requirements to establish whether it is contaminated and specialised handling and disposal is necessitated.

Soil Erosion
□ Measures to prevent erosion of bare soil, excavated areas and soil stockpiles shall be implemented in accordance with the specifications of the Environmental Consultant.

Control of Damage to Fauna and Flora
□ The Contractor to ensure that areas designated on the layout plan as being of ecological importance are not to be disturbed.
□ A buffer zone shall be established between construction activities and areas of ecological importance as designated by the Environmental Consultant.
□ Faunal species only to be removed from the site with the permission of the Environmental Consultant.
□ The Contractor to facilitate access to the site for the purposes of relocating plant/animal species prior to the commencement of the clearing of site activities.

Air Quality
□ Dust: The Contractor to ensure that control measures are applied to minimise dust, particularly in the windy season.
□ Engine, machine and other crude oil products may not be used to control dust.
□ Emissions: The Contractor to ensure that all vehicles and machinery (such as diesel generators) are well maintained to minimise exhaust emissions.

Waste Management: General Principles
□ Wherever possible waste that is recyclable to be recycled.
□ Waste that requires disposal to be disposed of at a licensed landfill site either by the Contractor or by an approved waste removal contractor.
□ Illegal dumping not to be tolerated under any circumstances.
□ Waste storage facilities to be positioned on site so as to minimise public nuisance.
□ Containers for different types of waste to be clearly marked. Minimum of four containers required: recyclables (glass, paper, cardboard, plastic and metal); construction waste, domestic waste; and hazardous waste.
□ No burning of waste on site to be permitted.
□ No disposal of waste on site, other than that agreed by the Environmental Consultant (such as compostibles and rubble) that may be disposed of on site.
□ The Contractor to ensure that no windblown litter occurs.
□ The Contractor to notify the Principal Agent in the event of any spills of fuels, chemicals or other hazardous substances that occur on site during the transport of materials to or from the site. Clean-up costs to be for the account of the Contractor. If specialist advice is required to determine clean-up requirements, these to be for the account of the Contractor.

Construction Waste
□ All clean construction waste (rubble, cement bags, waste cement, wire, nails and timber) to be collected and stored in the appropriate container.
□ If material is required for landscaping purposes, construction rubble may be used with the agreement of the Environmental Consultant and stockpiled in a suitable place as directed.

☐ Wherever possible construction waste that is not used to be recycled, with the emphasis on the opportunities for reuse by the informal sector or by the local authority.

Domestic and Office Waste
☐ The construction site to be kept tidy and free of litter at all times.
☐ Recycling of glass, paper, cardboard and metal is a minimum requirement.
☐ The Contractor to dispose of these waste products either by sale (e.g. to the small enterprise sector) or make them available to local communities or schools in order that they may generate income from these sources.
☐ The Contractor to be responsible for establishing an area for composting, as designated by the Environmental Consultant, where organic waste may be placed. The compost to be available for use in revegetation of the site or for use in community landscaping or other projects.

Hazardous Waste
☐ The Contractor to be familiar with those wastes that are legally defined as hazardous and potentially injurious to health. Hazardous wastes are usually proven to be toxic, flammable, explosive, carcinogenic, poisonous or radioactive.
☐ To be stored in an appropriate container which is to be clearly marked as a hazardous waste container.
☐ The Contractor to ensure that all potentially hazardous waste is removed and disposed of by an approved hazardous waste contractor.
☐ Potentially hazardous raw and waste materials to be handled in accordance with the manufacturer's specifications, legal requirements and specifications given on the Material Safety Data Sheet, where available.

Waste Water: Effluent
☐ Effluent may not be disposed of into stormwater drains, streams, rivers or any other water body unless agreed by the Environmental Consultant.
☐ Care to be taken in the washing of vehicles, particularly cement washings, to ensure that these do not enter stormwater systems, streams of wetlands.

Sewage
☐ Ablution facilities shall be maintained in good working order at all times.
☐ If sewage facilities are not connected to a reticulated system, the Contractor to ensure that it is removed on a regular basis by an approved contractor or by the relevant local authority.
☐ The Contractor to ensure that pollution of surface and groundwater resources is prevented.

Noise
☐ The Contractor to ensure that all equipment complies with the manufacturer's noise level specification. This means that equipment to be maintained and tested.
☐ Silencer units on plant and vehicles shall be maintained in good working order.
☐ The Contractor to ensure that all employees wear the appropriate noise gear when working in the vicinity of noisy equipment.
☐ The Contractor to notify the Principal Agent should it be necessary for construction activities to extend beyond given and agreed times, weekdays, Saturdays, Sundays and Public Holidays.

☐ The Contractor with the Principal Agent/Environmental Consultant to consult with residents located in the environs of the site construction activity need to exceed into overtime hours agreed as above.

Lighting
☐ Lighting of the site to be adequate for safety purposes but not to be intrusive for neighbours.
☐ Should overtime be necessitated, the Contractor to be responsible for ensuring that the associated lighting does not cause a disturbance to neighbours.

Public Safety
☐ The Contractor to ensure compliance with the requirements of the relevant safety legislation in force in specific locations.
☐ The Contractor to cordon off excavations and render them clearly visible.
☐ The Contractor to ensure that due care is taken when heavy vehicles or equipment enter public access roads.
☐ The Contractor to make appropriate provision for public liability insurance cover.

Community Relations
☐ The Principal Agent and the Environmental Consultant to assist in liaison with the neighbouring community. The Contractor to be responsible for providing information that may be required by the Principal Agent/Environmental Consultant. This could include project shedule, access routes, unsafe areas etc.
☐ The Contractor to liaise with the Principal Agent/Environmental Consultant in regard to specific activities that could cause inconvenience to neighbours (such as overtime work, disruption of services). Appropriate notification needs to be done timeously before such activities are carried out.
☐ The Contractor to make staff available for any formal consultation with affected parties for the purposes of explaining the construction process and to answer queries and/or complaints.

Third Party or Public Complaints
☐ The Contractor is responsible for assisting the Principal Agent/Environmental Consultant with response to queries and/or complaints.
☐ The Contractor to notify the Principal Agent regarding complaints.
☐ The Contractor is responsible for undertaking any remedial action as regards complaints, and as required by the Principal Agent/Environmental Consultant.

Site Rehabilitation
☐ The Contractor to rehabilitate the site as required by the Principal Agent/Environmental Consultant.
☐ Rehabilitation of the original site to an acceptable level prior to any formal landscaping activities, to be undertaken by an appropriate contractor approved by the Principal Agent in consultation with the Environmental Consultant.

BIBLIOGRAPHY

Alberts, T., *Buildings with a Difference*, Tour guidebook ING Building, Amsterdam, 1986.

Alexander, C., Ishikawa, S., Silverstein, M., *A Pattern Language*, Oxford University Press, New York, 1977.

Baker, I., Thomson J., Bowers, P., Research on post-Radburn housing areas, *Ekistics* 52 (312), 1985.

Batty, M., Longley, P., *A Geometry of Form and Function*, Academic, London, 1994.

Bauval, R., *The Orion Mystery*, Heinemann, London, 1994.

Begg, A., Mud Houses, In: *South African Country* Life No. 34 (Ed. Wasserfall, M.), 1998.

Bentley I., Alcock, A., Murrain, P., McGlynn, S, Smith, G., *Responsive Environments : A Manual for Designers*, Architectural Press, UK., 1985.

Bergamini, D., *Mathematics*: Life Science Library (Eds Life), Time-Life International, 1965.

Brady, I., Tobias, T., Eagles, P.,Ohrner, R., Micak, J., Veale, B., Dorney, R., A Typology for the Urban Ecosystem and its relationship to larger biogeographical landscape units, *Urban Ecology* 4, 1978.

Bramwell, A., *Ecology of the 20th Century – A History*, Yale University Press, New Haven and London, 1989.

Briggs, J., *Fractals - The Patterns of Chaos: discovering a new aesthetic of art, science and nature*, 1992.

Brundland Report: Our Common Future, published by the World Commission on Environment and Development, Oxford, 1987.

Calderwood, D., PhD Thesis, *Native Housing in South Africa*, Wits Univ. Press, 1953.

Chernushenko, D., *Greening our Games: Running sports events and facilities that won't cost the earth*, The Delphi Group, Centurion Publishing and Marketing, Ottawa, Canada, 1994.

Chaitkin, W., *Contemporary Architecture*, (eds.) Jencks, C and Chaitkin, W., Academy Editions, London 1982.

Ching, F., *Architecture: Form, Space and Order*, Van Nostrand Reinhold Co., New York, 1994.

Clifford Culpin & Ptnrs, Ove Arup & Ptnrs., Tym, R. & Ptnrs, *Urban Projects Manual* (Ed. Gerald Dix), 1983.

Colquhoun, I., *RIBA Book of 20th Century British Housing*, Architectural Press, Oxford, 1999.

Cremer, A., Stürmann, H., Cob Architecture In: *South African Country Life*, R. P. Publication, 1998.

Dantzig, G., Saaty, T., *Compact City: a plan for a liveable urban environment*, Freeman & Co. San Francisco, 1973.

David Clark's Album: Extract from *Time* - a rock opera, premièred London 1986.

Department of Forestry Services, Thimpu, Bhutan: Notification in the *Keunsel*, October 2001.

Dewar, D., Uytenbogaardt, R., *Housing: A comparative evaluation of urbanism in Cape Town*, Urban Planners Research Unit, 1977.

Dewar, D., Uytenbogaardt, R., Urban Poverty and City Development, In: *Architecture SA* March/April (1), 1984.

Doczi, G., *Proportional Harmonies in Architecture and Nature : the power of limits*, Shambala, Boston & London, 1985.

Douglas, I., *The Urban Environment*, Edward Arnold, UK, 1983.

Duffy, F., DEGW Partnership, Skyscrapers – Is the end nigh? Article in *World Architecture*, 1999 No. 79.

Editorial comment, Library joins Stirling shortlist, *Building Design* No. 1372, 6 November, 1998.

Esty, D., Chertow, M. (Eds), *Thinking ecologically – The next generation of environmental policy*, Yale University Press, USA, 1997.

Eubank-Ahrens, B., A closer look at users of woonerven, In: *Public Streets for Public Use* (Ed. Mouden, A.), Van Nostrand Rheinhold, New York, 1987.

Fletcher, B., *A History of Architecture on the Comparative Method*, Batsford Books, London, 1948.

Fonseca, R., *Shelter and Society* (Ed. Oliver, P.), 1976.

Frampton, K., *Modern Architecture: A Critical History*, World of Art Series, Thames & Hudson Ltd, London, 1992.

Fuggle, R., Rabie, M., *Environmental Concerns in Southern Africa: technical and legal perspectives*, Juta & Co., 1983.

Gans, H., *People and Plans: essays on urban problems and solutions*, Basic Books, Inc., New York, 1968.

Gerster. G., *Grand Design: the earth from above*, Weidenfeld & Nicolson, London, 1988.

Gibson, J., *Ecological approach to visual perception*, Houghton Mifflin, 1987.

Girardet, H., *New Directions for Sustainable Urban Living: the Gaie atlas of cities*, Gaia Books Ltd. 1992.

Gleick, J., *Chaos: the amazing science of the unpredictable*, Minerva London, 1997.

Goethert, R., Tools for the basic design and evaluation of physical components in new urban settlements, In: *Ekistics* (312), 1985.

Hall, E., *Silent assumptions in social communication*, Basic Books Inc, USA, 1972.

Hancock, G., Bauval, *The Mars Mystery*, Mitchell Joseph, London, 1998.

Heath, T., *Method in Architecture*, John Wiley & Sons, Devon, 1984.

Hill, R., Bowen, P., Current issues in sustainable construction, In: *Sustainable Construction – Environmental Supplement*, 1995.

Hillier, B., Hanson, J., *The Social Logic of Space*, Cambridge, UK, 1984.

Holm, D., Viljoen, J., *Primer for Energy Conscious Design*, Department of Minerals and Energy: Directorate Energy Development, 1996.

Hull, R., *African Cities and Towns before the European Conquest*, Norton & Co., N.Y., 1976.

Hulme, M., There is no such thing as a purely natural weather event, Article : *Mail & Guardian*, 17-23 March, 2000.

Jacobs, J., *The Death and Life of Great American Cities*, Cape, London, 1962.

Jencks, C., Non-linear architecture, In: *Architectural Design*, Vol. 67, No.9/10, Sept/Oct. 1997.

Jencks, C., Chaitkin, W., *Current Architecture*, Academy Editions, London, 1982.

Jensen, O., Environmental Accounting for Housing, Paper: *European Expert Meeting on Sustainable Urban Development*, June 1999.

Kibert, C., Sustainable Construction, *Proceedings of the First International Conference of CIBTG16*, USA, 1994.

Kidder Smith, G., *Italy Builds*, Architectural Press, London, 1956.

Knevitt, C., *Space on Earth: Architecture: People and Buildings* (Ed. Pheiffer, B.), Thomas Methuen, London, 1985.

Koenigsberger, O., *Manual of Tropical Housing and Building: Part 1 – Climatic Design*, Longman London, 1974.

Krier, L., *New Classicism*, Omnibus Volume (Eds Papadakis, A., Watson, H.), Academy Editions, London, 1990.

Lantz, H., Number of childhood friends as reported in a life histories group of 1000, In: *Marriage and Family Life*, 1956.

Levi-Strauss, C., *Structural Antholopology*, Penguin, Middlesex, 1968.

Lickindorf, E., Fractal geometry and ethnic art meet, *Monitor supplement to Mail & Guardian*, 7-13 Jan , 2000.

Lovelock, J., *Gaia: A New Look at Life on Earth*, Gaia Books Limited, Oxford Univ. Press, 1979.

Lynch, K., *A Theory of Good City Form*, MIT Press, London, 1981.

Mandelbrot, B., *The Fractal Geometry of Nature*, W. H. Freeman, San Francisco, 1977.

Mangin, W., *Peasants in Cities: Readings in the anthropology of urbanisation*, Houghton Mifflin, Boston, USA, 1970.

Marks, R., Palaces of Desire, *SA Architect* Nov./Dec., 2000.

Maxwell, R., Stern, R., *Venturi and Rauch: Architectural Monologues 1*, Academy Editions, 1978.

Meadows, D., The City of First Priorities, *Whole Earth Review*, Spring 1995., San Francisco, USA.

Melvin, J., Lifting the veil, *World Architecture*, 102, Jan 2002.

Mills, G., Recreating Urban Space, *Architecture SA*, July/Aug, 1988.

Mollison, B., Slay, R., *Introduction to Permaculture*, Tutorial Press Zimbabwe and Tagari Publ. Australia, 1974.

Mollison, B., *A Designer's Manual*, Tagari, 1997.

Morkel, M., Residential Densities – Quo Vadis (2) and (3), *Housing in South Africa* Nov./Dec. 1988.

Mound, L., *Insect*, Eyewitness Guides – Dorling Kindersley, London, 1990.

Munkstrup, N., Examples of urban ecology in Denmark, *Interplan* No.13, December 1995.

Naess, A., *Ecology, Community and Lifestyle*, (Ed. Rothenburg, D.), Cambridge University Press, 1989.

Neutra, R., *Survival Through Design*, Oxford University Press UK, 1954.

Norberg-Shultz, C., *Genus Loci: towards a phenomenology of architecture*, Rizzoli, New York, 1971.

Nouvel, J., *Architecture for the Future* (Eds Dubost, J., Gontier, J-F.), Editions Pierre Terrail, Paris, 1996.

Oliver, P., *Shelter and Society*, Barrie & Jenkins London, 1976.

Pawley, M., The Supreme Formula for Progress, *World Architecture* No. 67, 1998.

Pearson, D., *The Natural House Book*, Gaia Books Limited, 1989.

Pearson, D., *Earth to Spirit: in search of natural architecture*, Gaia Books Limited, 1994.

Pearce, D., Markandya, A., Barbier, E., *Blueprint for a Green Economy*, Earthscan Publications Ltd, 1989.

Pearce, M., New metaphors for the new millennium, *SA Architect*, March, 1999.

Peck, A., Agoric Planning, *Ekistics*, 49 (295), 1982.

Portoghesi, P., *Postmodern*, Rizzoli, New York, 1983.

Preston, G., Davis, B., *A case of tunnel vision*, Paper: The Palmiet phase 1 scheme versus water demand management and water catchment management, 1993.

Rand, H., *Hundertwasser*, Bendikt Taschen, 1991.

Rapoport, A., *Human Aspects of Urban Form*, Pergamon Press, New York, 1977.

Reekie, R., *Design in the Built Environment*, Edward Arnold London, 1972.

Roberts, D., Urban space planning in South Africa, and the need for a new approach, *Environment*, Oct./Nov., 1985.

Rogers, R., *Architecture for the Future* (Eds. Dubost, J-C., Gontier, J-F.), Editions Pierre Terrail, Paris, 1996.

Roodman, D., Lenssen, N., Paper: How ecology and health concerns are transforming construction, *World Watch*, 124, 1994.

Rose, G; Battaille, G; Till, J; *Occupying Architecture: between the architect and the user*, Ed Jonathan Hill, Routledge, London and NY 1998.

Rosenfeld, A., Hafemeister D., Article: Energy Efficient buildings, 1986.

Rossbach, S., *Fengshui – Basic Concepts*, Penguin Group, 1987.

Royal Fine Art Commission, What makes a good building?: an inquiry by the Royal Fine Art Commission (now: The Commission for Architecture and the Built Environment), Ed Cantacuzino, S., 1996.

Schaffer, D., *Garden Cities for America: the Radburn experience*, Temple Univ. Press, 1982.

Schon, D., *The Reflective Practitioner*, Basic Books, Inc., USA.

Schaffer, D., *Garden Cities of America: The Radburn experience*, Temple University Press, Philadelphia, 1982.

Schmuck, F., *Color Systems, Lexicon der Kunst Vol. 1, 1968*, Color in Townscape (Eds Düttman, M. et al.), Architectural Press, London, 1981.

Schumacher, F., *Color in Architecture*, Color in Townscape, (Eds Düttman, M. et al.), Architectural Press, London, 1981.

Sitte, C., *City Planning According to Artistic Principles*, Phaidon Press London, 1965.

Skaife, S., *African Insect Life*, Country Life Books, 1979.

Smithson, A., *Urban Structuring*, Faber London, 1967.

Spirn, A., *The Granite Garden: urban nature and human design*, Harper Collins, 1984.

Spring, M., Article: *Building*, Vol.262, No.8013 (43), 1997.

Stauth, R., *Environmental Economics, Environmental Concerns in Southern Africa* (Eds Fuggle, R., Rabie, M.), Juta & Co. Ltd., Kenwyn, 1983.

Steele, F., *The Sense of Place*, CBI Publishing Co. Inc., Boston, 1981.

Steen, A., Steen, B., Eisenberg, D., *The Strawbale House*, Chelsea Green Publ. Co., Vermont, USA, 1994.

Steiner, F., Zube, E., Ecological Planning, *Landscape Journal*, 7(1), 1988.

Talib, K., *Shelter in Saudi Arabia*, Academy Editions/St Martin's Press, 1984.

Terjung, W., *Process-Response Systems in Physical Geography*, 1973.

Thomas, D., Review: *The Work of Pier Luigi Nervi*, unpublished, 1958.

Thomas, D., Masters Thesis: *A systematic methodology towards creating spatial quality in urban settings*, unpublished, 1989.

Trancik, R., *Finding Lost Space*, Van Nostrand Reinhold Co., New York, 1986.

Tunnard, C., Pushkarev, B., Man-made America: Chaos or Control?: an enquiry into selected problems of design in the urbanised landscape, Yale University Press, New Haven, 1963.

Turner, N., Article: 4 Times Square, *World Architecture*, No. 83, Feb. 2000.

Underwood, D., *Oscar Niemeyer*, Rizzoli, New York, 1994.

UTC Fuel Cells: About Fuel Cells, Website www.utcfuelcells.com, 2002.

Uyanga, J., *Urban Planning in Nigeria*, Habitat International, 1989.

Vale, B., & Vale, R., *Green Architecture: design for a sustainable future*, Thames & Hudson, 1996.

von Frisch, K., with Otto, F., *Animal Architecture*, Harcourt Ltd., London, 1974.

van Niekerk, P., Essay on *Fractal Design in Architecture*, unpublished, 1999.

van Rensburg, B., Observer at Rio Earth Summit 1992. Unpublished diagram.

Visser, J., Article in KPMG, SA Newsletter, 1998.

Wates, N., *Community Architecture: how people are creating their own environment*, Penguin London, 1987.

Wheeler, M., *Roman Art and Architecture*, Praeger, New York, 1964.

Whyte, W., Small space is beautiful: design as if people mattered, *Technology Review*, 85(5), 1982.

Wigley, M., *Modern Architecture : A Critical History*, (Ed Frampton., K.) World of Art Series, Thames & Hudson Ltd. London, 1992.

World Commission on Environment, *Our Common Future 1 (Brundtland Report)*, Oxford University Press, 1987.

Wright, F.L., *Frank Lloyd Wright: collections of writings vols 1-4, 1893-1932*, Rizzoli in association with the Ford Foundation, 1992.

Yeang, K., Balfour, A., Richards, I., *Bioclimatic Skyscrapers*, Artemis, London, 1994.

Zerbst, R., *Gaudi 1852-1926: Antoni Gaudi: a life devoted to architecture*, Taschen Koln, 1993.

□ □ □ □ □

PHOTOGRAPHIC SOURCES
Acknowledged with thanks

Alice Wilkes: *Guggenheim, Bilbao, Spain.*

Argus Newspapers : *Crossroads, South Africa, aerial view.*

Barak Mizrachi: *Public spaces, Johannesburg, South Africa.*

Bernie Oberholzer: *Rotating solar panel on housing development, Denmark.*

BRE Marketing and Communications: *BRE Environmental Building, Garson, Watford, UK.*

Bridget van Rensburg: *Curitiba graphic.*

Chonat Getz: *Geometric wire basket patterns.*

Holm & Viljoen: *Photovoltaic array, South Africa.*

Ken Yeang : *Menara Mesiniaga Tower, Kuala Lumpur, Malaysia.*

Klaus Scheid: *Towns in Algeria and Yemen.*

Quentin Miller: *Buildings and urbanscape, Houston, Chicago, Dallas and New York, USA.*

Martine Ward: *Haj Terminal, Jeddah, Saudi Arabia.*

Mick Pearce: *Eastgate, Harare, Zimbabwe.*

Olympic Museum Lausanne, Switzerland: *Olympic Villages, Seoul, South Korea and Montreal, Canada.*

Paul van Niekerk: *Jewish Museum, Berlin, Germany; Badgirs, Dubai, Saudi Arabia.*

Roger Harrison: *ING Building, Amsterdam, Holland; Mill buildings, Holland & Spain; Carrè d'Art building, Nîmes, France.*

South African Country Life. Publication Editor and Herta Stürmann for *Cob Construction* material.

Suzanne Allderman: *Public spaces, Arequipa, Peru and Vancouver, Canada.*

□ □ □ □ □

INDEX

□ □ □ □ □